Sir Sigmund Sternberg

Sir Sigmund Sternberg

The Knight with Many Hats

EMMA KLEIN

VALLENTINE MITCHELL
LONDON • PORTLAND, OR

First published in 2012 by Vallentine Mitchell

Middlesex House,	920 NE 58th Avenue, Suite 300
29/45 High Street, Edgware,	Portland, Oregon,
Middlesex HA8 7UU, UK	97213-3786 USA

www.vmbooks.com

ISBN 978 0 85303 835 1 (cloth)

British Library Cataloguing in Publication Data

Klein, Emma.
  Sir Sigmund Sternberg : the knight with many hats.
  1. Sternberg, Sigmund, 1921- 2. Jews, Hungarian—Great
  Britain—Biography. 3. Jewish businesspeople—Great
  Britain—Biography. 4. Jewish philanthropists—Great
  Britain—Biography. 5. Council of Christians and Jews—
  Biography. 6. Three Faiths Forum (Organization)
  I. Title
  296.3'9'092-dc23

ISBN-13: 9780853038351

Library of Congress Cataloging-in-Publication Data

A catalog record has been applied for

Printed by CPI Group (UK) Ltd, Croydon, CR0 4YY

Contents

Foreword

In the contemporary world where religion has too often been a scene of conflict rather than conciliation, I know of no contemporary who has spanned the spectrum of interfaith as comprehensively and with such lasting impact as Sir Sigmund Sternberg – Sigi to all who know and love him.

He has been an indefatigable source for good, working at a pace that would exhaust someone a half or a third of his age. I once said that he is a one-man refutation of the Second Law of Thermodynamics – that all systems lose energy over time. Sigi has shown, to the contrary, that in the great words of Isaiah:

Even youths grow tired and weary,
and young men stumble and fall;
but those who hope in the Lord
will renew their strength.
They will soar on wings like eagles;
they will run and not grow weary,
they will walk and not be faint.

Throughout his life, and long before it became fashionable, he put his energy into developing, maintaining and enhancing relationships with individuals and organizations from across the world's main faith groups. This is a legacy that will stand the test of time.

Born in Budapest in June 1921, Sigi was forced to flee Hungary at the outset of the Second World War, arriving in Britain in 1939. By the time he became an official British citizen in 1947, he had built up a successful metal business.

But business was never the main goal in his life. It was a means to an end. It allowed him to become a generous philanthropist and a leading activist for the causes we all associate him so closely with today. This is what defined Sigi.

There is a story that someone once asked Sir Moses Montefiore: 'Tell me, Sir Moses. What are you worth?' Moses Montefiore responded with a figure. His questioner said, 'But that cannot be correct. I know you are worth ten times that amount.' Moses Montefiore responded in these words, 'You didn't ask me how much do I own. You asked me what I am worth. So I gave you the amount that I have given to tzedakah this year because we are all worth what we are willing to share with others.' By this definition, Sigi is worth a fortune, not only in respect of his generosity in terms of the tzedakah he has given, but also in terms of the time he has devoted to so many causes he has made his own. He truly is one of Anglo-Jewry's most treasured possessions, and has brought blessing to every great enterprise he has had a share in.

The Hebrew Bible contains the great command, 'You shall love your neighbour as yourself' (Leviticus 19:18), and this has often been taken as the basis of biblical morality. But it is, in truth, only part of it. The Jewish sages noted that on only one occasion does the Hebrew Bible command us to love our neighbour, but in thirty-six places it commands us to love the stranger. Our neighbour is one we love because he is like ourselves. The stranger is one we are taught to love precisely because he is not like ourselves. This is something that throughout his life Sigi has understood better than most. It is his love of both his neighbour and the stranger that has allowed him to be so successful.

Realising the importance of a world where there was not only dignity of difference amongst the world's major religions, but also a respectful understanding of their fundamental beliefs, Sigi was a pioneer not only of interfaith dialogue, but also of action, and in doing so he has brought the imperative of good interfaith relations to new generations. Through the establishment of the Sternberg Foundation; as one of the co-founders of the Three Faiths Forum; as chairmanship of the International Council of Christians and Jews; as Vice-President of the World Congress of Faiths; and as coordinator of the religious component of the World Economic Forum, Sigi has consistently placed the importance of interfaith relations at the heart of everything he does.

His efforts have not only made a lasting impact, but have

been recognised at the very highest level. Knighted in 1976, he was appointed a Papal Knight by Pope John Paul II in 1985, with a Star awarded in 2010. In 1998 he was awarded the Templeton Prize for Progress in Religion for his global interfaith work, and in 2005, he was promoted to the highest rank within the Royal Order of Francis I to the grade of Knight Grand Cross in recognition of his contributions to strengthening interfaith activities between the British and Irish delegations.

I have often argued that faiths are like languages. There are many of them, and they are not reducible to one another. In order to express myself at all, I must acquire a mastery of my own language. If I have no language, I will still have feelings but I will be utterly inarticulate in communicating them. The language into which I am born, which I learn from my parents and my immediate environment, is where I learn self-expression. It is an essential part of who I am. But as I venture out into the world I discover that there are other people who have different languages which I must learn if we are to communicate across borders.

A faith is like a language. I am at home in my own language as I am at home in my own faith. But I am not compromised by the existence of other languages. To the contrary, the more languages I can speak, the more I can communicate with others and the more I am enriched by their experience. Throughout his life, Sigi has become a master linguist, not only speaking his own so eloquently but reaching out across religious boundaries – and, at times, divides – to learn how to speak many others. He truly has become a true wordsmith of interfaith relations, building bridges where none previously existed and strengthening those already in place.

Sigi is unique, inexhaustible and the best source of renewable energy I know! Elaine and I are proud to be able to call him – and of course Hazel – cherished and beloved friends. Sir Sigmund deserves every honour that comes his way and this book is but one of a number of remarkable tributes to a great and transformative life. I wish him continued health and success in all his future endeavours.

Chief Rabbi Lord Jonathan Sacks
November 2011

Foreword

It is no exaggeration to say that Britain owes a great deal to the waves of Jewish refugees who came to the United Kingdom before the Second World War and after. Their intellectual, moral and cultural influence has been outstanding. If our nation has made a contribution in giving them a safe harbour and a tolerant and caring environment, we have been repaid many times over.

If that is true as a generalization, it is also no exaggeration to say that the subject of this book fits that description perfectly. Sir Sigmund Sternberg's remarkable career is the stuff from which legends are made. Forced to flee Hungary at the outset of war, Sigi came to Britain at the age of 18 as a 'friendly enemy alien'. Unable to work, Sigi assisted his cousin and developed skills in negotiating that were to become his hallmark in later life. Within a few years of war ending, and becoming a British citizen in 1947, he became a successful businessman in the metal industry.

However, from the beginning Sigi had a social conscience and was keen to help others and, without neglecting his businesses, he gave attention to the many causes where he felt he could offer assistance, as a philanthropist and as an activist. These included the Royal College of Speech Therapists; accepting the role as a magistrate; chairing the Society for Archaeo-Metallurgical Studies; Patron of Cruse; and many more besides.

Sigi Sternberg was knighted for his services to industry in 1976 but the trajectory of his life was already being shaped by his rich gifts in negotiation, diplomacy and advocacy. Ron Kronish, in this biography, describes him as 'a simple, sweet, loving and gentle soul'. There is a side of Sigi's character that echoes that description but more obviously Sigi was, and remains, a driven, disciplined and dominating man. He has astonishing reserves of energy, and if convinced that a course of action is required is not easily put off. Thus, he came to the rescue of the Council of Christians and Jews (CCJ) when it was in serious financial difficulties and injected cash, resolve and vision into its future. He was instrumental in getting faith onto the agenda of the World Economic Forum following 9/11, of which I became one of the faith leaders. In 1998, Sigi accepted the prestigious Templeton Prize for his exceptional services to inter-faith dialogue.

However, the Three Faiths Forum was perhaps his most significant creation. I recall when Sigi came to see me about the idea and, to this day, regret that I did not support it in the way I should have. I saw the beginning of a tripartite organization which included Muslims as well as Jews and Christians, as something that could undermine the CCJ. But I was mistaken. The Three Faiths Forum has not challenged the importance of the CCJ but, really, has enriched the United Kingdom by adding another dimension. Sigi was amazingly perceptive in seeing the need to include Muslims in dialogue and the Three Faiths Forum has become a central organ for interfaith cooperation in the country and a sign of hope in a broken and insecure world.

In my unswerving opinion, Sir Sigi Sternberg is one of the most important interfaith leaders in the Western world. In many impressive ways he has been a pioneer in the search for peace and reconciliation. Some have described him as someone in search of recognition and hungry for honours. Yes, there is something very tender and childlike in his pleasure when his great gifts have been recognized. That is a human characteristic shared by us all. But no one should be in any doubt that every honour he has received – and there have been scores with his Papal Knighthood as one of the most significant – has been richly deserved. He is one of God's children, a humble man of faith, a good friend to many, including myself, and one of the most able men I know.

This book by Emma Klein sets out so splendidly the

journey of this outstanding life but one thing must be added. Alongside him Hazel has been a gentle and strong influence, adding considerable wisdom to their common desire to bring people and faiths together. Through them both we have been blessed; to Sigi particularly our huge sense of gratitude for his magnificent contribution to the world. What a nonsense to call him a 'friendly enemy alien': he has earned his stripes ten times over!

George Carey
Lord Carey of Clifton, former Archbishop of Canterbury

Foreword: In Appreciation of Sir Sigmund Sternberg

The term 'indomitable spirit' appropriately describes the life and personality of Sir Sigmund Sternberg, who from having arrived in Britain as a refugee, rose to prominence as the pre-eminent Jewish personality of our times promoting relations and understanding between the different faith communities – in particular, between Jews, Christians and Muslims.

Never allowing voices of scepticism to deter him, he has not only been a key player in advancing these relationships, but he has forged new relationships and has also had the courage to take initiative where others feared to do so. Arguably this was most evident in the controversy over the Carmelite convent in Auschwitz, where his meeting with Cardinal Glemp proved to be the turning point in resolving the incident.

His role as a philanthropist for both Jewish and general causes as well as a bridge-builder between communities has, of course, gained him the highest recognition, making him unique as both a knight of the realm and a papal knight commander. Further recognition of his unique contribution to interfaith understanding came when he was awarded the Templeton Prize, the substantial prize money of which he donated to charity. In his generosity in the Jewish community and towards society at large he serves as a model for the ideal Jewish engagement that is both rooted in and dedicated to the creative continuity of Jewish heritage, while at the same time giving practical expression and commitment to the universal values of our Tradition. His achievements in this regard are nothing less than a *Kiddush HaShem*, a sanctification of the Divine Name.

Sir Sigmund has developed novel ways of pursuing these goals. As one who has been so remarkably decorated, he has been determined to see that others are duly recognized and the medallions and honours he has bestowed on others cover a stunning array of distinguished religious, political, civic and diplomatic leadership. In this regard, the saying in the Ethics of the Fathers (4:1), 'who is (truly) honourable? He who honours others', is particularly apposite.

While in recent years his interfaith initiatives have been devoted substantially to the Three Faiths Forum that he founded in Britain, he is perhaps best known internationally for his leadership of the International Council of Christians and Jews (ICCJ) over the course of the last three decades. This body embracing organizations devoted to Jewish-Christian friendship and understanding in some thirty countries is headquartered in Martin Buber House in Heppenheim, Germany. While local governments have contributed significantly to its operation over the years, without Sir Sigmund's support and devotion it would not have survived and played the valuable role that it does in combating bigotry and prejudice through spreading knowledge and mutual respect. In keeping with Sir Sigmund's encouragement, the ICCJ established an Abrahamic Forum to extend its operations to advance good relations and mutual knowledge with Muslims as well.

During the years as the ICCJ's President and Patron, he travelled the world together with Lady Hazel, extending the national membership of the organization. It was to that end that I was privileged to work with him in founding the Irish Council of Christians and Jews and then subsequently as President myself of the ICCJ.

While many family associations connect us, including Sir Sigmund's friendship with my late father, Rabbi Kopul Rosen of blessed memory, it has been my unique honour to collaborate closely with him since my tenure in Ireland; working together both in the ICCJ, on Christian-Jewish relations in general, and with the Catholic Church in particular. While I was privileged to be part of the small team that established full diplomatic relations between the State of Israel and the Holy See, the turf that enabled these relations to take root had been tilled effectively by Sir Sigmund and others, enabling our efforts to succeed accordingly. Among the many initiatives that prepared the way was the historic visit of Pope John Paul II to the Great Synagogue in Rome – the first ever visit of a pope to a synagogue – which Sir Sigmund helped facilitate. We have also worked together in bringing the interfaith dimension into the deliberations of wider world bodies, perhaps most notably the World Economic Forum.

In all these activities he has been and remains an inspiration to me. His instinctive wisdom and appreciation of what is right and good, his profound commitment to his faith and his people and at the same time to humanity at large, are ever a source of admiration and guidance, which I pray that we will be blessed to enjoy for many years to come.

Rabbi David Rosen, CBE, KSG

Preface and Acknowledgements

It was in the summer of 1988 that I first became acquainted with Sir Sigmund Sternberg. I had, for a few years, written articles on the subject of Christian-Jewish relations and was particularly keen to place such an article with the *Jewish Chronicle*. The forthcoming Lambeth Conference seemed a perfect opportunity, since various issues of considerable importance to the Jewish world were to be raised, relating both to the approach of the Anglican church towards Jews and Judaism and to the Israel/Palestine question, which had become particularly inflammatory in light of the recent Intifada. The Council of Christians and Jews had prepared a statement on Israel and the administered territories to be distributed to the bishops and other organizations were also involved in what was seen as a 'damage limitation' exercise.

My approach to *The Jewish Chronicle* received a 'wait and see' response, and a while later I received a phone call telling me that 'Sir Sigmund Sternberg will be contributing an article about the Lambeth Conference and you will be writing it'. I was somewhat taken aback, never having 'ghosted' an article, but my father was very pleased. I duly met Sir Sigmund, and we discussed the main points the article should cover. Sir Sigmund also invited me to a lunch he was hosting in central London with a focus on the forthcoming conference. After the meal was over, there were speeches and suddenly Sir Sigmund said: 'Emma Klein is writing an article about the Lambeth Conference. Tell them about it, Emma.' Once again I was taken aback but am quite comfortable with public speaking, so did my best.

That evening we had Friday night dinner with my parents and my father was delighted to hear all about this, saying, proudly, 'You are my daughter'. A few hours later he died, quite suddenly.

This was a terrible shock to us all. Sir Sigmund, with whom I had just become acquainted, was most kind and solicitous on hearing the news. He also invited me to a dinner at the Lambeth Conference two weeks later, a most enjoyable and stimulating occasion in the midst of a period of great sorrow.

The article itself was published two weeks after my father's death and generated four weeks of correspondence in *The Jewish Chronicle*. That made the 'ghosting' experience worthwhile for me as, had the article been under my name, it is likely to have initiated much less interest and controversy.

In the years to come, my acquaintance with Sir Sigmund furthered. He continued to invite me to a number of varied functions and I wrote one or two more articles for him and drafted a few speeches. I was then asked to write his biography and I did a considerable amount of research and interviewed a great number of people who had been involved in various areas of his life, particularly his interfaith work. At that stage, he was becoming increasingly involved with relations between Jews and Muslims and was soon to set up the Three Faiths Forum with the late Sheikh Dr Zaki Badawi and the Rev Dr Marcus Braybrooke.

For various reasons the biography was abandoned but two sample chapters were written, one of which, on the imbroglio over the convent at the Auschwitz death camp, was later expanded into a short book, *The Battle for Auschwitz*. Sir Sigmund played an important role in resolving the long-standing controversy.

This was just one of the innumerable achievements the young Jewish boy from Budapest was to accomplish in the course of his long and multi-faceted life.

When, in 2008, it was decided to go ahead with the biography, what interested me particularly was the work the Three Faiths Forum was doing with young Muslims, a crucial 'constituency' to win over in our time. This was another of his achievements. There will surely be more to come and I hope I have done justice to his story.

This book has had a rather unusual trajectory, having been written in various stages. There are some people whose backing throughout the period I would like to acknowledge with gratitude. Primarily I would like to thank Sir Sigmund's assistants, Elaine Shnieder and Maureen Greeves, for their invaluable help and support, without which I do not think I could have completed this work. I am indebted, too, to my husband, Chaim, a constant tower of strength, without whom I could never have contemplated a writing career. I must also thank my sons for putting up with me while I was so engrossed in this work.

On a more practical level, I thank Sheilagh Viviers for transcribing the few old tapes that were retrieved as well as the more recent interviews on my digital recorder. I would also like to thank Eric Muther, who worked in the Three Faiths Forum for some months in 2009 and who kindly allowed me to read his Masters dissertation, which provided me with much useful material about the Forum. I thank, too, the many, many people I interviewed since the project was originally conceived in the mid to late 1990s, most of whose voices remain unsung, because while their contributions were recorded on tape and even transcribed, so much of the material disappeared in circumstances quite beyond my control. There are others, too, I would like to thank, but their modesty precludes me from mentioning their names. Because so much recorded material was lost, the sources for much of the book have been provided by press releases, news reports and print-outs of speeches. The memoir of Sigi's sister, Suzanne Perlman, also provided extremely useful information about various incidents and events in Sir Sigmund's childhood and later career, for which I am most grateful. The source for the furtherance of the controversy over the convent at Auschwitz in Chapter Seven was my earlier book, *The Battle for Auschwitz*.

Emma Klein
November 2011

Plates

1. Sir Sigmund and Lady Sternberg.
2. Ruth, Michael, Sir Sigmund and Frances Sternberg.
3. Frances, Ruth and Michael Sternberg.
4. Hazel Sternberg with Ruth and David.
5. Frances Sternberg aged approximately 18.
6. Sir Sigmund and Frances Blane (née Sternberg).
7. Victor Sternberg.
8. Victor and Hazel Sternberg.
9. Robert Perlman, Hazel Sternberg, Sir Sigmund, Ruth Tamir, Noam Tamir and Jonny Tamir at Branksome, December 2009.
10. Lady Hazel and Ruth Tamir.
11. Sir Sigmund with great-grandson Jacob, March 2009.
12. David and Anna Sternberg.
13. David, Freddy and Nell Sternberg, August 2011.
14. Sir Sigmund with his sister, Suzanne Perlman
15. Bishop Jim Thompson and Rabbi Hugo Gryn, co-chairmen of the Inter Faith Network, receive the Sir Sigmund Sternberg Award in recognition of their work for 'cooperation between people of many faiths', 20 October 1987.
16. Presentation of Ashkenazi Haggadah to Pope John Paul II in Rome by Sir Sigmund, 1986.
17. Investiture as Papal Knight of the Order of St Gregory the Great, 4 March 1986.
18. Honorary Doctorate from Essex University, March 1996.
19. HRH The Duke of Edinburgh at the Sternberg Centre, November 1996.
20. Tamirs and Sternbergs.
21. Sir Sigmund with George Carey, Archbishop of Canterbury.

22. Sir Sigmund with Prime Minister Tony Blair at the Labour Party Conference.
23. HM the Queen and Sir Sigmund at the unveiling of the Wallenberg Memorial, London, 26 February 1997.
24. Presentation of the Templeton Award to Sir Sigmund at Buckingham Palace by HRH The Duke of Edinburgh, 15 May 1998.
25. Sir Sigmund with Oscar Scalfaro, President of Italy, January 1999.
26. Sir Sigmund presenting HRH The Duke of Edinburgh with a photograph of the tree planted at Yad Vashem in honour of his mother, Princess Alice, who was named a Righteous Gentile, Buckingham Palace, October 2002.
27. Sir Sigmund presents the Interfaith Medallion to Mary McAleese, President of Ireland, Dublin, 6 March 2003.
28. The Three Faiths Forum at Mansion House, 16 May 2003.
29. Visit of HRH Prince Michael of Kent to the Sternberg Centre, 4 May 2004.
30. Inauguration of a new Sefer Torah in Israel, 2005, in memory of Henry and Joseph Perlman.
31. Visit of the Papal Nuncio HE Archbishop Faustino Sainz Munoz to the Sternberg Centre, 11 October 2005.
32. HRH Prince Charles planting a tree in memory of his grandmother, Elizabeth the Queen Mother, at the Sternberg Centre, 22 June 2006.
33. Foreign Secretary David Miliband unveiling of a plaque in honour of British Diplomats who saved lives during the Second World War, Foreign Office, 20 November 2008.
34. Pim Waldeck, Suzanne Perlman and Sir Sigmund at the Presentation of the Royal Order of Merit to Suzanne Perlman, Embassy of The Netherlands, 29 April 2009.
35. Inauguration of the exhibition of the eighteenth-century synagogue Tzedek ve-Shalom from Suriname at the Israel Museum, Jerusalem, May 2010, made possible by Suzanne Perlman in memory of her husband Henry Perlman.
36. A selection of Sir Sigmund's medals.

1 Early Years

St Stephen's Basilica is the largest church in Hungary. Built over five decades in the latter half of the nineteenth century, it is in the classical style, not dissimilar to St Paul's Cathedral in London. The main portal boasts a bust of King Stephen, Hungary's first Christian king, while inside the church is Hungarian Catholicism's holiest relic, the *Szent Jobb*, the preserved right hand of the Basilica's patron saint.

It was during the 1980s that Sigmund Sternberg, together with his wife, Hazel, went to see the Basilica while on a visit to his native Budapest. A man who, for the past few years, had worked tirelessly to promote understanding and cooperation between Christians and Jews, Sigi was shortly to be honoured by the Pope with the award of Knight Commander of the Equestrian Order of St Gregory the Great. On this occasion, he had come to Budapest with the intention of setting up an association of Christians and Jews in Hungary, visiting hospitals and meeting the Papal Nuncio. Never before, however, had he entered St Stephen's, one of the glories of the city of his birth.

How different it had been, indeed, when he was growing up in the years before the Second World War. While there was quite a sizeable Jewish community in Budapest, Jews would not mix socially with Christians. The Basilica, too, had a particular significance: As Sigi recalls: 'We were living near by the Dome – the Basilica – on the Pest side. We saw a lot of priests there. It would never have occurred to me to go into the Dome. It was something unimaginable.' His reaction to seeing priests was 'to keep away from them, just keep away. It was the early 1930s, before Hitler. It would never have come into your mind that you would have any dialogue with them.'

The trouble with priests and with Christians in general was,

1

as Sigi sees it, that 'we knew, even as small children, that "the Jews killed Christ"'. It was later, as Sigi's sister, Suzanne Perlman, recalls in her memoir, that Sigi, then about 14, came home from the commercial college he was attending, 'white as a sheet', and refused to eat any lunch. He was the only Jewish boy in his class and was being constantly subjected to bullying by a Jew-baiter. The boy had beaten him up, telling him he had killed Jesus. Sigi replied: 'I didn't kill anyone.' Until he entered the college, he had attended a Jewish *gymnasium* but had recently transferred to the commercial college because it provided a superior education. Eventually, after being challenged to a fight by his tormentor, Sigi 'with supernatural fury' managed to floor him, even though he, himself, was far smaller. Sigi acknowledges that at this point he first became interested in Christianity and Suzanne sees this incident as a 'triggering point' for the interfaith work he engaged in later in life. At the time, however, any notion of entering the Basilica or any other church would have been quite unheard of.

But life in Budapest was good for the Sternberg family. Abraham (Abris) Sternberg was a prosperous antiquarian and patron of the arts and his wife, Elizabeth (Bozy) née Reiner, a very modern young woman who had no intention of being tied down with domestic and maternal responsibilities. These were left to household staff and governesses. Sigi was born, a beautiful baby, on 2 June 1921 and Suzanne about fifteen months later. While Elizabeth nursed her firstborn, her daughter was given to a wet nurse.

One of Sigi's earliest memories was walking to school with his governess. 'My mother was working and my father was working and I was very reluctant to go to school.' Sigi had started school when he was 6. 'It was a kind of kindergarten, I was always reluctant to go to school. School meant discipline. I was not very keen on discipline. I was a kind of entrepreneur – even at that early age. I liked to do my own thing.'

When the children were very young, most of the governesses they had were Jewish girls who had come to Hungary from abroad because, as Sigi explains, 'we were classed as a kind of Jewish aristocracy. We were always told, for instance, that when children came to our home they had to wash themselves first because the place was clean! They were not dirty children but the governesses made them wash. As children we were always told that we were sort of "better".' Sigi says he 'always felt a bit embarrassed when these children came – because of the bath. But they were quite happy to come to us. They had a good meal and we had a nice house.' He was particularly embarrassed when he and Suzanne were out in the snow and the governess they had at the time said that the poor children should pull their sledges and it would be an honour for them. 'This class distinction was with us all the time – we were different.' The governesses were also strict and insisted that the children needed to walk a lot, because that was healthy. 'I remember crossing the Danube in the cold winter time. It was snowing. I was very uncomfortable and couldn't understand why we couldn't go by bus but the governess said "this is very healthy".'

In her memoir, Suzanne speaks of her parents' romance. Abraham had fallen in love with Elizabeth when he spied her entering Antikart, the leading art and antique emporium in Budapest run by her cousin, Margit Sternberg, to take shelter from a storm. Margit was Abraham's sister-in-law and he begged to be introduced to the beautiful, mysterious stranger. Abraham had recently returned from a long sojourn in Germany, during which he had made his fortune, and was in search of a wife. Elizabeth's family was not as orthodox as the Sternbergs and therefore she was not considered a suitable match for him. Elizabeth's mother, Emelia née Schmidl, was the daughter of a prosperous forest estate owner and timber merchant. Since they lived in a more rural area, the Schmidl family was not connected to a Jewish community. Nevertheless, they had looked for a reasonably religious Jewish husband for Emelia, who eventually married her second cousin, Josef Reiner, from Budapest. The couple had established a business but then, as Sigi put it, 'struck bad times' and opened up a grocery business. As Elizabeth was seen as a grocer's daughter, that was not considered 'up to our standard'.

Undeterred by family objections and some hesitation on

Elizabeth's part, Abraham's determined pursuit prevailed and the couple were married. Suzanne recalls that despite her liberal attitudes, her mother, Elizabeth, committed herself to keeping a very orthodox household and every Friday afternoon, well before sunset, would be heard telling the family servants to make sure everything was prepared for the Sabbath. In contrast, Sigi remembers an occasion when he and Suzanne were 'looking through things' and found something that mentioned that their mother, who was very musical, had, prior to her marriage, performed in a concert on the Sabbath.

In the summer, the Sternberg family used to rent a cottage in the countryside. One day, when Suzanne was 5, she saw a gypsy woman wearing a many-layered multi-coloured skirt approach, holding a baby in her arms, with a small child in a sling on her back and a little girl walking next to her. The gypsy shouted out: 'Will you give me a jug of milk? For a jug of milk I will tell you your future.' Suzanne was mesmerised to hear and watch her. She had heard that gypsy women could tell the future. When she came up to her, the woman seized Suzanne's left hand and held it firmly in her grasp. 'Terrible things will be happening in this country and the living will envy the dead', she told the small girl, still clutching her hand very firmly, 'but your father will be looking down on you both and your mother and not even the skin of your hand will be hurt'. This prophecy, Suzanne recalls, was both for her and for Sigi. And, she recalls, what the gypsy had prophesied indeed happened.

The Sternbergs were members of the orthodox synagogue in Kazinczy Utca. Sigi speaks of his paternal grandfather, a bookseller, as 'a holy man, a learned man and people respected him'. It was his grandmother, 'a businesswoman' who kept the business going. Abraham was one of twelve siblings and Sigi and Suzanne had many cousins. Sigi recalls a special event in the synagogue when all the cousins, and others, had to kiss their paternal grandfather's hand. His mother Elizabeth, however, an independent woman, found the whole procedure ridiculous and refused to kiss her father-in-law's hand.

Among the cousins were Victor and Charles, the sons of a brother of Abraham. As Sigi sees it, they lived a more restricted life than he and Suzanne did, in a part of the city that was like a Jewish ghetto. Another cousin who was to play a prominent role in Sigi's life was Dr Solomon Schonfeld, the son of his father's sister, Ella, who had married a rabbi and moved with him to England. Sigi recalls the shock experienced by the family on hearing of the death of his aunt's husband when he was a young boy. Solomon Schonfeld, who was studying law when his father died, agreed to his mother's request to study for the rabbinate in order to follow in his father's footsteps. He returned to Hungary to train to become a rabbi. He later became a leader of the Jewish community, pioneered Jewish secondary school education and remained a great hero to the many Jews he rescued from Nazi-occupied Europe. One of Solomon Schonfeld's brothers was Sir Andrew Shonfeld, the economist and broadcaster.

Another of Abraham's sisters was Katherine Kato, who married Yair Weisz and moved to England. They had three children, Dr Olga Kennard OBE, a distinguished Cambridge scientist and Fellow of the Royal Society; Judith Weisz, a professor of endocrinology in the USA, and George Weisz. George Weisz, an engineer by training, founded a factory in Dunstable and later invented a handbag-sized resuscitator, which has been used all over the world. This unique device, 'an extremely sophisticated kiss of life', as it has been described, delivers twenty minutes worth of oxygen and has rescued many people. Some years ago, Weisz sold the patent to SmithKline Beecham. George Weisz and his first wife, Ruth Edith, have two daughters, Rachel, the Oscar-winning actress and Minnie, an artist and photographer.

Suzanne, too, has recollections of the governesses she and Sigi were left in charge of while their mother spent the week industriously and profitably engaged in a very large antique business in the centre of Budapest. She recalls that quite a number of the German and Austrian governesses were officer's daughters because her parents felt they would be able to teach the children discipline. The girls had come to Budapest to learn Hungarian. One governess was a very strict German lady, who, as she puts it, 'was never even supervised to ensure she was doing the right thing'. Indeed, the governess claimed that the children's mother was buying a small carpet beater for her to use whenever they were disobedient. And of course she did beat them, saying that this was what her father did to her. On one occasion, Sigi decided to take revenge and cut a big hole in the governess' new dress. The hole was in the back and she wore the dress without realizing this. Everyone laughed at her. When he was a bit bigger, Sigi jumped on her and hit her with a rolling pin. The final straw came on one occasion when Suzanne was crying out in pain after the governess kept beating her fingers because she was unable to tie her shoelaces. By chance Abraham was in the house and heard her. The governess was duly dismissed.

Another governess was Lola, a Viennese officer's daughter, who would dress the children in white and beat them if they dirtied their clothes. Not surprisingly, all normal play was forbidden. Suzanne recalls looking enviously at other children playing in the park. Not that Lola was particularly watchful of her charges. She would sit on a separate bench and flirt with one or other of the university students who would come and sit beside her. She once told Suzanne that she had decided to work 'with Jewish people who pay better and look after me although people say they really have horns'. On another occasion, a student came up to Suzanne and threw her some roses, saying 'this is for you, beautiful little girl'. Later, Lola took the roses away, saying: 'I cannot believe a Jewish girl can be beautiful'. Indeed, the Sternberg children would not infrequently hear casually expressed anti-Semitic remarks, such as those voiced by the farmer's wife at the house they rented for summer holidays: 'Not enough that you chase me out of my own beautiful home for a pittance ... You and your lot, all of you who killed our Lord the Saviour on the cross.'

Something special that the governesses and other household staff shared with the Sternbergs was Friday night dinner. What was particularly memorable was the way the governesses – Christian Austrian and German girls – would sing the *zmirot*, the Sabbath songs accompanying the Grace after meals, with great gusto. 'Hungarian was very difficult for them to learn but here they were singing away in Hebrew', Suzanne recollected. When they returned home, many of the governesses would write to the family saying how much they had loved being with them. They would sit round the Sabbath table with the family and it was Suzanne's duty to serve the dinner. As her father explained, 'Everybody has been working so hard during the week'. Suzanne used to sit next to her mother who would nudge her with her strong knuckles if she was too tardy in getting up to serve the next course. Sometimes it wasn't so easy. 'The soup was very hot and I was served last, so I hadn't finished when most of the others had', she recalls. The only person who was allowed to help her was the kitchen hand.

Sigi had no duties to fulfil. In Hungary at that time it would have been out of the question for a boy to engage in any domestic chores. It would have been considered in very bad taste or simply unacceptable had Sigi gone into the kitchen, brought food to the table or cleared the plates. All such tasks were left to the females of the family. The son of the family, the most important and cherished member next to their father, was geared to become a paterfamilias.

On Friday evenings, Abraham would sit at the head of the table and give explanations of the biblical passages from the Torah (Pentateuch) and the prophets which were read in the synagogue that particular Sabbath. These passages would be discussed with Sigi, when he was old enough to take part, and with the male visitors – wayfarers whom Abraham had met at the Sabbath Eve service in the synagogue, who were often Talmudic students. Suzanne recalls that she, too, would be asked for her opinion.

Sigi recalls that the children were not very pleased about the constant flow of visitors. 'This annoyed us as children. We didn't see our parents very much and then there were all kinds of strange people coming. They were hungry, they didn't have nice manners. We always had very clean tables and everything was nice and then these people come in and eat in our home....'

A governess of whom the children became very fond and with whom they maintained contact in later life was Regina Erlanger, from a Swiss Jewish family which had fallen on hard times. She eventually escaped to Israel and her son became the Israeli ambassador to Italy.

Many years later, shortly after Regina had died, Suzanne was at a brunch party in Israel when she met the Israeli ambassador to Italy. Finding out that she was originally from Budapest, the ambassador mentioned that his mother had once worked for a family there, who were so very kind and generous that she could never forget them. 'What was the name of the family?' Suzanne asked: 'The family of Abris Sternberg', the ambassador replied. 'He was my father!' The ambassador was amazed that Suzanne was the daughter of the family his mother had cared for.

Despite seeing their parents so little, Sigi can say that he and his sister had a happy childhood. 'Yes, we had a happy childhood. We had homework to do, we had lessons, we had discipline. There was no such thing as television. I had a Hebrew teacher coming to my home. He taught me Hebrew when I was a young child. My sister had piano lessons. It was a busy life.' It was apparent that constantly being occupied kept him happy.

With Elizabeth only putting in an appearance at weekends, it was Abraham who came every evening to see his children put to bed and to recite with them the *Shema* prayer. Though self-taught, he was a very cultured man and a great music lover, who would frequently put on gramophone records of arias from various operas. Suzanne recalls being deeply affected by the music. Sigi was not so fond of opera. He remembers that the family were given free tickets to the theatre and the opera. 'I found the opera very boring – long, long operas like Wagner – but we had to go because that was culture. We had to be cultured.' It was the clientele at the antique emporium who had given them the tickets. 'Our clientele were people who could afford antiques – aristocracy – so we met Hungarian aristocracy. We mixed with titled people, artistic people, artists and writers who came to the shop.' The relationship with this elite clientele remained on a business level, however. Sigi's parents were not invited to dinners, for example. Indeed, Sigi recalls an occasion in the 1990s when he met the wife of a former Austrian ambassador at a dinner. 'I never imagined I would be sitting next to an

Esterhazy and speaking with her – I spoke to her in Hungarian. They were aristocracy! They would never have mixed with us in the earlier years.'

Abraham was also eager for his children to be able to see how their Jewish faith was portrayed in literature. To take an example, he instructed them to read the play *Nathan the Wise* by Gotthold Ephraim Lessing. He then discussed the play with the children, wanting them to understand how people of other religions regarded Jews and how Jews thought of themselves. It was important, he felt, that Jews should defend their heritage and be proud of it. Since *Nathan the Wise* was essentially a plea for religious tolerance, it is intriguing to reflect that Sigi would later be carrying out Lessing's ideals in his many fervent endeavours to promote reconciliation and understanding between the faiths.

Suzanne recalls that in their home there were many engravings of family ancestors. A particularly notable ancestor was Rabbi Akiva Eger, the internationally renowned Talmudic luminary, who lived in the eighteenth and nineteenth centuries and wrote a commentary on the *Shulchan Aruch*.

A devoted father, Abraham was also in the habit of picking Suzanne up and carrying her around with great affection. He was obviously a man of deep emotions and might have found it easier to express his feelings with his daughter than with his practical wife. It is likely that the young Sigi resented this and would have wanted a greater show of affection from his father. As he was 'generally an obedient person', he didn't rebel or permit himself to get very upset, although he admits, 'I was a bit jealous'.

Suzanne believes that her father loved his son very much but felt that a boy needed to be treated differently. Both Sigi and Suzanne remember their father telling the young Sigi: 'Always remember to look after your sister.' However, Suzanne felt it was the other way round. She believed that she had to look after Sigi, that he was her charge. Since their mother was in business, Sigi needed to be taken care of. Sigi and Suzanne have remained close all their lives.

With such a large extended family and so many cousins, the

young Sternbergs rarely lacked for company. Sigi was popular and had a great many friends. He was also very good-looking and many of the servant girls took a fancy to him. Two tall, thin young men were also particularly devoted to him. One was Oscar and the other, Brody, the son of a physician. Suzanne recalls that their devotion to Sigi bordered on hero-worship and she always wondered what in Sigi's personality could have inspired this. Oscar, who predicted Sigi would do great things in life, escaped to Canada where he became successful in business and published popular books as a hobby, one of them being *How to be Successful in Business*. He remained a lifelong friend and would often comment: 'I told you so – he would make it'.

As Sigi recollects, the 1930s were 'very, very difficult times', with the rise of Hitler in Germany and an unstable financial climate. By 1933, he was already tri-lingual, in Hungarian, German and English. This he had learnt from an English teacher, an octogenarian, six foot three Irishman, and also from reading *The Times*, which, at the time, he pronounced 'Tim-es'. The children were taught with an Irish brogue which they took for the King's English. Sigi was also able to understand, first hand, the menace that was building up in Europe by listening on the radio to Hitler's broadcasts. 'I used to listen to the speeches in the dark on the world radio and I was absolutely frightened. And I knew what was going to happen. I remember hearing an expression which means "rub them out". I had no doubt in my mind that something terrible was going to happen to the Jews.' However, he felt safe in Hungary at that time. 'At 11 years old I didn't think that he would affect Hungary.' He was also regularly reading papers. 'I read with great interest what was happening in the English parliament. I remember a man called Attlee. What he said was very important.' From the age of 11 onwards, then, Sigi claims that he knew 'exactly what was going on in the world'. He was also interested in the business and would ask his father: 'What was the turnover? How much money did we make?'

Family life was tragically disrupted when, on 20 August 1935, Abraham died suddenly after suffering a brain haemorrhage on a train to Budapest. He was returning from his summer holiday in order to help Elizabeth in the antique business, although she had decided to take care of it for a week on her own. It was a terrible loss. Although Sigi understands how dreadful a shock it was for his sister, he can say for himself that it was 'very traumatic and a frightening experience'. Sigi was now the man of the family at the age of 14 and was forced to take on great responsibility and help in the business. His mother threw herself into the business with ever greater energy and spent all her time there. Sigi recalls constantly discussing business with her and giving her advice, not least about the importance of advertising in which he was a great believer. The first year was also a particularly difficult time for him as he would have to go early every morning to the synagogue to say the *kaddish*, the memorial prayer, before going on to his commercial college which was some way out of town.

The family was engaged in an important clandestine endeavour. It was possible, then, to go from Poland to Israel (or Palestine as it then was) through Hungary, along the Danube to Constanta in Romania, from where a boat would go to Palestine. The Sternbergs helped Polish refugees, who were illegally in Hungary, offering them shelter at their home and then bribing officials to allow them to take a boat on the Danube. From an early age, then, Sigi learnt how money could be used responsibly, to help others who were less fortunate. 'I was 15 or 16 at the time. I would bribe policemen to help these people on their way.' Earlier, from the age of 12, Sigi had joined Betar, a right-wing Zionist youth group, and it was members of Betar who had information about the movement of the Polish refugees. 'We knew we could bribe the policemen or gendarmerie because they were open to bribes.' And it was, then, at a very young age, that he came to understand the significance of money. 'That's when you knew that the most important thing in life is to have money because if you have money you can do anything. You can buy anybody or anything – including people, including girls, anything. That became my main aim in life, to be on my own. I mustn't be employed by anybody. I must only depend on myself.'

Belonging to Betar also confirmed Sigi's notion of his

identity. 'I never felt Hungarian at all in my life. I always felt Jewish. People ask about an identity crisis – there was no identity crisis. I never had any doubts because I always knew I was Jewish. I just happened to be in Hungary but I had no attachment to Hungary whatsoever.' Sigi affirms that it never occurred to him that he would have to live his life in Hungary. 'It was too small for me.' Palestine, however, was not an option. 'When people went off to Palestine it was a very moving experience. We sang Jewish songs at the station in Hungary to send them off – the Hatikvah, for instance. But I never thought of going to Palestine at all. It just did not arise. It would have been too small for me.'

As he says, now: 'I was a responsible person from the very beginning.' Indeed, while his cousin, Solomon Schonfeld, was in Hungary pursuing his rabbinical studies, Sigi, still a young teenager, had to play chaperone when Schonfeld had a meeting with an eligible young woman with a view to marriage. The couple did not marry, however. Schonfeld later married Judith Hertz, daughter of the renowned Chief Rabbi, Joseph Hertz.

With the threat of war looming, Sigi and his cousin, Victor went to Belgium in 1938. They both had visas to England through their cousin, Solomon Schonfeld. But while Victor went on to England, where his younger brother, Charles, was at school, Sigi returned to Budapest, not wishing to leave his mother and sister. At that time, Suzanne, although barely 16, had made a deep impression on a young man from a Jewish family in Holland, who was to revisit Budapest to pay court to her. But she was not yet engaged.

In August 1939, however, policemen came to the Sternberg home and asked for Sigi. He had a driving licence and this was registered with the police. Elizabeth, who opened the door, said Sigi was not at home. The policemen said they needed young men for 'voluntary work' and were rounding up all young men with driving licences. At that point, Elizabeth said she would let Sigi know when he came back. When the policemen had left, she told Suzanne to pack Sigi's case. 'He has to leave instantly for London', she said. Sigi did not agree. He would not leave on Friday afternoon and travel on the Sabbath. Suzanne then suggested that they go to the Chief Rabbi of Budapest and ask his permission. Sigi was sure the Chief Rabbi would not agree as he was extremely orthodox. When he heard the story, however, the Chief Rabbi told Sigi: 'When your mother tells you to go, you must go instantly. Run to the station with your packed case.' Sigi almost missed the train. He jumped on it when it was already moving and Suzanne waved him goodbye.

Sigi stayed on the train for about two hours, unsure that he was doing the right thing. How could he leave his mother in such a dangerous situation? At the next stop, he jumped out and took the train back to Budapest, arriving home as the Sabbath was under way. His mother was furious and after the Sabbath had ended, insisted that he leave immediately. The next day the police called for him again but Sigi was by then on his way to England. Days later the Second World War broke out.

Sigi arrived in England just before the outbreak. Still only 18 years old, he had just finished his matriculation. On arrival in London, he first stayed at a hotel in the East End and then, rather than reside with members of his family, he found lodgings in a small flat in Lordship Park, Stamford Hill.

At the time, members of the Schonfeld family were deeply involved in attempting to rescue Jews from Germany and Czechoslovakia who were in great danger, and lacked the time and energy to devote to the young cousins from Hungary. Charles was away at school in Shefford, Bedfordshire, but Victor might have felt somewhat slighted, before appreciating the importance of the work in which his cousins were engaged. Sigi affirms that the lack of a warm welcome from his family had not been upsetting for him because he understood that the rescue work was a serious priority.

This was characteristic of the 'stiff upper lip' tendency that was in some way native to him and which British mores would encourage to develop. However, his suppressed emotions were released in a number of letters he wrote at the time. These letters also revealed differing perspectives he entertained during the course of the war and its aftermath. One example is a letter written in 1942 in which he observed: 'The war's bound to end in a few months.' Another letter, written after VE Day, was notable for its absence of elation. In the letter he observed that everyone around him was 'going mad' but then stated: 'We've lost too much to be elated but Britain and Churchill have saved the world from Hitler.'

At the time of his arrival in England, then, his immediate family were deeply preoccupied in a worthy cause. However, a wish to distance themselves from new arrivals was characteristic of many British Jews at the time. Indeed, a large number of Jewish refugees were taken into non-Jewish homes. Sigi sees the attitude of British Jews of the time as 'denial', a refusal to acknowledge what was happening to their co-religionists in Europe and also 'fear', fear that the influx of new Jewish immigrants would endanger their standing and their livelihoods. He compares this propensity to the attitude of Jews in Germany towards Russian Jewish immigrants during the 1990s and to earlier resentment felt by established British Jews at the arrival of those fleeing Russia and Poland at the end of the nineteenth century and in the early decades of the twentieth century.

Since he owed his safe arrival in the country to his cousin, Solomon Schonfeld, Sigi felt obligated to help him in his various endeavours. Schonfeld and his family were active members of the ultra-orthodox Adath Yisroel community and Solomon himself had already set up the Jewish Secondary Schools movement. Sigi was made a governor of the school, later known as Hasmonean, in the early 1940s, as was William Frankel, a future editor of *The Jewish Chronicle*.

Sigi, who had begun to develop the negotiating skills he would use to such potent effect throughout his life, was, moreover, an invaluable aid to Schonfeld in his efforts to bring refugee children into Britain. It was Sigi who would accompany Schonfeld to the Home Office to put across Schonfeld's assertion that they would provide support for the children, once they were admitted. So great was their dedication to the task that one *Shabbat* the two of them walked the seven miles from Lordship Park to the Home Office and back, in order not to contravene the laws of travelling on the Sabbath.

Once the children had arrived, Sigi, together with Victor

and Charles, was kept busy ensuring that the children were entertained. It was when the children were later evacuated to the country that the cousins also left London and went to Brighton.

One condition of Sigi being admitted into England as a 'friendly enemy alien' was that he would not undertake any work, whether paid or unpaid. Volunteering to join the army was also out of the question. And further studies were not an option as he had no money. During the several months that he spent in Brighton, in order to support himself he would go to auctions, bid for goods and then put them up for sale again, usually for a profit. For example, one lot he bought by chance was equipment from a hospital and on another occasion fittings from a hotel. He had already developed a business sense from helping out in the family antique shop in Budapest and his shrewd bidding enabled him to make some money.

In 1941, after Sigi had returned to London, he was able to take advantage of the 'Essential Work Order' to get an unpaid government job in a metal firm. This was an opportunity that came his way and he duly seized it. Two years later, aged 22, he took over the company, in partnership with S.P. Lunzer, a Jewish businessman who brought some money in, and founded the 'Ingot Metal Company'. Sigi had taken an overdraft of £2,000 from Barclays Bank. When the bank manager, Mr Bodger, asked him for security, Sigi replied that he had no security but would pay him back. Mr Bodger trusted him and Sigi did pay back the loan.

The metal industry prospered greatly during the war years and played an important role in helping the war effort. In 1947, Sigi bought F.C. Larkinson, a loss-making scrap-metal company in Biggleswade in Bedfordshire. The Sternberg Group of Companies had come into being. At that time, F.C. Larkinson was only carrying out operations from the Biggleswade Star Works. Later, the Sternberg Group had ten premises and facilities at strategic points in the country. Another company Sigi bought and added to the Sternberg Group was Pinbrand, another scrap-metal company owned by Willy Pinkus. This he merged with a small company owned by Pinkus' son-in-law,

Siggy Reichenstein, leaving Reichenstein to run the joint company.

In a long memo to Sigi, Reichenstein recalled that his father-in-law always had a high regard for him and believed he would go far: 'He would have been delighted to have witnessed how right he was.' He, himself, was particularly touched by Sigi's help when Mr Pinkus died in 1954: 'We received the news late in the evening and wanted to get to Bournemouth as quickly as possible to be with my mother-in-law. That's when I first saw your very human side. You offered to drive us to Bournemouth, arriving in the early hours of the morning. Hanna and I will always remember this assistance, in our hour of need.'

Reichenstein was also very impressed with the manner in which Sigi conducted his business dealings:

> One of your special characteristics was that you were always able to get the very best out of people who worked for you. If something went wrong, your style was not to reproach but rather to offer good advice as to how to resolve the situation. Top traders behaved like prima donnas but you understood how to knead them into a group where all their strengths worked for the benefit of the organisation. You knew also when to delegate and give responsibility to those around you. You are a bit of a psychologist and find it easy to weigh people up – a useful trait in business. If you had a certain goal, you were always single-minded in your determination to bring your plan to fruition. In all, it was in so many respects an inspiration to have worked with you.

Reichenstein also recalls having been present with Sigi in negotiations with various foreign trading partners, including a meeting with a Nigerian minister who, a short while later, was assassinated. A particularly tricky venture concerned dealings with a Mediterranean country which was to provide monthly shipments of substantial quantities of metal against an irrevocable letter of credit. However, after an early shipment, it was discovered that the material contained detrimental impurities. On Sigi's advice, Reichenstein consulted two QCs as to the possibility of stopping the letter of credit but was told this would not be possible. A third QC said they had a 10 per cent chance of success. Sigi decided to take the risk of proceeding, despite the very slim likelihood of winning and the costs involved, and an injunction was, indeed, granted and the letter of credit stopped, subject to various conditions. Reichenstein recalls that, at the time, the ruling was quoted in law books as a precedent.

Another former employee of the Sternberg Group was David Reuben, now a Chief Executive of Reuben Brothers, together with his brother, Simon. The brothers built up their fortune during the 1970s and 1980s in metals and property and are well-known as businessmen and philanthropists. And in 1960, after his return from Ghana where he had served as Governor-General since 1957, the Earl of Listowel accepted a seat on the board of directors of the group, with the intention of using his experience and knowledge to promote Britain's export trade. Lord Listowel had served as Postmaster General, Secretary of State for India and Burma and Minister of State for Colonial Affairs in the Atlee government. Sigi was enthusiastic about his joining the board. 'His knowledge of economics and his services to the nation as Postmaster General and in other government offices give him great authority in his appreciation of export problems', he told a journalist from the *City Press*. By that time Sigi was a fellow of the Royal Economic Society and a corporate member of the Institute of Export.

Fred Ehrlich, who worked for Sigi in the metal business for many years, was impressed with Sigi's ways of pursuing his business activities. 'His genius was that he managed to persuade five or six individual non-ferrous metal merchants to work together.' Previously the merchants had worked individually, doing business in England and exporting some of their wares. Sigi convinced them that if they worked together, he would set up an office and all the exports could be handled from that office, saving money on the one hand and leaving the merchants free to pursue other avenues. Ehrlich remembers that people used to queue up outside Sigi's office, wanting to work for him. 'He has this incredible personality; everybody liked him.' Ehrlich also believes that Sigi had 'this incredible ability to look years ahead'. In the same way that the former Prince Louis of Battenberg became Louis Mountbatten – and was later given the title Earl Mountbatten of Burma, following his sojourn in India as the last Viceroy – Sigi changed the company's name from Sternberg to Mountstar, the English translation of the German 'Sternberg'. This foresight was also evident many years later when, after years of being a prominent activist in the field of Christian-Jewish relations, Sigi understood, well before it was generally accepted, that it was essential that Muslims should be included in interfaith dialogue. Moreover, Ehrlich recalls, when Sigi sold Mountstar, it was the beginning of the inflationary period and he had the ability to go into the property business at the best time.

On 1 January 1963, Sigi was appointed chairman of V. Kaye and Company, ring dealing members of the London Metal Exchange. Mountstar continued under his management until 1965, when he sold the concern to the Amalgamated Metal Corporation. While he retained shares in the new venture and was invited to remain on the board, he relinquished control and the new owners took over the operation. During the 1960s, he was voted onto the council of the Metal Traders Association and was later elected as president. He was also appointed by the Labour government of the time onto the Committee for Metal Recovery, founded in recognition of the importance of secondary metal. Sigi's assiduous activity in this sphere included many visits to prisons to involve prisoners in this vital work. On another level, his interest in metals led him to work with the Institute of Archaeology in the context of references to metal in the Bible. And his commitment to charitable work led him to set up the first metal traders' branch of the United Jewish Appeal (UJA), following the example of businessmen in every trade who collected money for the UJA.

While Sigi continued to see his cousins, Victor and Charles, there was less common ground between them. As Sigi recalls: 'My ways were not their ways. I was more of a businessman. I had a more luxurious lifestyle than they had. I had a bigger earning power. I had a flat.' He adds that although his cousins were only able to afford a room, 'they didn't have any sort of problem with women. They were more restrained.'

As for Sigi himself, it is not hard to imagine that he had become a most eligible young man, given his looks and charm and, not least, his success in business. His desirability was accentuated, moreover, by the scarcity of young men during the war years. Many families in Stamford Hill would try to interest him in their daughters and offer a substantial dowry, but he was not interested.

While Hungary had escaped some of the devastation of the war owing to its cooperation with the Axis powers, it was invaded by Germany in 1944 after Hitler had found out about secret peace negotiations that the Hungarian government was conducting with the United States. At that point, most Hungarian Jews were rounded up and deported to concentration camps where over 400,000 lost their lives. One of the rare occasions Sigi expressed considerable emotion during his recollections of his earlier life was in recounting the fate of Hungary's Jews at a time when the world was already aware of the systematic extermination of European Jewry being carried out by the Nazis. Indeed, a striking editorial in the Vatican newspaper, *L'Osservatore Romano*, in August 2009, accused the British and American governments of having detailed knowledge of Hitler's extermination plans and failing to do anything to halt them. Sigi, himself, became aware of the slaughter to some extent in 1942, being present as a spectator in the gallery in parliament when Anthony Eden read a statement and the house rose in silent tribute to those who had perished in Europe that year. However, as he acknowledges today, the full scale of the atrocities was not known till after the war.

While some members of his extended family were victims of the Holocaust, others managed to escape to Palestine. Fortunately, his immediate family was safe. Suzanne had married her admirer, Heinz Perlman, late in 1939, and the couple were now living in Curaçao together with their baby, Robert, the eldest of three sons. Elizabeth had obtained Christian papers through an important business contact in Sweden of her son-in-law, Heinz Perlman, and managed also to ensure the safety of her elderly mother. As Suzanne recounts in her memoir, her mother had a heroic war record, sheltering seventeen Jews in her home and disguising herself as a peasant woman in order to shop for food for the household.

It was later, when many of her lodgers had been rounded up and taken to the Jewish ghetto that Elizabeth went to find her mother, who was in hiding in the country. By now, the Christian papers she had obtained were no longer effective and she was assigned a place on the fifth floor of a 'Jewish House'. To carry her heavy and somewhat disabled mother up to the fifth floor and down to the shelters when there were air raids was, in Suzanne's words, 'saintly work'. When the situation became even more dangerous, she managed to prevail upon a gentile friend of hers to shelter her and her mother.

At a memorial ceremony in London in January 1994, marking the fiftieth anniversary of the deportation of Hungarian Jews, Sigi paid tribute to Catholics who had helped rescue Jews in Hungary during the war. He singled out Angelo Roncalli, at that time the Papal Representative in Turkey, who was later to become Pope John XXIII. And in November of the same year, the Hungarian Roman Catholic Bishops' Conference issued a fiftieth anniversary statement, confessing that 'the perpetrators of this mindless evil are not the only ones responsible. Faithful members of our congregations did not raise their voices against the humiliations, deportations and slaughter of their Jewish fellow citizens due to fear, cowardice or connivance', and expressing gratitude 'to those who, by risking their lives, saved their fellow human beings in those inhuman days'. The following year, Arpad Goncz, the President of Hungary, received the International Council of Christians and Jews Interfaith Gold Medallion at an international colloquium in Budapest devoted to the subject: Speaking of God Today.

Once the war had ended, Sigi was determined to return to Hungary to find his mother. As he had not yet been naturalized as a British citizen, he had no passport, only a laissez-passer. There was no way at that time that he could legally enter Hungary so he was obliged to travel as far as the border between Czechoslovakia and Hungary at Komarno, leave his laissez-passer there and get himself smuggled into Hungary, as it was not possible at the time to get a visa. He found much of the country destroyed but managed to travel to Budapest and look for his mother.

Elizabeth had lost her livelihood and her business but refused to leave for England. She felt her mother was too old and frail to make the journey and start again in a strange environment. However, she found a very kind distant relative to look after her mother and Suzanne and her husband regularly sent cheques for their maintenance and food parcels from Curaçao. Suzanne was in constant correspondence with her grandmother. As soon as Suzanne and her husband, Heinz, arrived in Curaçao, they helped refugees and before long Suzanne had established a branch of WIZO there, teaching Hebrew songs to a Dutch Protestant soprano and an Afro-Carribean Catholic pianist from a score she had brought from Hungary and splitting the proceeds of the funds received between the welfare of native children and charities involved with Israel, a novel idea later adoped all over South America. Suzanne recalls that the branch of WIZO in Curaçao was proportionately and continuously the highest contributor to Israel in Central America and when she finally reached Palestine, later to become Israel, she was given a rousing reception, with her brother-in-law, Pinchas Rosen, co-signatory of Israel's Declaration of Independence and Israel's first Minister of Justice, in attendance.

Elizabeth eventually left Hungary, joining her son in England for a short time, and then went to stay with Suzanne and Heinz in Curaçao, where she remained for fifteen years. She visited England only three times during that period, for short visits, and stayed for weekends with her son who wanted to see her after not having seen her for a long time. For the rest of her visit she rented a flat in Hendon.

Sigi became a British citizen in 1947, two years after the post-war general election in which he was ineligible to vote. As an admirer of Churchill, the hero of the war, he was surprised that he was not re-elected. As he recalls, 'Of course I would have voted for Churchill. He was a hero and it surprised me about the

British character that they could be so nice to the man and then throw him out of office. It was also very surprising to me when Churchill took Atlee with him to the Potsdam conference.'

His attitude towards Atlee's government, however, was very positive and he remembers meeting James Chuter Ede, the Home Secretary, who, he says, 'was nice to the Jews'. His cousin, Solomon Schonfeld, was now busy trying to get Displaced Persons admitted to Britain and, as before, Sigi was actively helping him. Indeed, Sigi continues to remember his cousin with great admiration, years after his death, and took it upon himself to defend his memory after a critic reviewing a biography of Schonfeld wrote disparagingly of him. In a letter published on 13 November 2009 in *The Jewish Chronicle*, Sigi wrote:

> The review seriously misplaces Schonfeld's place in Anglo-Jewry. He was the most effective leader in the community at a time when leadership and determination were essential. To describe this as 'bullying' or 'bombast' suggests that your reviewer regrets the saving of hundreds, perhaps thousands of lives in the Holocaust or from suffering under Communism, the building of Jewish schools at a time when few recognised the use of such things and the establishment of dozens of synagogues.

One particular function Sigi recalls was a reception Schonfeld had organized in Chuter Ede's honour at which Atlee was present. Indeed, Sigi was photographed with the Prime Minister. It was a foretaste of the dealings with the great and the good which would figure so prominently throughout his life.

2 Beatrice Ruth Schiff

At the time of Rosh Hashanah in 1949, Sigi married Beatrice Ruth Schiff, the middle daughter of a highly respectable orthodox Jewish family from Stamford Hill. They had met the previous Passover at the Winter's Boarding House in Hampstead where Ruth's recently widowed mother was spending the festival with her two younger daughters. At that time, Winter's was the home of Mrs Elizabeth Sternberg and, not surprisingly, her son joined her there for the Seder.

Whether the meeting was pure chance, or set up, as Sigi suspected, the couple fell 'head over heels in love with each other' as Ruth's sister, Zena Clayton, observed: 'It was very dramatic. The attraction was very strong.'

With her lovely face, pretty brownish hair, well-proportioned figure and tremendous sense of humour, Ruth was clearly very popular and had had the pick of numerous men friends. She had, in fact, by this time had at least twelve proposals of marriage. In this delightful young woman, Sigi had found 'everything I wanted. She was a beautiful woman. She came from a good family. Her father had been a very well-respected man.' In addition to her beauty, Ruth had studied French and German at university and had great refinement. As Zena saw it, 'Ruth was this beautiful English rose with an English education and English background. But it was an orthodox background, a background that was totally acceptable to his family.'

For the young Hungarian émigré who had spent the war years as a 'friendly enemy alien', unable, at first, to take a job, ineligible to join the army, unable to become a director of the company he was building up, the cachet of Englishness was, understandably, alluring. In contrast, the glamour of Sigi's exotic background obviously appealed to Ruth. As their daughter,

Frances Blane, put it: 'My father was a novelty, he was different.'
His lack of formal education at university or in the professions
appeared to be no disadvantage. 'There were doctors and
lawyers on offer', Zena recalled, 'but she didn't choose them'.

On the surface, it seemed an ideal match. Unlike many
British Jews who had remained remote from the sufferings of
their co-religionists in Nazi Europe, the Schiffs had been closely
involved and desperate to help. Mr Schiff had had sisters in
Antwerp and the family numbered among their friends 'many
people who'd come by difficult and awful ways out of Europe,
leaving horrors behind'. At the time of her marriage, Ruth was
working in an organization that was to become the World
Jewish Congress, using her linguistic skills to translate restitu-
tion papers.

While Sigi's experience as a refugee might have won him
sympathy, his 'fine background' also stood in his favour. Zena
recalls him as 'very charming, very attractive, very bright, just as
she was, and beautifully behaved and well-mannered'. During
the six-month courtship – 'much too quick' in Frances' opinion
– Ruth appeared to have given the matter a great deal of
thought, taking rational as well as emotional considerations into
account. The emotional pull was obviously very strong: 'She fell
in love with my father. He was handsome, gorgeous', is how
Frances sees it. But another factor affecting Ruth's judgement
may well have been her father's sudden death, which had come
as a dreadful blow. Sigi, at 27, was a young metal merchant and
had established the Sternberg group of companies. Later, with
others, he also established the Israeli section of the metal trade
which was instrumental in raising funds for Israel. He was
clearly a very capable young man and offered the prospect of
solidity and security.

While Ruth may have felt she had found someone she could
lean on, her vulnerability in her loss was likely to have charmed
Sigi, who often admits to 'a penchant for widows'. Having lost
his own father at a young age and marked indelibly by the
memory of his grief-stricken, distraught mother, he was sensitive to bereavement. Zena well remembers how understanding
he was at their father's tombstone-setting ceremony. 'He was

immensely supportive and caring and protective, demonstratively so.'

The Schiffs were a very close family, 'the sort of family that walks to *shul* holding hands', as Zena put it. Mr Schiff had evidently been a warm and loving father, doted on by his three daughters; his wife, a highly artistic woman, might have harboured aspirations to become one of the Bloomsbury Set but remained 'very much a mother at home', focusing her energies on her family and communal activities. Frances saw her mother's family as 'God fearing, idealistic people who weren't concerned with public accolades'.

Ruth had flourished within the safe space provided by the family. She was worshipped by Zena, her junior by seven years, who remembers 'hurtling up the road and throwing myself upon her' when her sister returned from school. Ruth would sing for Zena and invent 'the most wonderful children's stories', a foretaste of the literary talent she was later to demonstrate. She was successful academically, winning a State Scholarship to university. Since the Schiffs, like other residents of Stamford Hill, were evacuated to Cambridge during the war, it was in Cambridge that Ruth pursued her higher education. She was an undergraduate at Bedford College, one of the colleges of the University of London that had also been evacuated to Cambridge. The State Scholarship was a very rare bursary that covered all her fees and expenses. Only about twenty were awarded each year, and very few went to women, which makes the achievement of the graduate of the local girls' grammar school in Stamford Hill all the more impressive.

Up to the time of her marriage, then, Ruth had always lived at home, a 'very caring, strong, supportive, loving sister and daughter'. As far as Zena was concerned, she was a perfectly robust young woman, well-equipped for the brilliant, beautiful marriage that lay ahead of her.

Sigi and Ruth's wedding took place at the Egerton Road United Synagogue in Stamford Hill to which the Schiff family belonged. Dayan Abramski, the head of the London Beth Din officiated. Through his marriage, Sigi was entering the highest ranks of Anglo-Jewish orthodoxy.

After the honeymoon, the couple lived in Sigi's flat in West Hampstead. Before long, however, they moved to Hendon where Sigi purchased a large house in Goodyers Gardens, an exclusive cul-de-sac off Brent Street. The successful young entrepreneur paid £10,000 for the property, a very substantial sum of money.

For the unworldly Ruth, raised in the more modest surroundings of Filey Avenue in Stamford Hill, the transition to Goodyers Gardens was not easy. A kind, sensitive, dreamy girl, interested in the life of the mind, she lacked the toughness and the down-to-earth qualities which would have helped her fulfil the role of chatelaine of a palatial residence complete with staff at the age of 27. If she found things stressful, however, she did not communicate this. From Zena's perspective, her sister had gone into her married life with apparent happiness and success.

Sigi, of course, had never known domestic intimacy and was clearly unfamiliar with what his new bride might expect of married life, what constituted a 'proper marriage', as Frances put it. Like any young woman reared in a loving, sheltered family environment, Ruth was looking for emotional closeness, the ability to share thoughts and feelings as well as more practical, everyday concerns. Where Zena had found her strong and supportive, Sigi found her dependent, more dependent than anyone he had known. He, who had made a point since his early childhood of never being dependent, of relying on his wits to get by, found it very difficult to cope with a characteristic to which he was unable to relate.

In contrast, whenever anything of a practical nature was demanded, Sigi was right there, eager to help. He was a stalwart, supportive son-in-law and liquidated his late father-in-law's business. Zena, who has no brothers, saw him more as a brother than a brother-in-law, someone who was always there for her.

As a good son, it was natural for Sigi to ask his mother, who had returned from visiting his sister in Curaçao and had not yet put down roots in the new country, to share his spacious home whenever she was in England. Elizabeth Sternberg was very likely to have felt possessive of her only son, a sentiment fuelled by the belief that he and his bride were ill-suited. A strong, capable woman, Elizabeth was less than impressed by her new daughter-in-law. Later, Elizabeth bought her own flat in Hendon and visited Sigi and his family at weekends and festivals.

George Perlman, Sigi's nephew, recalls his grandmother as a 'formidable force, very intelligent, very dogmatic and very powerful in her opinions'. The latter trait is confirmed by Sigi, who speaks of his mother as having strong likes and dislikes. 'She formed opinions about people. Certain people she didn't like and they couldn't understand why she didn't like them.'

The young couple maintained an observant home and lifestyle. This was irksome for Sigi, who had lapsed in his religious observance during his bachelor years. 'I made up my own rules. Whatever suited me I did. I was quite willing to drive a car on a Saturday.' The new regime did not suit him. 'It didn't feel very good at all because it was a restriction which limited my life. The orthodoxy was very oppressive.' While he sensed that Ruth was carrying on what she had seen at home rather than experiencing the need to be orthodox for herself, he did not voice his objections in order not to upset her.

The move to Hendon brought him once again within walking distance of the Adath Yisroel Synagogue of his cousin, Rabbi Solomon Schonfeld. It was to please him that Sigi had continued to attend services at the Adath. Ruth, however, had other ideas. She had been raised in the United Synagogue and felt it would be preferable for Sigi to join the local synagogue in Raleigh Close where the congregation was more anglicised. As Sigi says: 'It didn't interfere with me. It wasn't an important part of my life.' The section of the service that did interest him was the weekly *Sedra*, the portion read from the Torah. While this was being chanted, he would read the commentary by Rashi in his *Chumash*. This, at least, was some residue of the religious education he had received during his childhood.

The Sternbergs kept themselves to themselves at home. While many of their neighbours in Goodyers Gardens formed a small community of their own, frequently visiting each other's homes, Sigi and Ruth were seen as somewhat aloof. Sigi was preoccupied with developing and expanding his business, no mean task in the cut-throat climate of the metal trade. He maintained some involvement in Zionist affairs but had little time or energy for other communal pursuits or casual social niceties. Ruth, a very private person with a keen interest in literature and philosophy, had little in common with the neighbours. Some may have been given the impression that as a Schiff she felt herself superior to them. As a former neighbour explained, the Schiffs were seen as an 'aristocratic Jewish family'.

Although Sigi could not share his wife's intellectual pursuits, they certainly impressed him. 'This was an endearing factor from my point of view. It was something very desirable for me. I wasn't an intellectual. My schooling finished when I was 18. But I was always very interested to learn and improve myself.' He was particularly impressed by her writing. 'She wrote articles. She showed me an article she had written in *Lilliput*. I was very impressed.'

The divergence in Sigi's and Ruth's interests need not have been a source of their difficulties, although many have asserted that this was the case. George Perlman is one who takes a different perspective. 'There are different levels of compatibility. The best is when people have different features that they can combine together to strengthen both and I think that that's what he saw in her when he married her, instinctively.'

That Sigi and Ruth loved each other very much is undisputed. Surely, then, a complementarity of attributes could have been achieved? Sigi has no hesitation in saying that 'there was a lot of love', something Zena Clayton equally unhesitatingly confirms; love, in fact, while binding them together may also have blinded them. As Sigi explained: 'If you fall in love, then you know what love is. You don't put everything under a microscope.' From a similar perspective, Frances sees her parents' love for each other as 'probably more of a passion'. Love, of course, needs time and space to grow stronger and more resilient. And time and space to develop their relationship was something Sigi and Ruth's marriage lacked. One attempt to remedy this was the couple's habit of taking a holiday alone together every year even after their children were born. These were times when

Ruth was able to blossom in the radiance of her husband's exclusive love and attention.

At home, Sigi was ever busier and more pressurized, striving to create a business empire and make the fortune which would ensure continuing security and prosperity for his family. Equally strong, though he may have been unaware of this, was the motivation to achieve great things and make a name for himself in his country of adoption.

Domestic life, too, was somewhat crowded. Ruth had to contend not only with the frequent presence at weekends of her indomitable mother-in-law but also, at school half-terms, with Sigi's young nephews who had come from Curaçao to receive a Jewish education in England. Robert Perlman, the eldest of Suzy's three sons, arrived at the age of 8 as a boarder at Carmel College, the recently established Jewish public school, founded by Rabbi Kopul Rosen. He was followed, a few years later, by his brother, Louis. George, the youngest, did not come to Carmel till he was 12, in 1963. Rabbi Rosen's youngest son, David, became one of the leading rabbis with whom Sigi later worked in fostering relations between Christians and Jews, and was awarded a CBE in 2010.

It was characteristic of Sigi to 'want to help as best I can'. Over the years, he formed a particularly deep relationship with his nephew, Robert, encouraging him at school and later at Cambridge University where he became President of the Union. Robert's success as a public speaker gave his uncle a special satisfaction since this was a sphere in which he, himself, failed to excel.

While Ruth had plenty of assistance to help cope with the busy household, it was her responsibility to organize and supervise the domestic arrangements, something that did not come easily to her. As Sigi acknowledges, 'it was difficult. It was not conducive to someone who was fragile.' The proximity of members of his close family placed demands of a different kind on Sigi and, consequently, on the marriage.

The birth of Michael in 1951 and of Frances three years later brought the couple great happiness. To the outside world, the Sternbergs seemed to have everything. Zena Clayton, for one, had no reason to believe her sister was anything but happy and fulfilled: 'As far as I could see and as far as I knew and as far as she disclosed she was happily married to a very nice guy, a very fine guy, who had a very successful life, was quite ambitious and achieving, all of which is totally acceptable, two gorgeous children, a very nice home and everything seemed to be going for her.'

A similar impression was conveyed by Suzanne Perlman, Sigi's sister, who met her sister-in-law for the first time on a visit to England when Frances was about one and a half. 'I was enchanted by Ruth, absolutely enchanted. She was the epitome of a very well brought up, very intelligent English-Jewish woman and very beautiful. She had such a radiance and such a noble appearance. She looked quite astounding.' The sisters-in-law hit it off immediately. 'We liked each other. She liked very much to discuss with me literature and books we had both read and opinions about plays and about Ibsen and Kierkegaard and various philosophers.' Suzanne was taken by Ruth's ability to articulate her thoughts, a talent which had stood her in good stead when she lectured, during her university years, to the Jewish Society in Cambridge on Zionism and other subjects. She, too, was under the impression that Ruth was perfectly contented. 'She seemed so easy and well-adjusted. She seemed to be very happy and she was very well married and looked after.'

In addition to her intellectual pursuits, Ruth was a loving, caring mother, adored by both children. As Michael recalls: 'My mother was tremendously dedicated to us and spent an awful lot of time looking after us and taking us to various orthodontists and doctors and all sorts of things.' The children also had a devoted nanny. Sigi, of course, was obliged to ration the time he could spend with his family. Michael remembers that

> he was working terribly hard. We would see him in the morning at breakfast, we would see him sometimes in the evening – he'd come back late. We'd see him on Friday evening when there was a traditional family meal, we'd see him obviously on Shabbat morning when we went to synagogue together as a family – my mother would come

later. On Saturday afternoons he would rest, on Saturday evenings he would go out with my mother. On Sunday mornings sometimes we would see him. On Sunday afternoons we would see him.

Within this somewhat regimented timetable, reminiscent of his boyhood days in Budapest when time spent with his parents was all too rare, Sigi found it hard not to repeat the patterns he had absorbed in his formative years and demanded the best from his children. As far as he was concerned, 'it wasn't strictness, just common sense'. The long walks across the bridges linking Pest to Buda were resurrected on the English coastline. 'I made the children walk. We were staying at Birchington, near Margate. To walk to synagogue was an hour and a half, there and back. They were about 10 or 11. I gave them a sweet to make them walk. It was very good, good for them.' Frances' recollections were decidedly less rosy:

> 'Had nice times with mummy, never had much fun with my father', that's what I always think. We were never allowed a biscuit or a cake because they were bad for your health. We couldn't drink with our meals and whenever we went to a restaurant, we always had to eat whatever was fastest. These were my father's conditions. He was really into being Spartan. We had to do exercise, there were long seaside walks and he'd say 'The children have been very good, they didn't ask for an ice-cream'. It was really miserable.

Significantly, however, Sigi was able to be more demonstrative towards his children than his parents had been towards him, as Michael reveals: 'I can remember as a very small child he would have a lot of pleasure in picking us up and throwing us up in the air and dancing around with myself and Frances. And whenever I felt sick the only person who would calm me down would be my father.'

Clearly, Sigi took his responsibilities to his family seriously and in the practical sphere, the sphere he understood and could relate to, he was assiduous in attending to their needs. Suzy Perlman has vivid memories of finding her brother immersed in domesticity when she arrived at his home in Goodyers Gardens:

> Ruth and the children were at the seaside. I arrived on Thursday and was going down with Sigi to the seaside for Shabbat. And I was amazed how caring he was. He made a long list of what he had to take, various household items, sheets and things for the children and food and some pots and pans. I arrived late at night and was amazed to find him rambling all around the house to find each item, to prepare each item, and then early in the morning, it must have been five-thirty, he got up to make sure he had every-thing together that Ruth needed. I thought for a young man, for a young husband, for a businessman to do that was quite extraordinary. It wasn't in his nature because he wasn't very orderly himself. I told him, 'Sigi, the way you are looking after everything, it seems you would like to bring down the stars for your wife.' I felt it was an extraor-dinary proof of love and care.

Such practical gestures, maybe, were not enough. Recalling that the whole family were equally vulnerable in their bereave-ment after the death of their father, Zena Clayton believes that 'given the right setting, one can grow up within it'. While Zena was under the impression that her sister was able, 'to a great extent', to make the transition to adulthood: 'She became a housewife and mother and worked very hard and successfully at it; she continued with things of her own mind as well', it is unlikely that the Sternberg ménage provided the nurturing environment that would have facilitated Ruth's development.

In contrast to her parents' home where expressions of affec-tion and the life of the mind were held at a premium, Goodyers Gardens, her marital home, might often have seemed an emotional and intellectual desert. Sigi makes no secret of the fact that emotions are something he can't cope with, not surprising in light of his own childhood experience. As Frances pointed out: 'My mother needed to be looked after and I think that my father was not able to do it probably because nobody had looked after him.' The emphasis on getting on with the task at hand rather than wallowing in feelings would have been reinforced by the presence of Sigi's mother. Suzanne Perlman recalls that in their childhood home, 'somehow it was not acceptable to show much affection as such. I think this must have come from my mother's side. She was a very practical person, very clever and very helpful during the war, but she didn't have the talent for being a mother.'

While Ruth found joy and comfort in her children, she was beginning to experience a degree of isolation in Goodyers Gardens that was only to increase. Sadly, she never sought to establish an independent niche for herself in which she could share her many gifts, such as establishing a literary salon at her beautiful home. It would seem that Ruth was seeking the reassuring love and closeness she had experienced in her parental home, an idyll of family life that had been shattered by her father's death. While the love she had received had enriched her and endowed her with a deep capacity for loving – Frances describes her mother as unwavering in her love, even in her darkest moments – it may, to some extent, have been over-protective and reduced her capacity for resilience. Sigi, in contrast, raised in the shadow of the Basilica of St Stephen and left from his earliest years in the care of a series of governesses, had imbibed resilience with the air he breathed. Childhood, for him, was a litany of incessant activity, duty and discipline: study Talmud, walk, study Gemara, walk, be good to Suzy, walk, wake up early, say *Kaddish*, help the refugees, help mother.

With inner worlds that were so divergent, a clash of temperaments was, perhaps, inevitable. Seeing his wife in what he might have thought to be a state of seemingly self-indulgent distress would prompt Sigi to recall the sterner virtues of his upbringing. 'I was always brought up that you don't show your emotions. That's what I like so much about the English people; they take things as they are. I find emotion – people crying, a lot of wailing – I find it disturbing.' Rather than bring the couple closer, Ruth's emotional SOS would activate her husband's underlying irritation.

Sigi admits readily that he 'was always looking at pretty girls', although he insists that he was never unfaithful during his marriage. This was for reasons of pragmatism as well as principle.

> It doesn't help if you have another woman, that's not happiness. If you don't get on with one woman, the answer is not to have another, then you have a further problem. If you start with a single woman, sooner or later they want to get married; if you start with a married woman it's even worse because then you have the husband coming after you. It's a messy situation. In my life I try to avoid difficulties, try to use common sense. I'm not passionate enough.

Flirtations, however, were something else. Sigi was a young, dynamic entrepreneur and it is not surprising if female members of his office staff made a play for him, if only on a light-hearted level. Christmas parties were one instance. 'I found it very strange indeed. The mistletoe, we had to kiss under the mistletoe. Ruth didn't like it at all. Probably she was jealous. I couldn't understand it because I wouldn't have done anything.' He maintains that, in principle, one should never have any relationship with an employee. 'That's how people get into trouble.'

During these social encounters, Sigi was not always able to detect his wife's reaction. 'If I'd seen it upset her, I would never have wanted to upset her. If I upset her, she would cry. It was no good for me.' He was perfectly relaxed, in contrast, when his beautiful wife excited the admiration of other men. On one occasion, Sigi was travelling on business with another woman in his car and Ruth was able to convey her anxiety. 'She said she didn't want it, she felt insecure. Not in so many words, but she made me understand.' He seemed unperturbed by his wife's fears. 'I expect all women are the same. Husbands are their possessions.'

Brushing aside matters of a personal nature that appear complicated or troublesome is characteristic of Sigi who recognizes this tendency, which could be called 'denial', as a weakness. 'I want to keep things simple. To walk away from trouble. I think that's probably a weakness in me. I don't deal with situations immediately, I let them slide and hope that things will mend themselves. Sometimes they do and sometimes they don't.' Clearly, the difficulties in Sigi and Ruth's relationship were not going to 'mend themselves' by being ignored. Sigi could understand that Ruth was a 'very deep person' and respect this but, as he says readily: 'I couldn't cope with it.'

One area of Sigi and Ruth's married life that should have remained free of tension was the material sphere. 'After we were married, she never had any financial problems. People quarrel over money and there is bitterness – it was never like that at all. Whatever she wanted she could have, married or not married. Ruth never needed anything.'

Sigi's mother is known to have commented to her daughter Suzanne, if not others, that had Ruth found herself in a marriage with fewer material trappings, it would have been better for her. Certainly Ruth grew to enjoy luxury and was a discerning purchaser. There is a story of her spending hours choosing a carpet from Sigi's cousin, Charles Sternberg, and driving him to distraction. Frances, her daughter, sees her as a 'bon viveur. She loved eating – she wasn't fat but she liked nice things – she liked clothes, she liked jewellery, she liked luxury basically.'

As in many marriages, Sigi's and Ruth's difficulties were, for the most part, undetected outside the privacy of their home. Colleagues and acquaintances of Sigi's have suggested that Ruth may have seemed 'erratic', 'highly strung', 'nervy' or 'moody' but the image of a successful, or at least satisfactory, union prevailed. One instance when the Sternbergs' domestic arrangements were on show and passed with flying colours was the Shabbat in 1959 that Chief Rabbi Israel Brodie and his wife spent at Goodyers Gardens. It was Ruth who organized all the necessary preparations for the visit. The spiritual head of the United Synagogue was visiting the Adath Ysroel Synagogue and Sigi and Ruth were chosen as his hosts.

Why the Sternbergs? After all, they were a relatively young couple and, according to contemporaries in Hendon, there were members of the Adath with equally grand houses. Sigi asserts that it was 'because we were members of the United Synagogue, we were prominent people, we were well-known people'. Maybe, but there were other members of the Raleigh Close congregation with links to the Adath. It is true that Sigi's connection to the United Synagogue went back to the days of the previous Chief Rabbi, Dr Hertz, whose daughter had married his cousin, Solomon Schonfeld. But it is not unreasonable to speculate that the Schiff association was a factor. In fact Brodie's inauguration as Chief Rabbi had taken place in Egerton Road Synagogue shortly before Mr Schiff's death, when he was on the rabbinical committee and sitting in the wardens' box. Zena Clayton attributes part of Sigi's progress and achievement in communal life to her sister. 'Anglo-Jewry was a new world to Sigi and Ruth was one of the keys to it.' Whatever her difficulties, Ruth rose to the occasion, undoubtedly radiating the charm and intelligence that had enchanted her sister-in-law.

Sadly, such occurrences were becoming increasingly rare. Sigi and Ruth's holiday in Israel in the summer of 1961 was the last holiday they took together. As Michael Sternberg recalls, within ten years his parents' marriage

> had turned into something which neither of them had contemplated. The marriage was in difficulties. Not that my father had anyone else or my mother had anyone else. They were just two completely different people leading separate lives. My mother was increasingly concerned about her own health, she knew she wasn't right, and she was unhappy and my father was unhappy and I think that neither of them was giving each other what they needed and there was a lot of tension between them and a lot of unhappiness.

Not surprisingly, neither Michael nor Frances were easy children and their schoolwork and general progress showed signs of suffering from the strain.

Undoubtedly, as Michael recognizes, Sigi's obligations to provide a base for his nephews as well as moral support and a place for his mother to stay when she wasn't in Curaçao, added to the burdens he faced within his own family; certainly 'he found shouldering that responsibility extremely hard'. Michael is convinced, nonetheless, that even without these additional factors his parents' marriage would, sooner or later, have come to an end.

George Perlman, who came to England late in 1963 when the marriage was foundering, remembers a Friday night dinner with the Sternbergs. 'It was quite formal. Sigi was sitting at the head of the table and Ruth at the other end. I remember feeling there was a coolness, a very structured environment.' The tension in the household was not improved when, on another occasion, George produced some fireworks he had brought from Curaçao for his cousin, Michael, lit one and threw it out of the window. 'Sigi was downstairs', George recalls, 'and he went absolutely spare.' Ruth, the 12-year-old boy observed, 'was a bit like a ship lost. The anchor was already beginning to drag.'

That same year, Sigi's attentions were needed in yet another quarter. His cousin, Victor Sternberg, had died suddenly, aged 43, after attending synagogue with his brother, Charles. Victor, who had been ill, walked to the synagogue with his daughter, Ruth, but then collapsed and died at his brother's home. Victor and Charles had been partners in a carpet/antique carpet business. Sigi was very close to both brothers and when Victor's widow, Hazel, sought his advice about her husband's business affairs, he was ready to help. Hazel, left with two small children, Ruth and David, would naturally have excited Sigi's compassion. A strong, practical young woman, she was very different from his highly-strung wife. It was hardly surprising if he was impressed by the courage and resilience of the young widow. Thrown together by tragedy, a deep sympathy developed between them.

The following year, when their son Michael reached the age of his bar mitzvah, should have been a time of celebration for Sigi and Ruth. Certainly the ceremony went ahead and, on the surface, everything seemed in order. Sigi's cousin, Miriam Ben-David, who was visiting from Israel, remembers Sigi and Ruth together and Ruth very elegant in grey. By now, however, Sigi could go on no longer. Despite the fact that he still loved his wife, their fundamental incompatibility was too great. As someone, who, as Frances has pointed out, had had no nurturing, it was impossible for him to nurture someone who desperately needed such attention. For Sigi, indeed, to make a mark in the world and achieve recognition was a profound aspiration. And, as Michael, himself, put it: 'I think he came to the conclusion that he just would not be able to function at all if he stayed with my mother. I'm sure he stuck it out as long as he could. So then he went. It was a tragedy for her.' Frances is equally succinct: 'After the bar mitzvah he left. And then my mother just got ill and got worse and then she was fed with drugs.'

Sadly, Ruth's many cultural and intellectual interests were unable to afford her much comfort. As her sister, Zena, sees it, 'The breaking-up of the marriage dented her self-confidence and her self-esteem to the extent that she wasn't able to produce and present.'

What seems particularly tragic about the illness that racked Ruth Sternberg during the thirty years that followed the breakdown of her marriage is that it could have been avoided. Sigi himself believes that Ruth would have been all right with a different husband. Frances is more specific: 'She needed to be with somebody who was kind, somebody who wasn't that interested in being so much in public life. She should have been married to somebody who would have looked after her, not been out making their way, making millions.'

Sigi had hoped that Ruth would remarry. She was still a very attractive woman and handsomely provided for. Whether or not there were candidates in the offing, Ruth had no eyes for them. Devastated by her husband's departure, she became, as Michael saw it, 'less and less able to cope. She was in love with my father and stayed in love with him till the day she died. She was a one man woman and that was it. That was her life and when it didn't work anymore, then as far as she was concerned there wasn't very much point to her life except she would do her best to see that Frances and I could have the best that was available.'

The best option for Michael was to join his cousin, George Perlman, as a boarder at Carmel College. Ruth, in her son's eyes, was a true 'heroine' in letting him go. But when it came to Frances, Ruth put her foot down. In the face of family pressure, she refused to have her daughter sent to boarding school. Frances went to Henrietta Barnett School in Hampstead Garden Suburb but was expelled at the age of 12 for swearing. There followed a long succession of tutorial colleges. It was an extremely difficult time for both mother and daughter. George Perlman, who was quite close to Frances, believes that 'she felt abandoned. What had been done to Sigi as a child, he did to his children. His kids felt they didn't get any emotional support. It was hard for him to give them.'

Frances, more than anyone, had the pain of witnessing at close quarters the deterioration of the mother she loved. 'She was really what you would call a good person. She couldn't say no, she was kind, she was weak in some ways, she'd rather hurt herself than hurt other people, which was probably part of her illness.' Yet instead of receiving the marital counselling or psychotherapy that may have helped and guided her, Ruth was, as her daughter sees it, 'the victim of psychiatric care. She actually had the wrong doctors. They just dished out barbiturates. The drugs made her worse.' The tragedy is compounded by the fact that Ruth was attended by the top psychiatrists of the day. 'She had all the fashionable chemicals of the time, largactil, lithium – the side effect of lithium was death. It's no wonder she became absolutely deranged. An ox couldn't have survived the quantity of drugs my mother was taking – about twenty or thirty different pills a day.'

But there were rays of light in the bleak picture. Ruth was not constantly unwell. As Frances says: 'She was either well or she was ill. When she was well she was fine.' She enjoyed a close relationship with both her children and derived great joy from her grandchildren – Michael's children – Rachel, Daniel and Sarah. And as well as taking care of her financially, Sigi's attachment to Ruth never wavered, even after he remarried in 1970 and his life spiralled faster and faster in wider and wider directions. As he says, 'She always said I looked after her, discussed things with her. Hardly a week went by without us talking to each other on the phone.' Michael, too, agrees that his father 'always had a special relationship with my mother. She would ring him or he would ring her on festivals and on each other's birthday. When he got his knighthood, she came to his house for the party and from time to time he would visit her. He always asked to be reminded of her birthday and if he forgot he was mortified and he'd rush round with flowers.'

Although one part of her never ceased longing for Sigi to come back, Ruth's love for him was such that she delighted in everything he did and achieved. On the occasion of Sigi's 75th birthday celebration at the Sternberg Centre in 1996, Michael spoke of his regret that his mother was no longer there to see that happy day, a remark that might have surprised anyone who was not party to the complexity of Sigi and Ruth's relationship. As Zena Clayton sees it, 'She was a very loving woman and she only wanted to love and give and care. She always loved him and she had worked to help him make himself and she would have the satisfaction and pleasure of seeing his various arrivals and his various achievements, she would have shared in them. She would have pleasure for herself and him.' Michael confirms this: 'She was always pleased to hear about his successes and it meant a great deal to her when he got the knighthood and the Papal knighthood.'

In their different ways, then, Sigi and Ruth still loved each other and, as Michael sees it, 'cared passionately' for their children. They stood under the *chupa* together when Michael married Janine Levinson in 1975 and later when Frances married Neil Blane in 1984. 'They both behaved in a very dignified and civilized way and both were very happy to be there together.' When, some years before his marriage, Michael had a terrible eye accident at Cambridge, Ruth was moving house and had her hands full. She sent a telegram to Sigi who was chairing an industrial conference in South America.

> My father left in the middle of the conference. He took a plane to New York and another to London and he drove up to Cambridge to see me because he was concerned that I was in danger of losing the sight of one eye. He was the one who came, not my mother. When things got really, really bad my father would pull the stops out but it required something like that to happen for him to do it

because he was just so bound up in whatever he was involved in.

Sigi will always assert that his family comes first with him. In another age, when men had more than one wife, he may well have shone as a patriarchal figure. Michael tells this story of a joke his parents shared. 'My mother used to say to him, "Actually, what you really want would be to have a whole series of wives. We'd all sit around the table with our families." And my father used to laugh and say, "Yes, you'd be the chief wife."' Sigi vigorously scorns such an idea. Nevertheless, he is noticeably reluctant to give precise details about his divorce from Ruth. Michael sees his father as 'a very traditional man in that respect. He had more than one family, he has more than one wife and his idea of a good time is really to have everybody round the table and really to try and gloss over the difficulties that may exist between the individuals concerned on the basis that "We're all here together. Let's all try and get on."'

As the years went by and her children had their separate lives, Ruth was frequently in and out of nursing homes as she did not appear to find a satisfactory carer to look after her at home. In August 1994 she was diagnosed as suffering from cancer. Shortly after, she was moved to the Royal Free Hospital in Hampstead.

To Sigi, her illness came as a terrible blow. Despite the many achievements and satisfactions that his life afforded him, Ruth's unconditional love for him remained a gift he valued as he did the qualities he had seen in her at the time of their marriage. As George Perlman put it, 'People unconsciously gravitate to each other for reasons they don't necessarily understand and I think that maybe later on, having had a certain distance, he was able to appreciate that better and what happened and what was lost along the way.'

Sigi's devotion to Ruth in the weeks preceding her death was such that the hospital staff couldn't believe they were not married. Although it was difficult for Zena to witness this – 'He was there in such a loving, caring, husbandly way' – it was a blessing for Ruth. 'It gave her great comfort because it was what she'd always wanted. Him to be there as a loving husband. And that's how he appeared to be.' In the last week or two, he was at the hospital every day, sometimes for as much as ten or twelve hours. Frances had never seen him so distressed. 'We were all together, Michael, myself and mummy and daddy around the hospital bed. Daddy held her and daddy stroked her and he spoke to her. Daddy brought the *siddur*. It was very sad, it was very touching. He said when she died that he should have stayed with her, things should have been different.'

Sigi was unable to sleep and would ring the hospital in the small hours. His last call was on the day of Ruth's death. As Michael recounts,

> The day my mother died she had been in a coma for about twenty-four hours and in effect had ceased to communicate. A nurse told us that my father had phoned the hospital at something like two in the morning to find out what was going on and how she was doing. According to the nurse, she went in to see my mother and was speaking to my mother although she was unconscious and the nurse said to my mother who was in this coma, 'Sigi rang to find out how you were.' Whereupon she sat up in bed and said 'That's nice' and that was the last thing she ever said.

Ruth's death at six o'clock that evening, on 21 September, fell during the Jewish festival of *Succot*. With her death she managed to achieve what had eluded her in life. As Frances put it, 'She had the people around her that she loved that she didn't have in her life. It was good that my mother, who didn't have much of a life, had a rather fulfilling death.'

It was a vindication of the love Ruth had never renounced. To Sigi she remained 'a valuable, precious person' and for all his mistrust of emotion, he can say with his heart that he loved her all his life. Indeed, Frances believes that 'he loved her more than he loved anybody'. And Zena, too, feels that 'to the maximum of his capacity, as much as he's ever loved anyone, he loved and maybe still does love her'.

3 Various Involvements

At the time of the breakdown of his marriage, Sigi was becoming ever more deeply involved in communal and public affairs outside his immediate business interests and was developing an interesting circle of acquaintances, which was rapidly widening. While his involvements were very varied, there were three principal areas – health, the Labour Party and metal work for prisoners. Sigi had made a very good impression on Sir Keith Joseph, then Minister of Health in the Conservative government of the early 1960s and since Joseph was keen to bring in business men and women to help the National Health Service, Sigi, who had achieved considerable success in less than twenty years, was one of those to whom he turned.

An institution in which Sigi took particular interest was the Royal College of Speech and Language Therapists, to which he was introduced by the neuropsychologist, Edna Butfield, in the early 1970s and of which he is now Senior Life Vice President. He would often quote the case of the biblical Moses who had a speech defect – he was 'not eloquent ... slow of speech and slow of tongue' (Exodus 4:10) – and yet became a great leader, as an illustration of the importance of helping people with speech impediments to communicate. Sigi facilitated the college's move to larger premises, taught the staff how to make use of publicity and introduced them to many of his friends and acquaintances in public life who were also able to assist the college in its work. Years later, he was to present staff at the college with the Sternberg Award for Clinical Innovation on more than one occasion. As he said at the award ceremony in October 1997 in relation to children suffering from a cleft palate: 'You are giving children with this harsh affliction a real opportunity to communicate with the world around them.' At another award ceremony nearly three years later, he praised the winner for using the technique of story-telling to facilitate communication: 'By utilizing the precision of structure, the relevance of classroom activities and some of the more common expressive and language difficulties, she has created what is not just a clinical innovation. I think we could even call it an art form. And with it, she is helping uncertain young people to acquire the tools and confidence to become storytellers.' Sigi himself received an honorary fellowship from the Royal College in 1989 for his twelve years of service as Vice President and twenty years later, in 2009, was presented with a Special Award in recognition of his long service and unstinting commitment to the College.

One colleague at the college was Mrs Audrey Callaghan, wife of the future Labour Prime Minister, who was, herself, very interested in speech therapy. She and Sigi were both patrons of AFASIC, a charity which supports children and young people with speech and communication impairments together with their parents and carers. Sternberg remembers that during Callaghan's premiership, Audrey Callaghan did not have a car or driver at her disposal and he had to chauffeur her back to Downing Street from the meetings they attended, something, as he puts it, 'that would be unimaginable today. Unlike today', he adds, 'there was no gate outside 10 Downing Street and anyone could just walk in.'

Sigi was appointed a magistrate in 1965, at the age of 44. He is still on the supplementary list of magistrates and is entitled to do everything except sit. And with the return of the Labour government in 1964, his experience in the metal business led him to be appointed on to the Committee for Metal Recovery, as the government recognized the importance of secondary metals. In this context, Sigi supplied the government with materials to be used for stripping cables and made frequent visits to prisons. At that time, the principal activity of prison inmates was sewing mailbags, and stripping cables for metal recovery was obviously more productive. Sigi bought electric meters from the Coal Board and the Electricity Board and took the meters to the prisons to be dismantled. Today Sternberg recollects seeing prison life as a very interesting experience and says he visited prisons more than anyone else. Indeed, it was to Sigi that prisoners complained, demanding to know why they got so little pay. He tried to explain that the remainder of any profits went to the Prison Commission. One occasion, however, turned out to be particularly frightening. Sigi was surrounded by prisoners who were blaming him for the meagre pay they were receiving. It was, as Sternberg recalls, 'a pretty rough prison in Liverpool', and no prison officer appeared to be around at the time. As he says today: 'What I learned from that situation was that you should never show you are frightened and try to run away. You should just stay put.'

Sigi's interest in metals was not restricted to a business or functional context. He became a trustee and later Chairman and Lifetime President of the Institute of Archaeo-Metallurgical Studies at University College, London, through the encouragement of Professor Beno Rothenberg. Not surprisingly, perhaps, in view of his dedication to inter-religious affairs, a fascinating insight he made in a speech some years later about the excavations at Timna in southern Israel was the connection between archaeo-metallurgy and belief. 'One of the great surprises of this research programme was the discovery of the close link between metal mining and smelting – and religious beliefs. It may be stated that there is not a single ancient metallurgical site without a religious shrine and in Timna there is a close connection between mining and metallurgy and early Biblical traditions.'

While Sigi had sold his metal business in 1965, he was already dealing in property and in 1972 set up an investment property business with Martin Slowe, who continues to run the business from an office in Star House, the building housing the Sternberg Foundation and other organizations with which Sigi is involved. Martin Slowe recalls their partnership appreciatively:

> It's a pleasure to work with him. He established himself in property long before he involved himself with me. We've always been partners but he has always been busy

with his charitable work. He has never been dealing day to day with the properties. I've been dealing with the day to day side. He's not a completely silent partner. He's one who speaks to me at least once a day. I just observe what he's doing. I've had a very happy relationship with him over the years.

Sigi's involvement in health affairs continued during the 1970s when he made great efforts to reorganize health services for the Camden Area Health Authority. Mrs Callaghan, his colleague from the College of Speech Therapists, was also a member of the Health Authority. Some years later, however, during the 1980s, he resigned, believing that too little time was devoted to patients and too much to management. By that time, he was chairman of the North West Regional Area Health Authority, which embraced, among other institutions, the Royal Free Hospital and St Mary's Hospital. Also within the Health Authority's aegis were the Tavistock Clinic and the Portman Clinic, which specialized in improving mental health and emotional wellbeing.

Through his connections in the hospital group, Sigi got to know the psychiatrists Cecil Todes and Ismond Rosen. Indeed, he was chairman of the interviewing board when Todes, who had previously been a dentist, came for an interview. Sigi asked him why he had changed his profession. 'I want to heal minds, not teeth', was Todes' response. Sigi maintained friendly relations with Dr Rosen, who was also a distinguished sculptor, and his actress wife, Ruth. He spoke movingly at a memorial service for Rosen, who died in 1996:

> I will always be proud that I was chairman of the appointments committee when Ismond came to Paddington – although I am sure we were not aware of the whirlwind which had arrived in our midst!
>
> Running an innovative psychotherapy centre, conducting a busy private practice and working like a fury to complete a huge collection of new sculptures for an exhibition, Ismond displayed incredible energy and an intensity of dedication to everything he did.

That dedication showed, most especially, I think, in his Holocaust Triptych, the crowning work of his art which took a decade to complete. It is now permanently housed in the Heilig-Kreuz Kirche in Berlin. This was just one of the ways Ismond built bridges between religions, between peoples, by his art.

I know his work was highly valued in the Vatican. I know of the deep impression the Triptych made when displayed here in London at St Paul's Cathedral.

He will be remembered by this work, especially, as a major sculptor of his time, one who sought to heal the wounds between Christian and Jew, German and Jew by his art.

And he will be remembered by countless others – his patients – as a doctor who brought them personal healing, assuaged broken hearts, mended tormented minds.

Some years after Rosen died, an entry on his life in the National Dictionary of Biography described him as 'Renaissance Man, polymath, genius' and a special exhibition of his work was held, as a tribute, at the Cork Street Gallery in 2008. Another exhibition – Psychoanalysis and the Creative Mind – was on display at the Wellcome Collection in 2010.

To help people suffering from bereavement was another area to which Sigi paid considerable attention. Hazel, his second wife, the widow of his cousin Victor, whom he married in 1970, was a dedicated counsellor with Cruse, an organization involved in bereavement care, which was initiated in 1959. Sigi became a patron in Cruse and supported its important work. In 1984, Hazel wrote an article in the Cruse journal, *Bereavement Care*, about Jewish mourning practices. In October 2009, a Golden Jubilee reception was held at St James's Palace, hosted by the Queen, who is the Royal Patron of the charity. Sigi had made a special donation to sponsor the reception. Other patrons include members of parliament, Trevor Phillips, the Chief Rabbi, Lord Sacks, and both Cardinal Cormac Murphy-O'Connor and the Archbishop of Westminster, Vincent Nichol.

In the course of her work as a bereavement counsellor, Hazel comforted relatives of the victims of the Kings Cross fire in 1987, when an old wooden escalator was engulfed by a flash fire at Kings Cross Station, killing thirty-one people. Two years later, in 1989, she offered counselling to the relatives of those killed in the Marchioness disaster, when the pleasure boat sank after a collision with the dredger, Bowbelle. More than fifty people died in the tragedy. Her commitment to her work was so great that she set up Highgate Bereavement Counselling, which she funded from her own pocket and ran from her home, engaging a team of ladies who were sent out to numerous clients near and far.

One of Sigi's most prominent associations was with the Labour Party. His involvement dated from the days of Atlee's premiership after the war. Indeed, he furthered his acquaintance with Atlee, with whom he had been photographed at an earlier function, when, some years later, he brought him and his wife to a fund-raising dinner organized by the Jewish Secondary Schools Movement at which the former prime minister was the guest of honour. He also became acquainted with Harold and Mary Wilson and remains good friends with Mary Wilson. While Wilson was Prime Minister in the 1970s, the Labour Party was keen to encourage business people to contribute ideas. At the time, Sigi was part of a Labour party group together with Tony Benn and Harold Lever, working on company law reform, and his contribution was greatly appreciated.

Sigi also provided funds for a special research department Wilson had requested while leader of the opposition. Steve Bundred, a previous chief executive of the Audit Commission, recalls that shortly after graduating from Oxford University he had been invited by a former tutor, recently ennobled by Wilson, to set up this research department to provide Wilson with support as Wilson was not satisfied with the advice he was receiving from the official Labour Party research department. As Bundred points out, Sigi's help was instrumental in forming the department which gave support, not only to Wilson, but to other opposition front benchers.

The research unit was disbanded, however, when Labour came to power. Bundred had moved on to work in Transport House once the election was called and then became a special advisor to the Secretary of State for Energy. Bundred still remembers how helpful Sigi had been to him and was able to express his appreciation again, many years later, when they met at a Mansion House dinner. Sigi, in turn, on reading of Bundred's appointment to the Audit Commission, and remembering everyone with whom he had come into contact, wrote to congratulate him and said he had always known he would go far.

For his invaluable support to projects dear to the prime minister, his contribution to the Labour Party and his important work in using his experience of the metal trade for social purposes, Sigi was awarded a knighthood for services to industry in Wilson's resignation honours list in 1976.

On 14 July 1993, Sigi announced his resignation from the Labour Party after forty years of active membership. He disagreed with the policies the leadership had pursued which, he believed, had lost the party the election the year before. In his resignation announcement he did pay tribute to the leadership of John Smith, who had taken over from Neil Kinnock and remained leader until his untimely death the following year. Sigi was then invited to join the Social Democrat Party but declined. He remained a member of the Fabian Society, the Labour think-tank, and is still a member today, although he has expressed disappointment that policies promoting interfaith dialogue have not been put forward. He rejoined the Labour Party after Tony Blair became leader and introduced an updated version of 'Clause Four', which recommended the nationalization of British industry. This, many believed, had hung like an albatross around the Labour Party's neck. The virtual abandonment of nationalization was the point at which the Labour Party became 'New Labour'. Sigi remains an admirer of Tony Blair.

An important Labour Party politician with whom Sigi has worked is Frank Judd, now Lord Judd, a former Director of Oxfam. Judd is particularly appreciative of Sigi's support for Oxfam and his effective handling of tensions between Oxfam and the Jewish community which were evident during the late 1980s when Oxfam spoke out on some of the injustices in the Middle East. As he recounts:

> The misunderstandings and accusations of bad faith or worse began to escalate ... Sigi set to work, almost day and night, to build bridges. He would not countenance a breach in relations. He arranged meetings with the Chief Rabbi, with the Board of Deputies and others. The bridges were effective. A potentially disastrous breach was averted. He and a few others deserve great credit. And what is more, after the whole episode subsided, Sigi increased still further his already considerable personal contribution to Oxfam.

Sigi's multiple involvements ensured that his renown had spread behind the Iron Curtain. One telling example of this was a call he received from the British ambassador in East Berlin in 1988. He was told that he had been invited to the city by the President of East Germany, Erich Honecker. On asking why, it appeared that as a 'prominent British Jew', his visit to Berlin, which was ostensibly to attend the fiftieth anniversary commemoration of Kristallnacht, might also be used to pave the way for a visit by British Premier Margaret Thatcher. Another reason Sigi had for visiting the city was to meet Klaus Gysi, the State Secretary for Church Affairs, who had previously served as East German ambassador to Italy, the Vatican and Malta. He was also the father of Gregor Gysi, one of the few free lawyers in East Germany who had defended dissidents and citizens wishing to emigrate.

On the journey, Sigi was surprised to find that he was accompanied by a private detective – 'for his protection'. 'I don't need protecting', he protested. Nevertheless, he found the detective most helpful, taking care of his luggage and making the journey very comfortable. While most of the guests stayed in Honecker's hunting lodge, Sigi insisted on staying in a hotel. And he defied his hosts to the extent of crossing through Checkpoint Charlie to attend a similar commemorative event in Frankfurt.

The following day, Sigi was told that he was to receive an award from President Honecker. As a knight of the Queen, protocol demanded that any award from a foreign country should be cleared with the British authorities. So Sigi consulted the British ambassador who told him he could receive the award. Sternberg today remembers the occasion clearly. It was rare, indeed, to receive an award from a Communist country – as East Germany then was. As it happens, when President Honecker was presenting Sigi with the award, the subject of the Berlin Wall came up in their conversation. Sigi advised Honecker to tear the wall down. 'It will last another thousand years', the president assured Sigi. The following year the wall came down.

Sigi also told Honecker to erect a museum at the location of a bombed-out synagogue and recommended beginning talks with Israel. The following year, both these requests had been fulfilled. However, when Honecker asked Sigi to arrange to set up a Rotary Club in East Germany, since Sigi had already set up Rotary Clubs in many parts of the world, Sigi was obliged to explain to the East German president that it was only possible to set up these clubs in a free society where there was complete freedom of speech and no one need fear that what they were saying would be recorded. At that particular time, the necessary circumstances did not exist in East Germany, and therefore it was not possible to set up a Rotary Club there.

After the collapse of the communist regimes, however, Rotary Clubs were set up or re-instated in many countries in Eastern Europe, in part due to Sigi's 'tireless efforts in expanding the Rotary movement in Eastern Europe and elsewhere', to quote *The London Rotarian*. In 1989, Sigi went to Budapest for this purpose. The Budapest Rotary Club, like many others in Central and Eastern Europe, had been struck off the Rotary International's list during the Second World War and the subsequent communist era. Sigi met Bertalan Tamas, an ecumenical officer of the Reformed Church in Hungary, who helped him and other colleagues from Rotary to re-instate the Budapest club. In Hungary there is also an affiliate of the

International Council of Christians and Jews and a recently established Christian/Jewish/Muslim organization.

Sigi was originally introduced to Rotary by Siggy Reichenstein. At a special ceremony at the London Rotary Club in June 2005, both he and Reichenstein were awarded centennial certificates for having been members of Rotary for more than twenty-five years. Indeed, Sigi is listed among the 100 eminent Great Rotarians, a list that includes the Duke of Edinburgh and Margaret Thatcher. He has received two awards in the name of Paul Harris, the founder of the Rotary movement, one of which was for introducing new members. A report in the autumn 2005 edition of *The London Rotarian* mentioned that he had introduced more than thirty members to the London club alone. One member he introduced was Venetia Newall, a distinguished author and journalist, who went on to become the first woman president of the London Rotary Club. Others have included Gillian Walmes MBE, the Executive Director of the Anne Frank Trust, of which Sigi was one of the founders, Lord Raj Loomba of the Loomba Trust and many ambassadors.

In 1999, Sigi was presented with the Rotary International Award of Honour, usually only presented to heads of state, for his work in promoting inter-religious dialogue. Before presenting Sigi with the award at this 'unique event', Bill Huntley, Rotary International's past president, announced that 'tonight we are to have the first presentation of the Rotary Award of Honour to someone who is not a head of state or head of government. It will be my privilege, on behalf of all Rotary, to honour Sir Sigmund Sternberg with what is truly Rotary's highest award. Sir Sigmund … is the epitome of all that Rotary stands for, having worked all his life to further world understanding and peace.' In his reply, Sigi said, 'This Rotary Award of Honour brings me immense pride. Rotary is now more than 1.2 million strong with 29,000 clubs on every continent and we are one of the world's greatest voluntary forces for good.'

Philip Lader, the US Ambassador in London and himself a member of Rotary, who hosted the reception at the US

Embassy, expressed his pleasure in being associated with the award:

> Occasions such as this serve to demonstrate the truly international aspects of Rotary and the genuine achievements which are possible in furthering international understanding ... As in so many aspects in life, it is the vision and dedication of a few individuals who can make change happen. Sir Sigmund Sternberg is one such man and it is salutary that he should be the first person who is not a head of state to receive the Rotary Award of Honour.

A special event organized by Sigi on behalf of Rotary was a 'Rotary Shabbat' at West London Synagogue in October 2005. In his address, he reminded his audience that Nazi Party members had been banned from being members of Rotary precisely because of Rotary's conviction that, united in international solidarity, men and women could do much to relieve the pains of modern society through voluntary action, a belief shared by most Jews. With members of Rotary striving to help those in need and working towards world understanding and peace, how, Sigi asked rhetorically, could Jews not be involved? Sigi spoke, too, of the activities of Rotary in Israel, where youngsters of all religions who could not afford to stay on at secondary school were awarded scholarships by the Rotary branch in Jerusalem to complete their studies. Rotary branches in Israel were active in promoting Arab-Jewish reconciliation as were, Sigi pointed out, Rotarians in Norway who, through their Shalom-Salaam project, invited groups of university students, half of them Israeli and half of them Palestinian, to an 'all expenses paid' summer programme in Oslo. 'They work together, eat together, learn together, play together and return home with a new perspective on those they once thought of as enemies.'

An article about Sigi in the Spring 2008 edition of *The London Rotarian*, in which he is heralded as 'Member of the Moment', reports that he sees Rotary as 'a wonderful forum for different people with different ideas and faiths to meet' and believes he has introduced more new members into the Club than anyone else, as well as setting up many Rotary Clubs in Eastern Europe. And at a special reception in June 2011, to mark his 90th birthday, Sigi emphasized how keen he was for religion to be discussed in a Rotary forum.

4 Hazel

Lady Hazel Sternberg, Sigi's second wife, was the widow of his cousin, Victor. Victor Sternberg's sudden death in 1963 was a terrible blow for Hazel, and their two small children, Ruth and David. Before marrying Victor, Hazel had converted to Judaism with the encouragement of Victor's cousin, Rabbi Solomon Schonfeld, who had also taught her Hebrew.

Victor and Hazel had married in 1954. Theirs was, as Hazel's friend, Nin Saunders, expressed it, 'a quiet, embracing love'. Victor, a keen bridge player was, as many remember him, a serious, intelligent, caring man – 'fantastic, so nice, a great father', as Nin Saunders recalls. Ruth Edith Weisz, at the time married to Victor's and Sigi's cousin, George Weisz, also recalls Victor's great kindness and how he had paid special attention to her when she and her husband were visiting him. 'He was such a lovely man. Hazel adored him and would do anything for him', she said.

Born in December 1927, Hazel was the daughter of Everett Jones, the owner of a very large and successful advertising agency. Hazel attended North London Collegiate School, amongst other schools, and later studied sociology at the London School of Economics. At the LSE, Hazel had met a fellow student, Reuven Gavriel, known as 'Kuno', who became her boyfriend. After graduating from the LSE with a degree in Social Work, Hazel went with Kuno on a trip to Israel. While in Jerusalem, she was invited to the home of Joseph and Miriam Ben-David. Miriam was the younger sister of Sigi's cousins Victor and Charles Sternberg. She and her husband, Joseph, had become friends of Hazel's and Kuno's in London. Joseph Ben-David, an Israeli of Hungarian origin,

had been studying at the LSE, after being awarded a scholarship by the Palestine Mandatory Authority. Before he finished
his earlier studies in Palestine, Ben-David had been working
as a probation officer for the British government and had also
worked with children in the Old City of Jerusalem. He was
sent to the LSE to qualify, on a course specifically designed for
students from the British Empire, the colonies and mandated
territories. At the LSE, Ben-David also attended other lectures
and met Hazel, who was keen to mix with the Jewish crowd,
as recalled by Miriam. In 1955 Ben-David completed his
doctorate at the Hebrew University and went on to become a
distinguished professor of Sociology and the History of
Science at the university. He was also a visiting professor at
the University of Chicago on a regular basis and also held
visiting appointments with several other illustrious American
universities. When in Chicago, he would stay with Saul
Bellow, who would also visit Ben-David in Jerusalem.

While in Israel, Hazel worked as a volunteer at a hostel for
new immigrants in Mevasseret Zion, near Jerusalem. The new
immigrants couldn't pronounce her name and called her
'Yochevet'. At that stage Kuno had joined the Israeli army and
when Hazel visited the Ben-Davids, she met Miriam's brother,
Victor, who was also there. Shortly after that, Hazel went back
to London, at that stage planning to marry Kuno. Victor also
returned to London and Miriam asked him to send her a
raincoat from there with Hazel, when Hazel returned to
Israel.

In London, Victor was staying with his aunt, Ella Schonfeld.
He met Hazel again at the home of another aunt, Kato Weisz.
Hazel and Victor fell instantly in love but shortly after that
Victor fell ill with flu. Hazel visited him at his Aunt Ella's, and
seeing him lying there sick, with such a compassionate visitor,
his aunt told Victor that he should marry Hazel. 'Okay', Victor
is thought to have replied, 'but there's a little problem'. Hazel
was not Jewish. She had already started to take an interest in
Judaism during her relationship with Kuno and once she and
Victor decided to marry, she underwent a thorough conversion
with Victor's cousin, 'Solly'. Miriam, of course, did not get her

raincoat! But Victor and his family greatly appreciated the fact that Hazel was willing to marry Victor, knowing that he could not have children. They later adopted Ruth, born in 1959 and David, born in 1961.

Hazel's family took her conversion to Judaism very badly; indeed, her brother refused to speak to her any more. However, the two were reconciled before her brother's death from cancer. Hazel's parents, too, grew much closer to her after years of separation. Interestingly Kuno, who later made a life for himself in the United States, kept in touch with Hazel and, in fact, Hazel and Sigi visited him in the USA before he died some years ago.

Nin Saunders, Hazel's friend, recalls first meeting Hazel and Victor during the late 1950s, when they were neighbours at Corringham Court, near Golders Green. Victor ran a business in antiques and objets d'art together with his brother, Charles. They had a large shop in South Audley Street near Grosvenor Square, with a workshop downstairs in the basement for repairs of the tapestries and carpets. 'Charlie', Nin says, the opposite of his quiet brother, 'was very jolly and funny'. Later Hazel and Victor moved to a house in Cranbourne Gardens in Temple Fortune. They gave the leasehold of the flat in Corringham Court to Victor's cousin, George Weisz, who moved in later with his then wife, Ruth Edith.

In Cranbourne Gardens, Hazel and Victor lived round the corner from Charles and his wife, Klara. On 11 October 1963, which was the festival of *Simchat Torah* (Rejoicing in the Law), Victor had gone to synagogue with Charles and taken his small daughter, Ruth, to the service. Afterwards they had walked back to Charles' house where Klara was setting up a *Kiddush* table. Ruth remembers how her father was coughing and spluttering and holding his chest on the walk from synagogue. Shortly after they reached the house, Victor collapsed. Hazel was at home with David when somebody came round and told her Victor was ill. By the time she got to her brother-in-law's house, Victor's body was laid out on the floor (the customary place to put a dead body, according to Jewish law) – an image she could not get out of her mind.

Even now Hazel has told her friend, Nin, 'I know it is the custom but it was so awful to see him there on the floor.' Hazel was devastated. As Nin recalls, 'she would frequently say in her great distress: "I don't know if there's a hell in the brain, I don't know." She was quite lost and everybody else took charge, including Charlie and Sigi.'

Hazel inherited Cranbourne Gardens and half the business. At that time Ruth and David were attending a local nursery. She wanted to help her widowed mother, who was living in Wimbledon, but her mother was a tough, independent woman – 'like Hazel', as Nin puts it – and would not accept any help. Noam Tamir, Hazel's son-in-law, recalls her mother as an elegant woman who lived on her own till the age of 94, when she moved to a care home in Liverpool, where she had come from. Sigi, Hazel and the family would visit her there, while staying at a house Hazel owned in North Wales.

At the time of Victor's death, Sigi's support provided great comfort to Hazel and the children. By that time his marriage to Ruth was encountering considerable difficulties and they were divorced in 1969/70, the Decree Nisi in October 1969 and the Decree Absolute in 1970. Sigi married Hazel in 1970 and moved with her and the children to Branksome, a large house in Courtenay Avenue, a private road off Hampstead Lane between Hampstead and Highgate. It was Hazel who had found Branksome, while house-hunting.

As her daughter, Ruth Tamir, who was just 11 years old at the time, points out, Hazel was a very strong person, having had to cope as a young widow bringing up two small children on her own in a community in which single mothers were often ostracized. Initially she developed a career in marriage guidance counselling, later turning to bereavement counselling with Cruse. Ruth feels she really 'came into her own' as an experienced counsellor at the time of the King's Cross fire in November 1987 and nearly two years later after the *Marchioness* disaster on the River Thames. Later Hazel set up her own Highgate Bereavement Counselling. She had wished to become a speech therapist but accepted that Sigi did not want her to, understanding that she would need to make compromises to live with 'such a driven, powerful man', as Ruth puts it.

While Hazel has always been a great support to Sigi in all his endeavours, it was none too easy to take on the role of 'Sigi's second wife'. Inevitably, perhaps, she and the children frequently encountered considerable resentment from Sigi's own family and Hazel was obliged to shield the children from this as much as possible. Ruth, her daughter, believes this 'took its toll', particularly as Sigi, never one to relish confrontation or delving into emotions, had no wish to face up to what was going on. In her opinion, Sigi, who found the fact that the two families were not united extremely painful, has remained ambivalent and torn about the situation all his life.

Before their mother's remarriage, Ruth and David had had a very 'normal' childhood and weren't spoiled in any way. Ruth saw her mother as a very grounded woman, hard-working, modest and practical. Now, suddenly, their mother was constantly busy and they had to get used to spending less time with her. They also had to get used to a new stepfather and a new home, which was a difficult transition for them. Sharing their mother with a new father was none too easy, not least because Sigi was a 'strict, rather formal father who ran the home with very rigid meal times and rules'. Now Ruth appreciates that Sigi's tendency to be 'prim and proper' was very likely to be the result of having been forced out of his home and arriving as a refugee in an alien culture, an experience he would have shared with many men of his generation.

At the time of the transition, however, Ruth felt that the big house was 'miserable'. She recalls that, previously, they used to live in Temple Fortune, a small, friendly neighbourhood. In contrast, they felt quite cut off in Courtenay Avenue, where there were no children to play with and the only form of transport was the 210 bus. Ruth and David spent most of their early years at Branksome playing together.

Both Ruth and David recall the lifestyle Sigi imposed on them as strict and regimented. Weekends were spent walking across the Heath and riding their bicycles. Sigi would call these 'educational walks'. David remembers him saying: 'You mustn't waste time, you must learn something', and when the children returned from school he would ask them, 'What did you learn today?'

The family often went swimming – particularly in the sea when they were staying at their weekend home in Bournemouth. The sea was very cold and David, who was then about 10 years old, didn't want to go in and cried when he was in the water. Sigi called this 'water laughter'. By the time it was all over David was glad he had gone in. They also went on a lot of walks in Bournemouth, which were not always enjoyed. Hazel, however, loved exploring and would often drive off with the children to a local beauty spot or National Trust property. Many summer holidays were spent in Mediterranean seaside resorts.

Sigi taught David how to play golf and also taught him his first swing. He was unable to join Highgate Golf Club because at that time Jews were not permitted to become members, but instead took David to the Hampstead Golf Club where they were allowed to play after Sigi had paid a 'green fee'. In Bournemouth Sigi would play at the Parkstone golf course and David, who was about 9 at the time, would 'caddy' for him. David had his own set of 'chopped down' golf clubs. Although he had a 'natural swing', he didn't like playing golf at that time as he was much more taken with football and remains a keen Chelsea fan. Sigi never accompanied him to a football match.

David also recalls Sigi's own lifestyle as extremely regimented. After he had read the papers, which he would do before anyone else was up, he would carry out his morning exercises. He would put out a blanket or a sheet on the floor on which to exercise in order to keep clean. He also used a rowing machine, dumb-bell weights and a skipping rope. He would then eat grapefruit and muesli for breakfast. Sigi continued to row and exercise on his treadmill well into his 80s. David joined in the exercise sessions and was glad that he had done so because he was surprised to find he had a good physique compared to the others in his class.

Ruth recalls that she remained close to her Uncle Charles and his family, who lived in Golders Green. In contrast to Sigi and Hazel's household, where, as Ruth points out, 'we never entertained family', Charles and his wife did a lot of entertaining and also hosted cousins from Israel. Hazel, too, had remained very close to Charles and Klara and she and Sigi enjoyed attending their Hungarian-style tea parties. David also remembers Charles and Klara with great fondness. They were very important to him and gave him a lot of love and support that he will never forget. He appreciates how much they always used to help people from all walks of life. Sadly Charles died in March 1992 and Klara five years later in 1997. Ruth spent most of her holidays with family and friends in Israel. While Branksome was 'never a home where family stayed', visitors included business associates and religious dignitaries. Sigi, Ruth observes, was 'totally absorbed in his work' and never one for 'chit chat'.

For his part, David admits to having been unimpressed 'with all the archbishops and popes and synagogues' that made up such a large part of Sigi's work. It was much more interesting, he felt, when they would go on walks together and Sigi would 'think out loud, as if he was having a business discussion in his head'. David also remembers going to the courts with Sigi when he acted as a magistrate. 'You'll see what happens to miscreants', he would tell him. David would sit at the back with the families of the 'criminals'. Sigi, who was sitting in the centre, would look up at him 'with a little grin', a 'warning in his eyes'. He had a sense of humour and often had a 'twinkle in his eye'.

All the time he was at home, David only heard Sigi swear once, when they hired a motor boat and couldn't start the engine. David was quite 'shocked' to hear him swear. David was also somewhat taken aback at having been persuaded to concur with Sigi's propensity for charitable donations. Around the time of his Bar Mitzvah, Sigi had asked him: 'What do you feel about donating all the money you get for your Bar Mitzvah?' At that point, David was so looking forward to getting his Bar Mitzvah over that he said 'Fine'.

Only afterwards he felt, 'It's ridiculous. I didn't get a penny!'

The family had become members of the Reform synagogue in Alyth Gardens and attended services regularly. This was something Ruth enjoyed and she remains a member together with her husband and children. She sees the fact that Sigi had joined the Reform movement as quite unusual, for at that time the *machers* – the leading members – in the Jewish community tended not to be Reform.

Ruth, who went to the Jewish Free School, never felt she was one of the 'suburb set', the teenagers from Hampstead Garden Suburb who tended to be more showy in their dress and behaviour. Her main hobby as a teenager was drama and she kept busy attending drama classes and appearing in productions. She was delighted to be accepted to drama school after she had finished secondary school. She spent part of her gap year in Israel and several happy years there as a 'new immigrant' after leaving drama school. One motive for wanting to spend more time in Israel was to escape from the tensions at home as she never really felt 'part of Sigi's new family'. She never doubted Sigi's 'overwhelming love' for her but realized that his divided loyalties made it very difficult for him to express this love openly. Moreover, when his family visited, she, her mother and David felt 'very excluded'. She recognizes that family life was anything but relaxed and feels, in fact, that the family was 'quite driven', something she believes must have been particularly difficult for her brother, David, and her step-sister, Frances, who were more bohemian in their outlook and career pursuits. Indeed, Frances regards herself and David as 'black sheep' as they were more unconventional. Ironically, it was the two of them and not the other children who were at Buckingham Palace when Sigi was awarded his knighthood.

Ruth, clearly, had many reasons for being keen to get away. Sigi, however, was not happy that she was so far away and in 1982, at the onset of the first Lebanon War, phoned her in Israel, saying, 'I want you to come home'. Ruth refused. She was making a new life for herself, it felt like a 'natural step'. That year she had met Noam Tamir, her future husband, and she introduced him to Hazel and Sigi the following year. Noam recalls that they met at the King David Hotel in Jerusalem. Sigi and Hazel came to Israel at least once a year, to attend meetings at the Hebrew University where Sigi was a governor, and this was their first visit since Ruth and Noam got together. Ruth was very concerned that Noam would be cross-examined by Sigi and then leave her, but Noam reassured her. As it happened the first thing Ruth mentioned was that Noam was fortunate enough to have been one of the fighters at the raid on Entebbe – he was, in fact, the youngest officer – and Sigi was duly impressed and asked Noam about Entebbe. He then said to Ruth: 'I know now why you love Noam; he's so similar to me.' Everyone burst out laughing. After that they had a good discussion and then Sigi asked: 'When can we meet your parents?'

The first meeting with Noam's parents took place a few months later. Both Hazel and Sigi felt very comfortable. Hazel was fluent in Hebrew – she is, in fact, a very capable linguist – and was able to communicate immediately with Noam's mother, which was very pleasing for Mrs Tamir. Noam's father spoke good English and got on very well with Sigi. He was from Teplice in Bohemia and Noam had a great-uncle living in Budapest. Sigi and Noam's father had a lot in common with similar cultural backgrounds and have maintained a close relationship over the years. Noam's mother, who died of cancer some years ago, aged 86, remained very close to Hazel.

Sigi's first 'man to man' talk with Noam about 'life' was on the morning of Noam and Ruth's wedding, on a fine day in September 1984, at the Accadia Hotel in Herzlia. Sigi started to tell Noam about the whole family and the various relationships. He also spoke about Victor and Hazel. As Noam recalls, the talk went on for several hours and was very emotional. A close bond was formed. Ruth and Noam were married 'under the stars' at Tel Aviv University that evening.

At the time Noam was finishing his degree studies at the Haifa Technion and was working for a large firm of insurance brokers in Ramat-Gan. In this context he can say of Sigi that when Sigi sets his mind on something, he doesn't give up and usually the person or people concerned will do what he wants as the pressure would be so intense. In fact Sigi said to Noam, 'I've always had my own company. One day you will, too. How about buying some shares in the insurance brokers?' Noam explained that this area, though profitable, was not of particular interest to him as he was more interested in computer science and systems analysis. Not long afterwards he moved to a public company where he worked in computer systems.

Elinor, Ruth and Noam's eldest child, was born at home in Givatayim, near Tel-Aviv, in January 1986. It was an easy birth and Hazel arrived from London shortly afterwards and Sigi two days later. In the intervening years, Ruth and Noam had visited London frequently while Hazel and Sigi would come to Israel two or three times a year to see them. Even at the time of Elinor's birth Sigi said to Noam, 'You need to have your own company', a topic he pursued in the course of their frequent telephone conversations.

At this stage, the company Noam worked for wanted to expand into Europe and asked Noam to open a branch in London. This was a 'dream come true' for Sigi. He told Noam, 'let's meet the boss'. Noam's boss was a highly successful woman and she, Noam and Sigi met several times in Israel to discuss the plans. Sigi's idea was very simple. He told Noam's boss: 'Rather than represent you, Noam could represent you and other companies.' Sigi assured Noam, who had grown up on a kibbutz and had no experience in business, that he would help him.

Ruth and Noam decided to come to London for a trial year to see how things worked out. Ruth was not so keen. It was the winter of 1986 and the weather in the UK was not very good and Elinor was only nine months old. In Israel, Ruth had been working for the British Council and she didn't know what she would do in London. They stayed for a few days at Branksome, in Ruth's old room. Noam remembers Sigi coming to their room while Ruth and Elinor were with Hazel. Sigi started to talk to Noam about his life and his difficult first marriage. What had attracted him to Hazel, he said, was her independence. However, he confessed, it was not always so easy for two such strong-minded people to live together. Noam felt a little strange as he was not accustomed to his own father talking to him at such length. He also remembers that Sigi would talk to him as they walked across the garden to the Highgate Golf Club, where Sigi had a key to the back entrance.

Sigi was a partner in Noam's first company for some years, and Noam recognizes that he was trained by Sigi. He later set up a new company. At Friday night dinners Sigi would invariably ask Noam how business was going. He would always say: 'You are like my son so it's my duty to ask you questions.' Indeed, it was Sigi who held Ruth and Noam's baby son, Jonny, at his circumcision ceremony.

Ruth greatly appreciates Sigi's support for Noam in his work and recognizes that he has mellowed in recent years. It was obviously difficult for him, she realizes, to bring up two teenagers for a second time. Now their families are extremely close. Sigi and Hazel were there 'minutes' after her younger children, Deborah and Jonny, were born, also at home. Hazel was a very active grandmother and spent a lot of time with the children and would frequently pick them up from school. They attended the Akiva School, the Progresssive Jewish primary school at the Sternberg Centre in Finchley, and all found it a wonderful experience. For Ruth, herself, as a woman, it was very important having a father with an active Reform affiliation and she is pleased that she and her brother grew up with very progressive and liberal values.

Ruth and her family have enjoyed joining Sigi and Hazel at the Alyth Gardens Synagogue every Sabbath and spending Friday night dinner with them, listening to them speak about all the exciting people they have met. Ruth and Noam have also enjoyed attending the important events in Sigi's life and have been gratified at the opportunity of meeting such a wide variety of interesting people. Ruth feels a great deal of pride in all Sigi's achievements. She also recalls that Sigi told Noam: 'I could have made much more money but I'm so delighted that I was able to contribute to interfaith activity'.

Together with Noam's parents, Sigi and Hazel were on the

bimah when Ruth's daughters had their Bat Mitzvah ceremonies and when Jonny had his Bar Mitzvah, and all the family enjoyed the celebratory parties. At Elinor's Bat Mitzvah, the family presented Sigi with a chocolate gold medal as a joke! The children are very close to Sigi and Hazel and feel lucky to have grown up with four wonderful grandparents.

While Ruth had originally been reluctant to return to London from Israel, she developed an absorbing and fulfilling career in antenatal education and breastfeeding counselling. She finds it quite amusing that Sigi, who has always been an extremely busy man, often phones her and Noam and tells them that they work too hard. She is touched that he frequently phones her daughters, Elinor and Deborah, who have left home, and is also pleased that Elinor and Deborah get on well with Sarah, the younger daughter of her stepbrother, Michael. The family all meet on Sigi's birthdays and at the various events he is involved in.

David, meanwhile, became an actor and appeared in plays at the National Theatre, including Mike Leigh's *2000 Years*. He also had a small part in the film, *Notting Hill*, and has appeared in many commercials. He met his wife, Anna, at drama school where they did a three year diploma. They have two children, Freddy and Nell. Anna works as a psychotherapist and also with the charity, MIND. David is now building up a thriving business dealing in vinyl records.

Hazel has remained very busy. For Noam, her son-in-law, it was interesting to see such an active woman. As he recalls, she would always be 'rushing around, juggling so many balls in the air'. There was her work, her family and Sigi's constant demands. On the social scene it would be Hazel who remembered everyone's name and would consequently inform Sigi. 'It was a bit like briefing the queen', Noam joked. Of course, Sigi and Hazel would have arguments from time to time as Sigi would have preferred his wife to be with him all the time.

Ruth is very proud of what her mother has achieved. She is particularly impressed that Hazel was able to get on with her own life, since it could not have been easy to live with a powerful man. She admires her mother for the fact that she has always had her own mind and would not 'suffer fools gladly'. While it is evident that Hazel enjoyed the opportunities to travel and meet so many interesting people, she, herself, helped Sigi in that she was very easy to talk to and always found something to say to whoever she was with. And what Ruth found particularly special was that while supporting Sigi in all his endeavours, her mother remained 'her own person – independent, stubborn and free thinking'.

Nin Saunders is of the same mind. Hazel, she feels, was brilliant and really pushed Sigi in his career. 'Sigi recognizes that she was the driving force behind him. She had the ability to take charge of situations and also to show great kindness.' What is more, Nin points out, each time Hazel's name was mentioned at various ceremonies, for example at the palace, there would invariably be a standing ovation, something that, for all his achievements, would rarely greet Sigi.

5 Introduction to Interfaith

It was in the latter years of the 1970s that Sigi, almost by chance, was directed towards a field of endeavour that was to play a major role in his life. He was asked by Lord Sammy Fisher, then president of the Board of Deputies of British Jews, of which he was a member, to 'save' the Council of Christians and Jews which, at that time, was in a parlous state due to lack of funding. As Fisher put it, 'I've got a *mitzvah* for you'. This *mitzvah* was to prove the overriding passion of Sigi's life, something he refers to now as his *meshuggas*. He commends his wife, Hazel, for putting up with his obsession with interfaith relations and for her constant support and help. Because of his central European background and the suffering endured by many of his family during the Holocaust, he was quick to appreciate the crucial value of good relations between Christians and Jews, to which he was to dedicate much of his life, on an emotional as well as an intellectual level. Indeed, it was the horrors of the Holocaust that inspired prominent figures in the Christian world to seek reconciliation with Jews and thereby make amends, not only for the atrocities perpetrated by the Nazis, but for centuries of Jewish suffering and persecution inspired by the Christian 'teaching of contempt' towards Jews, the 'Christ killers', and their religion.

An early declaration in 1947 was 'The Ten Points of Seelisberg', an 'address to the churches' put forward by the Christian participants at the second conference of the recently formed the International Council of Christians and Jews (ICCJ), which affirmed the Jewishness of Jesus, his disciples and the apostles and expressed strong disapproval of any attempt to denigrate Jews or Judaism. Some years later in 1962, the Second Vatican Council, opened by Pope John XXIII, focused on relations between the Catholic Church and non-Christian religions, culminating in the declaration, *Nostra Aetate*, promulgated by Pope John's successor, Paul VI, on 28 October 1965. The Jewish people were absolved of the charge of deicide, from which they had suffered for centuries and which Sigi, himself, had heard voiced on several occasions as a child, and the Jewish religion with its roots in the Old Testament was accepted as valid in its own right rather than superseded by Christianity. This seminal date in the history of Christian-Jewish relations was deeply affecting for Sigi. Indeed Sternberg, today, wishes to see it commemorated every year as a *Nostra Aetate* Day.

Despite these historical landmarks, however, the day to day affairs of the Council of Christians and Jews (CCJ) were governed by more mundane concerns. As the Reverend Marcus Braybrooke states in his book, *Children of One God – A History of the Council of Christians and Jews*, the annual report of 1975/76 claimed that this was the year 'which saw the Council in its most precarious situation since its inception'. Plans were made for a major appeal and Sigi became Appeal Chairman and later Joint Honorary Treasurer. He was soon able to announce that pledges of about £100,000 had been made. This news was welcomed by Dr Donald Coggan, the then Archbishop of Canterbury and a joint president of the Council. It was a 'fine start', he proclaimed at the Annual General Meeting in 1977, and he hoped it would lead to a 'flying finish'.

The late Lord Coggan, as he became after his retirement in 1980, who recalled 'coming across' Sigi first while he was Archbishop of York, was impressed from the first meeting that Sigi was 'unique! He is an enthusiast for his causes and he was very anxious that I should be to the forefront in these things. As the years went by we had a little joke – "for every ten things he has asked me to do, I would do one".' This became a standing joke between the two men 'down the years'.

Coggan, whose own interest in 'things Jewish-Semitic' was inspired by his study of Hebrew at school and Hebrew and Aramaic at Cambridge, was conscious that 'so many of us Christians are so unenlightened in this sphere and we don't realize how deep our debt is to Judaism. After all they gave us the Old Testament, the Tanach; they gave us our Messiah – what greater debt can we owe them than that?' He believed that Sigi's experience of anti-Semitism in his youth, albeit that he escaped the Holocaust, 'had bitten deeply into him. He's absolutely genuine about the fear, the danger of an uprising of anti-Semitism. I think if you scratch you would find very near the surface this overwhelming desire that there should be no occurrence of this either in Britain or, indeed, in the world.'

Sigi's contribution to the advancement of the Council's activities took many forms. In 1979 he established the Sir Sigmund Sternberg Award for distinguished contributions to Christian-Jewish relations. As Braybrooke explains in his book, the awards, which were to become an annual event, 'helped to give a higher profile to the Council's work, as well as being an acknowledgement of remarkable service'. The first winner was Carl Witton-Davies, Archdeacon of Oxford and a Canon of Christ Church, who had retired the previous year as chairman of the Executive after twenty years' service. Movingly, fourteen years later, Sigi wrote an obituary of Witton-Davies in which he lauded him as a 'staunch defender and friend' of Israel and the Jewish people: 'He was renowned as a Hebrew scholar and Christian Zionist, with a world-wide reputation.'

While many branches of Christianity were now involved in fostering good relations between Christians and Jews, the Catholic Church was the one with the greatest global outreach. It was also the dominant church in most countries in Europe, including Hungary where Sigi had grown up. While Sigi has cultivated numerous connections with important members of the Anglican Church and others, much of his activity has involved relations between Catholics and Jews.

In 1980, Sigi was one of the members of the CCJ to be received by Pope Paul VI in Rome at a public audience. He sat in the front row and was greeted by the Pope. The trip to Rome included a visit to the Rome Synagogue, and provided in some ways a foretaste of events a few years later when Sigi would be awarded a papal knighthood and would escort the Pope – in this case Paul VI's successor, John Paul II – to the synagogue. Through his connection with the Council, Sigi also became involved with other institutions which reflected its aims and concerns. He was elected to the executive board of Keston College, a human rights charity reporting on 'the plight of Jews and Christians behind the Iron Curtain and in other countries where the free expression of religion is suppressed', and gave generous backing to the Interfaith Network for the UK, which links together representatives of the various religious communities in Britain as well as national and local interfaith organizations and groups.

Sigi's support for the CCJ was not confined to the United Kingdom. He played a prominent role in the ICCJ, becoming chairman of the Executive Committee and Patron, after the Executive Committee was abolished. Ruth Weyl, the ICCJ's consultant, recalls meeting Sigi in 1978 after learning about him from Moshe Davis, then PA to the Chief Rabbi, and finding a suitable position for him in the ICCJ, which, at that time, was in a state of flux. Dave Hyatt of the American National Conference of Christians and Jews had just been elected president of the International Council and envisaged a more global role for the organization, which was then active only in America and Europe. Indeed, when Sigi was brought on board, there were branches of the Council in only eleven countries. However, as his sister Suzanne recalls in her memoir, he has been active in establishing almost forty branches of the Council in countries all over the world.

Sigi, together with Ruth Weyl, the Rev. Bill Simpson, the general secretary of the ICCJ who was then nearing retirement, Dave Hyatt and the German rabbi, Professor Nathan Peter Levinson, established useful contacts with various departments within the German government and with the German Conference of Catholic Bishops. This led, ultimately, to the venue of the headquarters of the ICCJ being transferred from London to the Martin Buber House in Heppenheim, a gift from the government of Hesse. Moreover, in his role as Chairman of the Executive Committee, Sigi made it clear that in order to make a real impact, the ICCJ needed to improve its finances and its international outreach. He was aware that many of the officials in charge of the member organizations were erudite and well-intentioned but had little experience of political and financial realities. As Ruth Weyl recalls, one of his first steps was to commit himself to generous financial support of the International Council, in negotiation with Professor Martin Stohr, later president of the organization. Stohr, a theologian, academic and peace activist, dedicated to the cause of Christian-Jewish dialogue, was a very able man and very helpful to Sigi. Sigi also established an annual international ICCJ Sir Sigmund Sternberg award, which was first presented in 1985. As well as recognizing sustained intellectual contribution to inter-religious understanding, the award looked for achievements of international significance beyond the recipient's own country. The award, accompanied by a cheque for £2,000, was last presented in 2007, in Australia, to Sister Dr Marianne Dacy, national secretary of the Australian Council of Christians and Jews and an eager proponent of interfaith dialogue and reconciliation between the religions. The award has subsequently been discontinued as Sigi is no longer chairman of the ICCJ.

As Patron of the ICCJ, Sigi addressed a reception at the Board of Deputies of British Jews in January 2006 in honour of the German Ambassador, Thomas Matussek, who was leaving the UK to take up a new posting as Germany's ambassador for the United Nations. The then President of the Board, Henry Grunwald QC, presented the ambassador with the Friendship Award in recognition of his personal contribution to fostering and promoting friendship between Germany and the British Jewish community, while Sigi described the ambassador as 'an open and true partner in the still necessary dialogue between Jew and German', and pointed to the ambassador's visit to a service in memory of Kristallnacht held at the Central Synagogue, the first such visit by a German envoy to a British synagogue. In his response, the ambassador stressed the many points of similarity between Germany and Jewish communities throughout the world and emphasized, too, the importance of continued teaching about the Holocaust in schools, as well as the value of teaching children in schools in both Germany and the UK about contemporary society in each other's country.

Sigi also created the ICCJ's Interfaith Gold Medallion. Prominent recipients have included King Hassan II of Morocco and King Carl Gustav of Sweden, as well as several presidents. Both women presidents of Ireland, Mary Robinson and Mary McAleese, have won the award, as have President Arpad Goncz of Hungary, President Michal Kovac of Slovakia, President Carlos Menem of Argentina, President Eduardo Frei Ruiz-Tagle of Chile, President Johannes Rau of Germany and President Julio Maria Sanguinetti of Uruguay. Shimon Peres, now president of Israel, received the award several years before his appointment and another important Israeli winner was Teddy Kolek, the former Mayor of Jerusalem. Others who have received the Gold Medallion include former Archbishop of Canterbury Lord Runcie, Archbishop Gregorios of Thyateira and Great Britain, several cardinals and bishops and some rabbis. There have also been parliamentarians, including former Speakers Betty Boothroyd and Bernard Weatherill, several ambassadors and figures in the business and academic worlds including Sir John Templeton, Lord George Weidenfeld and Ferenc Glatz, president of the Hungarian Academy of Sciences. Most poignant was the award to Pope John Paul II shortly before his death in 2005.

This particular award was remembered a month later when a special service to commemorate the life of the recently deceased Pontiff was organized by West London Synagogue and the Three Faiths Forum. Sigi, as a co-founder of the Three Faiths Forum, sent a written tribute describing how John Paul II was the first Pope to make reconciliation between the Church and the Jews a central feature of his Papacy. He was, said Sigi, 'a man of immense moral stature, humanity and courage; all sections of the Jewish world will mourn his passing'.

Not all Sigi's initiatives met with approval, in the first instance, from his colleagues in the International Council, though, in retrospect, these initiatives turned out to be very positive. Ruth Weyl, who has also won the Interfaith Gold Medallion, speaks of 'his unfailing instinct to find and bring along personalities he considered of value to the work and outreach of the ICCJ'. One of these was the Archbishop of Paris, Cardinal Lustiger, a Jewish convert to Catholicsim., who accompanied him, 'to raised eyebrows', to the first meeting of the ICCJ at Martin Buber House. In the event, as Ruth Weyl testifies, Lustiger was to become an outstanding leader in the field of Christian-Jewish relations and was presented by Sigi with the Interfaith Gold Medallion. Sigi also brought along Dr Gerhart Riegner of the World Jewish Congress (WJC) and created lasting ties between the ICCJ and the WJC. It was also thanks to his influence that the ICCJ at its annual meeting in Rome in 1997 had an audience with the Pope.

It was Sigi, too, who, despite considerable opposition, insisted that interfaith dialogue should be extended to include Muslims. Due to his determination, the ICCJ created an 'Abrahamic Forum'. Eventually, together with Sheikh Zaki Badawi and the Rev. Marcus Braybrooke, Sigi set up the Three Faiths Forum, now one of the ICCJ's most active members. While Sigi could ignore objections when he felt he knew best how to promote the interests of the ICCJ, he was also capable of accepting the opinions of others rather than his own if the matter in question was not too important. Moreover, as Ruth Weyl points out, Sigi's advice with regard to interfaith relations has been sought by leading personalities throughout the world and he has received much acclaim and numerous honours. In Germany, for example, he was given an award by the Prime Minister of Hesse, where the ICCJ is located.

Sigi's first priority, on joining the ICCJ, was to extend its outreach. Indeed, the visit to Budapest in the early 1980s, when he visited St Stephen's Basilica for the first time, was for the purpose of setting up a Hungarian branch of the Council. He was accompanied by the Papal Nuncio who was in favour of the endeavour and they needed to obtain the permission of the local cardinal. To add weight to his request, Sigi wanted a rabbi to accompany him on his visit to the cardinal but found no rabbi willing to go. Ultimately, Rabbi Istvan Doman, a prominent Budapest rabbi, reluctantly agreed. In the event, the result of this attempt to build bridges between the communities was enormously successful.

Sternberg recalls the anxiety and tension leading up to the successful encounter. The weather was bad, the party travelled by car and Sigi had the feeling that he was the *capora hundl* – the chicken sacrificed on the eve of the Day of Atonement to absolve the pious Jew from his sins – the equivalent, perhaps, of the sacrificial lamb.

Not only was the Council set up in Hungary, the first Communist country to engage in Christian/Jewish dialogue, but also over the next decade in several other countries in eastern and central Europe – in Slovakia, for example, in 1993 and in Rumania in 1994. Sigi had even attempted to open up a branch of the Council in Russia before Perestroika, in conjunction with Oliver McTernan, co-founder and director of Forward Thinking, an organization that facilitates dialogue. McTernan at that time was the parish priest at St Francis of Assisi in Notting Hill and a member of the international Christian peace-making movement, Pax Christi. He had done a great deal of work with the Eastern Orthodox churches. Their project was not going to be easy; as McTernan recalls: 'I said to Sigi one day, "If you're going to get involved with Russia, you're going to need a lot of patience" and he looked at me and said, "the problem is that I haven't the time for patience".'

In the event, the Council was not set up but a meeting to discuss the matter with the Russian Orthodox Church was scheduled for October 1991. However, owing to the coup that took place in August that year, the project had to be abandoned. As McTernan explained: 'The fact that it was on the church's agenda was an achievement. Then the post-coup atmosphere was so negative with the emergence of the nationalistic forces.' McTernan expressed admiration for Sigi's determination to 'expand boundaries, to push to see how far we can go', and recalls that after he arranged meetings between Sigi and diplomats in the Russian embassy in London, Sigi continued to work behind the scenes to provide political protection for the church in Russia.

One upshot of Sigi's endeavours to build bridges with faith groups in Russia was a meeting a few years later at the Sternberg Centre for Judaism, the largest Jewish cultural centre in Europe, between the Russian Ambassador, Anatoly Adamishin, and Sigi, Oliver McTernan, the late Dr Zaki Badawi, then Principal of the Muslim College in Ealing and some leading Reform rabbis. It was at a time of great unrest between Russia and Chechnya, when the Chechens were seeking independence. The ambassador emphasized that 'once the dust had settled', it would be necessary to seek the advice of representatives of the Jewish, Christian and Muslim faiths with experience in interfaith dialogue and conflict resolution in helping to re-establish peaceful relations between the conflicting parties.

It is important to note that, to further his aspirations, Sigi was prepared to work in a confidential setting. While he has frequently had to contend with the charge that he is eager for publicity and recognition in his numerous endeavours, McTernan, for one, sees things very differently:

> People are always critical of activists, whatever the motives. Maybe, too, because Sigi is single-minded when he tackles something, some people just can't cope with that or with his energy. He actually makes himself vulnerable and exposes himself to criticism and, like everyone else, looks for affirmation. When someone is pursuing things and being criticized and seen in negative terms, it is quite natural that he should like to be affirmed in what he is doing. If he didn't, there would be something wrong with him.

McTernan also sees the desire for media attention as legitimate: 'People need to know that there are interfaith groups. People need to know that there are people who break down barriers and develop friendships and trust. To keep your light under a bushel isn't always a good quality and it's often important to make statements in the press.'

Sigi was also obliged to refrain from seeking publicity in his work with the Israel-Diaspora Trust, of which he remains a trustee. He was invited to become a patron of the trust by its founder, the late Rabbi Sidney Brichto, after Brichto became acquainted with him when they were both working with the Oxford Centre for Hebrew and Jewish Studies at Yarnton. Sigi was then the Governor of the Centre and later Governor-Emeritus. At the time, Sigi was very active in the Centre and a great help to David Patterson, the Founding President; Brichto was involved in the Centre's development programme.

The aims of the Israel-Diaspora Trust were, in Brichto's words,

> to create an elite group of Jews who were influential in their own right to discuss matters of concern to Israel and Jews in the diaspora, and to use their influence with their friends and associates who were the opinion makers. The purpose of the group was not to have any agenda and not to give any publicity to those people involved and not to support any faction in Israel or out of Israel but to enable intelligent Jews to let their hair down in a confidential atmosphere and ventilate and cross-ventilate their feelings.

Sigi became a donor to the Trust and through his efforts ecumenical meetings were held from time to time. On one occasion, the Chief Rabbi and Cardinal Koenig were among the guests. On such occasions, Sigi was 'desperate' to have some statement or photographs in the press but Brichto always 'put his foot down'. Later, as he pointed out, Sigi, who was also instrumental in arranging meetings with the then Archbishop of Canterbury, George Carey and Cardinal Basil Hume, the then Archbishop of Westminster, 'began to realize that just talking could be very productive because it could lead to things'.

Oliver McTernan also attended a dinner organized by the Israel-Diaspora Trust focusing on Catholic-Jewish relations and the anti-Semitism that still existed in the Church. As he recalled: 'That meeting exposed just the surface of things and showed the desperate need to continue that discussion. A lot more needed to be said. I find the tendency to make the Jewish race responsible for the activities of the Israeli government disturbing. I think Sidney Brichto pointed that out and the matter needed to be pursued further.' McTernan credits Sigi for facilitating 'that sort of dinner. He has an extraordinary ability to create friendships and bonds.'

Another guest at the dinner at the Royal Overseas League was Father Michael Seed, Ecumenical Advisor to the Archbishop of Westminster, who was accompanying Cardinal Hume. He recalls that at times 'the conversation did get a little bit heated' and that some of the guests admitted that the Catholic Church had been quite anti-Semitic. 'People were talking about their early concepts of having Jewish neighbours and similar experiences. Some of the stories were very positive, others were not.' Sigi, Father Seed recalls, was 'almost like a chairman. He never really gave his views or his opinions' and showed no sign of emotion.

As if to 'return a favour', Rabbi Brichto was persuaded by Sigi to become an executive on the Council of Christians and Jews. He also expressed admiration for Sigi's energy and persistence in trying to get as many people as possible involved in interfaith work. 'He is so focused on achieving what he wants to achieve, he will dirty his hands. He rings up people, he does the work, he goes right for it and no one's too small and no one's too unimportant. Every time he sees somebody, he feels he can get them involved.' Brichto did feel that, at times, Sigi was preoccupied with too many objectives, but considered that interfaith was his primary cause. 'He likes to be a unifying force; he wants to be recognised as the motive behind the unifying force.'

Brichto accepted Sigi's desire to receive credit and recognition for his work and acknowledged that to obtain results, it was sometimes necessary to be a 'pusher'. 'You can't have it both ways. If Sigi were more subtle, he would have to accept that sometimes subtlety doesn't achieve what you want to achieve.'

Sigi's deep commitment to interfaith activity has also been commented on by Lord Weidenfeld in his autobiography, *Remembering My Good Friends*. Weidenfeld recalls that when the Waldheim affair erupted during the 1980s, bringing Austria into disrepute for its failure to admit the degree to which its people had condoned Hitler and its inadequate compensation of the victims of Nazism, he had discussions with various Austrian ministers as to how the damage could be repaired. One suggestion he put forward was to bring together Christian and Jewish thinkers to discuss how public opinion could be made more aware of the changes initiated by the Second Vatican Council. It was agreed that Weidenfeld could organize a conference on 'Jews and Christians in a Pluralistic World' in the Vienna

Hofburg with Cardinal Koenig as a co-convenor. As Weidenfeld recalls: 'I prepared it in close cooperation with Sir Sigmund Sternberg … who, as chairman of the International Council of Christians and Jews, has devoted his life to ecumenical causes with stubborn single-mindedness'. Sigi, Weidenfeld pointed out, enlisted the help of a number of American and European clergy, including the former Archbishop of Canterbury, Lord Coggan, while Weidenfeld himself invited Bernard Lewis, the Islamic scholar, and Conor Cruise O'Brien, the writer and political commentator.

Sigi was also involved with interfaith relations in Israel, initially with the Israel Interfaith Association. When this organization was floundering, he gave his financial and moral support to Rabbi Dr Ron Kronish and Rabbi David Rosen, who were setting up a new body, the Interreligious Coordinating Council in Israel (ICCI). Sigi's award of the Interfaith Gold Medallion to Archbishop Montezemolo, then the Papal Nuncio in Israel, was, in Dr Kronish's opinion, 'an important stepping stone in the whole development of Catholic-Jewish relations in Israel'. Sigi also influenced Cardinal Cassidy to speak at a seminar at the ICCI.

Kronish admired Sigi's networking skills which helped people get together to further their work. One example he gave was that he had been contacted by someone who was involved in pursuing contact with Jordan and Muslims. This man had met Sigi in England and was advised by him to get in touch with Kronish so that they could cooperate on various projects. Kronish was also appreciative of Sigi's role in the ICCJ as Chairman of the Executive.

> It's a complicated organization because it's a collection of people from so many different countries, all of whom have very different ideas of how it should be run but he's given it leadership, he's given his vision of the kinds of things he'd like to do … This huge international organization which he has tried to build up over the years has been beset with internal problems but nevertheless he stayed with it. Despite its imperfections, this organization still has a noble cause and a noble vision. Sigi tries to take the high road and

doesn't allow himself to get bogged down with all the details of the internal conflicts.

Sigi, Kronish felt, was like a 'roving ambassador', 'very good with the media' and 'his own PR man, one of the best', important qualities for furthering a cause which deserved greater support.

> From what I can see, his motivation is sincere. He believes in the cause. There aren't many people in this movement and there are relatively few Jews in the world who care much about it. He's one of a handful so I think he's come to believe in being the informal ambassador to Jews in the world.

Sigi was also instrumental in initiating contact between Kronish and Monsignor Michel Sabbah, the Latin Patriarch in Jerusalem and the first Palestinian in that role. Sabbah had frequently been outspoken about the Israeli occupation of Palestinian land. As Kronish explained:

> Sigi wanted to see Sabbah so I set up the meeting and went with him and I found that he was very warmly welcomed and so was I and since that day I've kept up my contact with Sabbah. As a matter of fact Sabbah came and spoke at a big international colloquium we hosted in Jerusalem. So, as I say, one thing leads to another. Sigi would go to someone who is a controversial figure and meet informally and be a catalyst for change.

Sigi had also met Bishop Samir Kafity, another leading Palestinian Christian, but Kafity was nearing retirement age and did not become involved with the ICCI.

Kronish, who perceived Sigi as 'a simple, sweet, loving and gentle soul', also praised his wife, Hazel, 'who keeps him on track'. He doubted whether Sigi could have done so much without her support. He also recalled an occasion when he was with Sigi in Budapest: 'I have a picture of myself standing with him and the President of Hungary. He's recognized by presidents and ambassadors all around the world and in a sense he's what I call "larger than life". He's become a symbol, a symbol for the good natured improvement of Christian-Jewish relations.'

6 The Papal Knighthood

In late 1985, there was a certain buzz in the circles associated with Westminster Cathedral. As Peter Bander van Duren, an expert on heraldry and orders of knighthood, recounts in his book, *Orders of Knighthood and of Merit*, he was asked by Cardinal Hume, Archbishop of Westminster, to devise a ceremony for the investiture of the award of Knight Commander of the Equestrian Order of St Gregory the Great to a prominent member of London's Jewish community for his work in Catholic-Jewish relations. 'I was informed that it would be a public function attended by members of the Government, the upper and lower Houses of Parliament, ambassadors and public figures.' The man to be honoured was, of course, Sigi.

Father Michael Seed, who had arrived at the Cathedral in January that year, recalls that there was some gossip about the award as it was so unusual, almost unique at the time. Father Seed did not feel, however, that people were too surprised. 'Things had changed so much. It was 1985 and we were in modern times, twenty years since the end of the Vatican Council and twenty years since *Nostra Aetate*, so I think, in a sense, it was just overdue.'

Why Sigi was chosen rather than another prominent figure in the Jewish world was, naturally, a matter of interest. While his involvement in Christian-Jewish relations had spanned barely a decade, what he had achieved in that time was quite remarkable. As well as rescuing the Council of Christians and Jews in the United Kingdom, he had taken on important roles in the International Council and had been instrumental in expanding the ICCJ's outreach in many countries. It is quite likely, too, that perceptive senior Catholic clergymen were of the belief that by awarding Sigi with a Papal Knighthood, he would be able to use this to ever greater interfaith endeavours.

Father Seed looks at it this way:

> Sigi is almost like a Scarlet Pimpernel. He's involved in just so many things, so many activities. But, if you think about it, the award could have gone to a Jewish scholar, an academic or a rabbi. It could have gone to a Chief Rabbi. I just think that by that point Sigi had been the means of so much interconnection, whether it was to do with issues relating to Israel, issues with the Council of Christians and Jews and the International Council and, of course, all his projects.

Father Seed assumed that it was Cardinal Hume who had recommended Sigi for the honour. His recommendation would have gone to Cardinal Agostino Casaroli, the Secretary of State to the Vatican, who would have had to approve the nomination before consulting the Pope. Casaroli was known to be interested in inter-religious affairs and was, in Father Seed's view, 'a very saintly man'. It is likely that he was supportive of the nomination and would have worked hard to remove any difficulties which may have stood in the way of its going ahead.

While Catholics who had become Papal Knights had had the award conferred upon them in a private ceremony, either at the house of a bishop or after a mass in church, Sigi's award required a full investiture – 'a ceremony more like a state occasion than a spiritual ceremony', as Bander van Duren put it. Bander van Duren found himself 'inundated with letters from all over the British Isles as well as the continent of Europe', as Catholic Knights voiced their resentment at having been deprived of such a ceremony.

It was also virtually unprecedented for Knighthoods of the Equestrian Order of St Gregory to be awarded to non-Catholics. The Order of Pius IX had been awarded to diplomats accredited to the Vatican, irrespective of their religion and the Order of the Golden Spur had been given to non-Christians until Pope Paul VI decreed that it should be given only to Christian Heads of State as it was dedicated to the Virgin Mary. While it was always acknowledged in Vatican circles that the award honouring Sigi was well deserved, some officials were of the opinion, as Bander van Duren noted, that an even higher rank in the Order of Pope St Sylvester would have been more appropriate. As it happened, over ten years later, in 1997, Sigi's wife Hazel was awarded the honour of being appointed a Dame of the Equestrian Order of Pope St Sylvester.

Organizing Sigi's investiture ceremony was no easy task. The award he was to receive was a Pontifical Equestrian Order and there appeared to be no precedent for functions of this kind. Bander van Duren was obliged to consult the late Bishop Gerald Mahon, the then representative of the Bishops Conference of England and Wales for interfaith relations, and to study programmes of investitures of other Orders of Knighthood. Eventually, he succeeded in devising a ceremony of induction and investiture, even though he was confronted by another, more fundamental problem. Since Sigi was not a Catholic, the investiture could not take place as part of a Mass as was customary. Moreover, as a non-Catholic and non-Christian Knight, Sigi would not be requested to make an oath of unswerving and continued obedience to the Pope, the Apostolic See and the Catholic Church. Despite – or perhaps because of – the unusual nature of the occasion, a large number of Papal Knights of various orders accepted the invitation to attend the occasion, all to be dressed in their uniform. The ceremony itself was to take place in a large assembly hall adjoining Westminster Cathedral but not in the Cathedral itself.

The award came as a great surprise to Sigi. When he received a letter from Bishop Mahon informing him that he was to be made a Papal Knight, he telephoned Dr Immanuel Jacobovits, the Chief Rabbi, who told him that he should accept the award. The two men, who were contemporaries, were good friends. Sigi later visited the Pope in Rome and told the Pontiff that he would make every effort to arrange for him to visit the Holy Land, an occurrence that took place eventually in 2000.

Before the investiture ceremony on 4 March 1986, Sigi had acquired the uniform of a Knight Commander of the Order of St Gregory. As well as the sizeable delegation of Papal Knights, the guests included a large contingent of public figures headed by the Lord High Chancellor of the United Kingdom and leading politicians. There were also diplomats from many countries, in particular Israel, and many representatives of the Vatican, several bishops, the Chief Rabbi and members of the Board of Deputies of British Jews. Lord Coggan, the Archbishop of Canterbury and many other important dignitaries were also present. As Bander van Duren recounted, there was wide international press and television coverage and the question of security was of paramount importance.

In a letter to Sigi in October the following year, presenting him with an advance copy of his book, Bander van Duren wrote:

> As you will see, you are making history, and two juridical chapters concerning precedence of a Jew receiving the Pontifical Equestrian Order of St Gregory the Great and to be invested, as well as the detailed account of your investiture, culminating in your attendance upon His Holiness during the first visit of a Supreme Pontiff to a Synagogue, are here as a historical record and guideline for the future. It is a new and historical record of Catholic-Jewish relations nobody can undo!

Sigi's sister, Suzanne, recalls in her memoir that after Cardinal Hume, the Archbishop of Westminster, had bestowed the Papal Knighthood on him, Sigi made a speech of acceptance in which he said that he did not consider that the award was for himself but for all Jews today and for those who had perished in the Holocaust. He went on to relate how surprised he was that he, a Hungarian Jew, should receive a Papal Knighthood. He recalled that as a 6-year-old boy in Budapest, when he had gone out for walks with his sister under the care of a Catholic nurse, whenever a Catholic priest had approached the nurse told the children that they must cross the road because they were Jews and had killed Christ. The children could not understand and asked: 'When did we kill Christ?' Suzanne relates that Cardinal Hume, who was standing next to Sigi, was very moved by his words and said that the Christian Church had to take full responsibility for all the decades of suffering of the Jewish people and for the Holocaust.

After Sigi was appointed a Papal Knight, he heard from the Vatican's representative on the ICCJ that the Pope had blessed the Jews coming out of synagogue in Rome. Sigi's response was that the Pope should go to the synagogue. This was not something that was simple to organize. Sigi had to discuss the matter with some leaders of the Jewish community in Italy and with Bishop, now Cardinal, Jorge Mejia, secretary of the Pontifical Commission for Relations with the Jews, who represented the Holy See on the International Council of Christians and Jews. Mejia, too, had urged the Pope to visit the Rome synagogue, after Sigi had put the idea to him, and he and Sigi met so that the necessary arrangements could be made. Indeed, the preparations for this unique occasion were very difficult. Nevertheless, barely a month after Sigi's investiture ceremony, the visit took place. On 13 April 1986, Pope John Paul II visited Tempio Maggiore, Rome's Great Synagogue, the first visit of a pope to a synagogue since apostolic times. Once again there was a great deal of international media attention, the event being covered by the BBC, NBC in America, by an Australian television station and other major media outlets. A memorial stamp was also issued to commemorate the visit.

Sigi, of course, was one of the prominent guests at the occasion. Suzanne, whom he had invited to accompany him, gives a vivid account of the experience. On arriving in Rome during a downpour of rain, she and Sigi 'were dashed off to the nearest entrance of the synagogue by a waiting limousine'. Sigi was wearing his full Papal Knight's regalia.

As Suzanne recounts, a new protocol had been invented

for this unique occasion. Rabbi Elio Toaff, the Chief Rabbi of Rome, decreed that there should be two thrones, one for the Pope and one for him. Twelve cardinals in carmine robes accompanied the Pope and twelve rabbis in white with white skull caps attended the Chief Rabbi.

The Pope spoke first, in Italian and Latin but with his distinctive Polish intonation. In his speech he referred to the Jews as 'Christianity's beloved elder brothers'. 'As we all well know', he went on to say, 'the relationship of brotherhood that could and should typify relations between the Church and Jewry has ... throughout our common history been tragically perverted into one of internecine enmity and oppression.' The Pontiff was followed by Chief Rabbi Toaff, a classical scholar and professor, whose address had an electrifying effect, as Suzanne remembered:

> It was permeated with the influence of Roman antiquities, like those of the founding fathers of Rome, Romulus and Remus. His eloquence carried the tones of Virgil and Homer. Evidently he had unconsciously been imbued with the great oratorical skills of Cicero. All these were present in his delivery. I could see the cardinals at close range overcome by total amazement and awe. Possibly none could have surpassed the brilliant performance of their host.

In a gesture that symbolised a new era in Catholic-Jewish relations, the Pontiff and the Chief Rabbi shared an embrace. And after the service Sigi was invited to a private audience with the Pope in the Vatican. The Pope asked Sigi about his opinion of his visit to the synagogue. Sigi's reply was one he was, sadly, all too frequently to use in many different contexts: 'Holy Father, it was a wonderful, memorable occasion. If we had been able to arrange it a couple of thousand years earlier, just think how many millions of innocent lives might have been saved.'

What Sigi was determined to do was to use this unique award to further his work in writing a new chapter in the relations between Christians and Jews. There remained many

significant areas in which Sigi would make a valuable contribution. In Father Seed's view, his most notable achievement
was his work in furthering the process which led to the
Vatican's recognition of the State of Israel. While Sigi would,
by no means, have been the only figure involved in the
complex negotiations prior to this historic landmark, Seed
'always suspected that Sigi's mark was behind that'. It was
something, Seed added, that Sigi had dearly wanted. 'It was
the ultimate restoration and, in a way, the ultimate forgiveness for all the problems he had had in the past.'

Rabbi Mark Winer, former Senior Rabbi at West London
Synagogue, recalls that he and Sigi got to know each other
while working on the treaty between the Vatican and Israel.
At the time, Rabbi Winer was still in America and President of
the National Council of Synagogues, the umbrella body for
American Jewry, with a special brief to oversee interfaith
relations between American Jews and Christians and
American Jews and the US government. Indeed, it was Sigi
who was instrumental in persuading Winer to apply for the
position at West London Synagogue after the death of the
much-loved Rabbi Hugo Gryn. Once the signing ceremony
for the treaty between the Vatican and Israel had been
arranged to take place in Jerusalem, Winer, together with Sigi,
his wife, Hazel, and Gerhart Riegner, the former secretary of
the World Jewish Congress, were the four diaspora Jews
invited by the Israeli Foreign Ministry to witness the signing
of the momentous document.

Sigi has spoken of the long struggle between the Catholic
Church and recognition of the Jewish State. He recollects
reading an account by Theodor Herzl, the founder of modern
Zionism, of his visit to Pope Pius X in 1904 to ask his support
for a Jewish homeland in Palestine. The reply he received was
hardly encouraging. 'If you go to Palestine and settle your
people there, we will have priests and churches ready to
baptise all of you.' Some sixty years later, when passing
through Israel, Pope Paul VI refused to meet the country's
Chief Rabbi and would never utter the word 'Israel' in public.

As the late Chaim Bermant wrote in *The Independent* in

December 1993, the Vatican's commitment to sign an agreement with Israel by the end of the year, granting the Jewish State official recognition, would mark an end to the enmity between Rome and Jerusalem that went back 2,000 years. And three months later, in March 1994, the signing of the agreement was celebrated at a reception for many distinguished guests in the Throne Room of Archbishop's House, Westminster, hosted by Cardinal Hume and Sigi. At the reception, the Cardinal was presented with the ICCJ Interfaith Gold Medallion for his outstanding contribution to interfaith dialogue and Chief Rabbi Jonathan Sacks praised the Roman Catholic Church for being courageous enough to abandon some harmful ideas which had contributed to its enmity with the Jewish people. This new approach, he said, had made possible the Vatican's historic agreement with the Jewish State. A sad note to the occasion was the need for both the Chief Rabbi and the Israeli ambassador, Moshe Raviv, to strongly denounce the murder of twenty-nine Muslims at the tomb of the patriarchs in Hebron the previous week by the extremist Jewish settler, Baruch Goldstein.

The new agreement was the subject of the Bishop Mahon Memorial Lecture given two months later by the Editorial Director of the Catholic Herald under ICCJ auspices with Sigi in the chair. In his talk, 'The Holy See and Israel – A New Era?', Gerard Noel pointed out that the agreement 'implicitly reverses the 2,000-year-old Catholic claim that – because of their supposed "crime" of killing Christ from which they have been absolved by a decree of the Vatican Council – the Jews could never again exist as a united people or as a sovereign nation. We thus truly enter "a new era".'

This 'new era' was also marked by a remarkable event that had taken place in Rome the previous month. A concert was held at the Vatican on 11 April 1994 to commemorate the Shoah. Those who attended included a number of Holocaust survivors, Chief Rabbi Elio Toaff, the Israeli ambassador and members of the College of Cardinals and of the Diplomatic Corps accredited to the Holy See. Sigi led a group of dignitaries from Britain including Bishop Charles Henderson,

1. Sir Sigmund and Lady Sternberg.

2. Ruth, Michael, Sir Sigmund and Frances Sternberg.

3. Frances, Ruth and Michael Sternberg.

4. Hazel Sternberg with Ruth and David.

5. Frances Sternberg approximate age 18.

6. Sir Sigmund and Frances Blane (née Sternberg).

7. Victor Sternberg.

8. Victor and Hazel Sternberg.

9. Robert Perlman, Hazel Sternberg, Sir Sigmund, Ruth Tamir, Noam Tamir and Jonny Tamir at Branksome, December 2009.

10. Lady Hazel and Ruth Tamir.

11. Sir Sigmund with great-grandson Jacob, March 2009.

12. David and Anna Sternberg.

13. David, Freddy and Nell Sternberg, August 2011.

14. Sir Sigmund with his sister, Suzanne Perlman.

15. Bishop Jim Thompson and Rabbi Hugo Gryn, co-chairmen of the Inter Faith Network, receive the Sir Sigmund Sternberg Award in recognition of their work for 'cooperation between people of many faiths', 20 October 1987. From left to right: Chief Rabbi Immanuel Jakobovits, Bishop Jim Thompson, Sir Sigmund, Rabbi Hugo Gryn, Archbishop of Canterbury Robert Runcie. Copyright Henry Jacobs, LMPA.

16. Presentation of Ashkenazi Haggadah to Pope John Paul II in Rome by Sir Sigmund, 1986. Copyright L'Osservatore Romano Citta' del Vaticano.

17. Investiture as Papal Knight of the Order of St Gregory the Great, 4 March 1986. Left to right: Cardinal Basil Hume, Archbishop of Westminster, Sir Sigmund, Brigadier Viner of the Papal Knights Association. Copyright Peter Fisher.

18. Honorary Doctorate from Essex University, March 1996. Back row: Noam Tamir, Ruth Tamir, Daniel Sternberg, Vice Chancellor; front row: Michael Sternberg, Hazel Sternberg, Sir Sigmund, Suzanne Perlman. Copyright Official Photographer for Essex University.

19. HRH The Duke of Edinburgh at the Sternberg Centre, November 1996. Copyright John Rifkin.

vice-chairman of the Council of Christians and Jews. The audience was addressed by the Pope, who recalled his visits to Auschwitz and Dachau:

> During the first year of my Pontificate I again went to Auschwitz and before the memorial stone with its Hebrew inscription I sought to express the profound emotion evoked in me by 'the memory of the People whose sons and daughters were destined to total extermination'. It is precisely this People who had received from God the commandment, 'Thou shalt not kill', who have experienced to a particular degree what killing means. No one may pass by this inscription with indifference. Once again, today, I express a word of abhorrence for the genocide decreed against the Jewish people during the Second World War.
>
> The concert this evening is a commemoration of those horrifying events. The candles which will burn as we listen to the music will keep before us the long history of anti-Semitism which culminated in the Shoah. But it is not enough that we remember, for in our own day, regrettably, there are many new manifestations of the anti-Semitism, xenophobia and racial hatred that were the seeds of those unspeakable crimes. Our shared hope is that the music we shall listen to together will confirm our resolve to consolidate the good relations between our two communities so that, with the help of Almighty God, we can work together to prevent the repetition of such heinous evil. Humanity cannot permit that to happen again.

The Pontiff paid tribute to the many Christians in his homeland and across Europe who had made every effort 'to help their brothers and sisters of the Jewish community, even at the cost of their own lives'. He was conscious of the dangers the current generation was obliged to confront and urged 'Christians and Jews together' to offer guidance 'to a world struggling to distinguish good from evil'. Later, in an interview with the press, the Pope acknowledged that the Jewish people now had a land of their own 'after two thousand years of being scattered among all the nations of the world'.

The Vatican had also appointed a commission of nine German theologians to draw up a document which would attribute co-responsibility for the Shoah to the Roman Catholic Church. At a meeting in May 1994, Sigi welcomed a draft of the document which stated that 'the anti-Jewish theological tradition of the Church was an important component of the Holocaust', although he emphasized that it was only at a provisional stage and had not yet been approved by any Church authority.

Since receiving the award of a Papal Knighthood, Sigi has clearly devoted much of his energy into furthering the cause which had become of such importance to him. Whether he could have achieved so much without the constant support of his wife, Hazel, is doubtful. Father Seed saw her as 'the powerhouse behind him. She's very sensible and would protect him a great deal and advise him considerably. I think she is the biggest influence in his life and her calmness in an almost therapeutic style is excellent.' Seed felt Hazel had not had any serious acknowledgment for what she had done and hoped that one day she would be recognized. Oliver McTernan was of a similar opinion: 'One of the people who is overlooked in Sigi's life is Hazel and I think that Sigi would not be able to function in the effective way he does if it weren't for the tremendous loyal support and love that Hazel gives him.' And Dr Ron Kronish in Jerusalem spoke of her as 'a wonderful wife who keeps him (Sigi) on track. She's a wonderful lady, very interested in things, very up on the issues, knows what's going on.' Kronish also doubted whether Sigi could have done all he had without Hazel and saw her as a great help, not least on the diplomatic side of his work.

On 7 September 1997, Hazel was presented in Rome with the award many of her admirers had been hoping for. Cardinal Edward Cassidy, who headed the Commission of the Holy See for Religious Relations with the Jews, conferred on her the title of Dame of the Equestrian Order of Pope St

Sylvester. In her speech after receiving the award, Hazel joked that as she and Sigi were both members of Papal equestrian orders, it was obviously the Vatican's intention that they should 'continue journeying side by side'. She paid tribute to Cardinal Cassidy for his tireless work in promoting interfaith dialogue and, in particular, for 'masterminding' the concert commemorating the Holocaust.

> You will recall the many thousands who were there, the splendid sight of the Holy Father flanked by the President of Italy and the Chief Rabbi of Rome. In front of them, dressed in the never to be mistaken striped pyjamas of the concentration camp inmate, were several hundred survivors who had come back to Europe from America for the occasion. They had been received in a Papal audience and for them, for us, it was an emotional experience never to be forgotten.

Some years later, the St Robert Bellarmine Medal was presented to Sir Sigmund Sternberg and Lady Sternberg for promoting interfaith dialogue by the Rector of the Pontificia Universita Gregoriana in Rome on the occasion of the launch of the Gerhart Riegner Memorial Fund.

Pope John Paul's visit to Israel in March 2000 was the source of further deeply emotional experiences. There had been a gradual build-up to the visit. In 1998, the Vatican issued a significant statement – *We Remember: A Reflection on the Shoah* – presented by Cardinal Cassidy, who had been nominated earlier in the year as the recipient of the ICCJ's Sigmund Sternberg Award for Interfaith Endeavour. The statement was accompanied by a personal message from the Pope, who had personally requested that the document should be prepared. In some ways this could be seen as a follow-up to *Nostra Aetate*, in which there is no mention of the Holocaust, or of the establishment of the State of Israel. The new document was 'addressed to the Catholic faithful throughout the world, not only in Europe where the *Shoah* took place, hoping that all Christians will join their Catholic brothers and sisters in meditating on the catastrophe which befell the Jewish people, on its causes and on the moral imperative to ensure that never again such a tragedy will happen.' At the same time, the document asked 'our Jewish friends to hear us with an open heart'.

The Vatican statement failed to placate those in the Jewish world who would have wanted an outright apology for Church leaders who failed to speak out against Hitler, in particular Pope Pius XII, whose silence had long been a subject of controversy. Rabbi Yisrael Meir Lau, the Chief Rabbi of Israel and himself a Holocaust survivor, claimed that 'a clear condemnation from the Vatican at the time could have prevented the terrible things that were done', while Lord Greville Janner, chairman of the Holocaust Educational Trust in Britain was 'deeply disappointed' at what he termed 'this unworthy document'. Many Jews objected to the document's insistence that Nazi anti-Semitism 'had its roots outside Christianity'. Sigi, in a more balanced appraisal, acknowledged that 'the last word has not been said on the silence of those in the Church who knew well what was happening to the Jewish people' but asserted that 'Jews everywhere' would share the Pope's hope that the Vatican document would help heal wounds.

This aspiration was voiced in a letter incorporated in the document in which the Pope stated that it was his 'fervent hope' that the document 'will indeed help to heal the wounds of past misunderstandings and injustices. May it enable memory to play its necessary part in the process of shaping a future in which the unspeakable iniquity of the *Shoah* will never again be possible'.

At this point, it may be relevant to point out the contribution of the young Bishop Wojtyla, as Pope John Paul then was, to the debate during the Second Vatican Council about the proposed declaration, *Nostra Aetate*. As Sigi related in an article he wrote at the time of the Pope's visit to Israel, while some participants in the Council found it difficult to accept that the Jews should not be held responsible for the death of Jesus, the unknown Polish bishop began to speak of the Church's responsibility to change its relations with the Jews.

Some thirty-five years later, Sigi's article continued, 'on the eve of his visit to Israel, Pope John Paul led his cardinals and a huge flock of the faithful in a solemn mass confessing to a litany of sins with which he believes the Church to be burdened and for which it seeks forgiveness. Primary among these sins was one declared to be a "Confession of Sins Against the People of Israel".'

As 'a Jew to whom the epithet "Christ-killer" still rings down the years', Sigi confessed himself particularly moved by the prayer the Pope then offered:

> God of our fathers, you chose Abraham and his descendants to bring your Name to the Nations. We are deeply saddened by the behaviour of those who, in the course of history, have caused these children of yours to suffer and, asking forgiveness, we wish to commit ourselves to genuine brotherhood with the people of the covenant.

Aharon Lopez, Israel's ambassador to the Vatican, was also greatly moved, feeling that with him during this historic mass stood his ancestors from the Crusades, Spain and the Holocaust. The papal apology was produced by twenty-eight theologians and scholars under the guidance of Cardinal Joseph Ratzinger, who was to succeed Pope John Paul II as Pope Gregory XVI.

This act of repentance did not pass without controversy. There were those in the Church, including a number of hardliners among the cardinals, who argued that while certain individuals within the Church over the centuries may have sinned, the Church itself should not be held responsible. Excessive penitence and self-questioning, they claimed, could undermine faith in Christianity and its institutions. On the other side, various Jewish voices posited that the Vatican's apology did not go far enough. Rabbi David Rosen, however, a member of the Permanent Bilateral Commission that had negotiated the full diplomatic normalization of relations, put the Vatican's Day of Forgiveness text in perspective: 'While the content does not go as far as past statements of the Pope, the significance lies above all in the inclusion of a statement of contrition for sins committed against the Jewish people, in

Catholic liturgy.' Rabbi Rosen, whom Sigi had known since he was a boy at school with his son Michael, had worked closely with him to further the process of reconciliation between the Vatican and Israel. The papal apology was also praised by Israeli Prime Minister Ehud Barak as a noble act that had 'raised the flag of fraternity to full mast'. And certainly many, like Sigi, were greatly affected by the Pope's contrition, not least by his desire to seek forgiveness for the Church's wrong-doings against the Jews, as voiced in his prayer.

It is this prayer that Pope John Paul inserted between the stones of the Western Wall in Jerusalem during his visit, a sight which Sigi found particularly affecting as he related in a speech at a Millennium Conference in London two months later. 'To see the Pope standing there, where the tears and prayers of Jews have been offered down the ages, was indeed a moving occasion ... Indeed, I have known few occasions which filled me with so much emotion as when I sat before the monitor at the BBC TV centre that day commenting on the Holy Father's visit to the Kotel.' The Pope's prayer was later enshrined at Yad Vashem, the memorial in Jerusalem to the millions of Jews murdered in the Holocaust.

Pope John Paul's visit to the Hall of Remembrance at Yad Vashem was another profoundly moving occasion for those who were there. He first laid a wreath at the massive granite slab that covers the cremated remains of some of the uniden-tified Jews killed in the death camps, and then lit the eternal flame. Ron Kronish recounted in a report for the Interreligious Coordinating Council in Israel, 'As a cantor sang "El Maleh Rachamim", the traditional memorial prayer chanted for the dead and especially for the martyrs of the Jewish people, we could see the Pope's face straining to take everything in at this highly personal and intensely emotional occasion.' Later during the ceremony, the Pope's own prayer moved several of the witnesses to tears:

> The words of the ancient Psalm rise from our hearts: 'I have become like a broken vessel. I hear the whispering of many ... as they scheme together against me, as they plot to take my life. But I trust in you, O Lord ...".

In this place of memories, the mind and the heart and soul feel an extreme need for silence. Silence in which to remember. Silence in which to try to make some sense of the memories which come flooding back. Silence because there are no words strong enough to deplore the terrible tragedy of the Shoah …

Here, as at Auschwitz and many other places in Europe, we are overcome by the echo of the heart-rending laments of so many. Men, women and children cry out to us from the depths of the horror that they knew. How can we fail to heed their cry? …

The honour given to the 'Righteous Gentiles' by the State of Israel at Yad Vashem for having acted heroically to save Jews, sometimes to the point of giving their own lives, is a recognition that not even in the darkest hour is every light extinguished. That is why the Psalms and the entire Bible, though well aware of the human capacity for evil, also proclaim that evil will not have the last word.

When the ceremony was over, Kronish recounts,

the Pope … slowly got up from his seat and walked across the Hall of Remembrance to greet the Jewish Holocaust survivors who were standing there, one by one. As he shook each hand, the commentator on television revealed that many of these survivors had been saved by Righteous Gentiles … including one woman who was saved by Pope John Paul II himself long before he became Pope, during the days when he was a young priest in Poland.

Indeed, according to a report in *Ha'Aretz*, 'Edith Tzirer wept as she told the Pope how he had saved her in 1945, when he was a young priest, by giving her food and carrying her on his back for three kilometres when she was drained of strength'. And Israeli Prime Minister Ehud Barak told the Pope that his visit to Yad Vashem marked a 'climax of this historic journey of healing'.

It is the very human quality of these events that

contributed to the success of the papal visit, which had been threatened, at its outset, by an agreement signed barely a month earlier between the Vatican and the Palestinian Liberation Organization, which provoked considerable anger in Israel and led the Israeli government to accuse the Holy See of interfering in peace negotiations between Israel and the Palestinians. David Rosen, however, who in 2005 was made a Knight Commander of the Order of St Gregory the Great, foresaw the moment when the Pontiff would pay his respects to the President of the Jewish State as 'the ultimate symbolic act of the historic transformation in Catholic teaching towards the Jewish people'. And a report in the *International Herald Tribune* spoke of Vatican officials, who had been somewhat anxious about the visit, leaving feeling a stronger bond with Israel:

> They were impressed by Prime Minister Ehud Barak ... by the gracious and uplifting speech he gave at the Holocaust memorial and by the way his government turned the other cheek to Palestinian provocations. In contrast, the Palestinians, whose cause they support, somewhat disappointed them by failing to take advantage of the worldwide platform they had been afforded by the Pope's visit.

This included a visit by the Pontiff to Bethlehem and to the nearby Dheisheh refugee camp with Yasser Arafat at his side.

During the visit, indeed, the Pope was confronted by political disputes and a variety of publicity stunts, yet managed to keep the focus on spiritual matters. As an admiring Israeli diplomat told a correspondent from *The Daily Telegraph*: 'He seems to be able to walk between the raindrops without getting wet.' And while there had been disquiet among some Jews about a Christian leader with a cross round his neck going to the Western Wall, the text of the message the Pope inserted between the stones reassured them. As Rabbi Michael Melchior, who had welcomed the Pope to the Wall explained: 'I think what's important is not the cross. It's that he touched the wall and the wall touched him.'

The papal trip to the Holy Land, culminating in the visit to the Western Wall, was hailed as a major triumph in the Italian press. *Il Messaggero* quoted Israeli cabinet minister Haim Ramon as saying that there was 'nothing else the Jews can ask this great leader. A long era of conflicts between the Christians and the Jews has come to an end.'

Ramon's conclusions may be seen to have been a little premature since later in the year certain Vatican initiatives caused considerable unrest in the Jewish world. The announcement in June that the nineteenth-century pope, Pius IX, would be beatified in September alongside the universally admired Pope John XXIII was denounced by the Italian Jewish community, provoked anger in Jewish circles worldwide, and was opposed by many liberal Catholics and other Christians. Commentators pointed out that Pius IX had scarcely concealed his anti-Semitism and spoke of Jews as 'dogs of whom there are too many present in Rome, howling and disturbing us'. John XXIII, in contrast, had instigated the Second Vatican Council and, during the Second World War, as Monsignor Angelo Roncalli, had exerted whatever influence he possessed to save Jews from persecution and death during the Nazi years. Initially, the Vatican had proposed to beatify Pope Pius XII alongside John XXIII, but had decided against this because of the controversy over Pius XII's role during the Second World War. The resolution to beatify Pius IX instead was regarded by some observers as a gesture to placate the more extreme conservative voices in the curia.

Then in early August, the Congregation of the Doctrine of the Faith, headed by Cardinal Ratzinger, published a declaration, *Dominus Iesus*, which included a paragraph intimating that all non-Christian religions were 'gravely deficient' as far as salvation was concerned. Even non-Catholic Christian communities were held to have 'defects'. The effect of this declaration, which was seen by many to go against the spirit of ecumenism which had characterized much of John Paul's papacy, was exacerbated after extracts were leaked from a new book by Cardinal Ratzinger which stated that the Catholic Church was 'waiting for the moment' when Israel and the Jews embrace Christianity. Chief Rabbi Jonathan Sacks, in a broadcast on Radio 4, felt that the Vatican was sending out mixed messages. 'On the one hand there have been the personal initiatives of the Pope, high among those being his visit to Jerusalem, which did a great deal to heal the scars in the relationship between the Church and the Jewish people. On the other hand you have this very conservative voice coming from the Vatican, which does seem to belong to an earlier age.' The Chief Rabbi, who had attended a Millennium World Peace Summit of Religious and Spiritual Leaders at the UN in New York, together with Sigi, Sheikh Zaki Badawi and Rabbi Tony Bayfield, considered that since interfaith relations had moved into the global era, there was no longer a place for 'monopolistic claims'.

Sigi's own statement in a press release in response to *Dominus Iesus* was indicative of his unfailing aptitude for diplomacy:

> The Catholic Church, speaking through its Congregation of the Doctrine of the Faith, has told its followers that there is no compatibility between it and other religions and varieties of the Christian faith. That is neither new, nor surprising, and I would be astonished to hear a rabbi say that you could just as well be a Christian as a Jew. I do not believe this means the Catholic Church will not continue to seek for a decent and respectful relationship with other faiths, especially the Jewish faith, to which Pope John Paul II has more than once referred to as the 'older brother' of Christianity.

Sigi's sentiments were not dissimilar to those voiced some days later by Dr Eugene Fisher of the United States Conference of Catholic Bishops, who was then based at the headquarters of the ICCJ in Heppenheim. Fisher claimed that 'theologically, *Dominus Iesus* does not affect Catholic-Jewish relations adversely at all. For the most part it simply restates, albeit in very strong language, what the Church has taught all along … Does this mean that everybody needs to become a Catholic in order to be saved? Absolutely not.' Nevertheless,

Dr John Pawlikowski, a prolific author, professor and leader in the field of Christian-Jewish dialogue, sent a copy of his response to Dr Fisher's statement to Sigi, in which he indicated that Cardinal Edward Cassidy and other church leaders had been embarrassed by *Dominus Iesus* and had tried hard to block the publication of the document. They intended to do everything possible to overcome the document and marginalize it as the prevailing document for inter-Christian and interreligious relations. Pawlikowski also quoted from a pastoral letter read by Cardinal Carlo Maria Martini of Milan in his cathedral, in which the Cardinal said that 'salvation is possible for everyone, outside of any church, so long as they follow the will of God, the Holy Spirit and their moral conscience'. Ending his communication on a particularly positive note, Dr Pawlikowski spoke of a consultation in Moscow hosted by the Russian member unit of the ICCJ at which it was anticipated that the Russian Orthodox Church would issue its first ever declaration on Christian-Jewish relations in the presence of Patriarch Alexy II, the Chief Rabbi of Russia and the head of the Muslim communities in Russia.

Sensitive to the reaction *Dominus Iesus* had provoked, the Vatican was anxious to mend relations with other religions. Cardinal Cassidy hoped to reassure representatives of other religions at the 13th International Meeting of Peoples and Religions held in Lisbon that the Vatican remained committed to improving relations with non-Catholics. While *Dominus Iesus* was not referred to in the planned discussions, the leader of Portugal's Jewish community said the meeting needed to directly address the Vatican Declaration. The Vatican had also planned a symposium on Christian-Jewish dialogue, but was obliged to cancel it after two leading Italian rabbis announced their decision to withdraw from the meeting since they believed that *Dominus Iesus* undermined the mutual respect necessary for interfaith discussions to continue.

In Britain, the CCJ issued a statement in response to *Dominus Iesus* in which they recognized that despite the 'remarkable progress' that had been made in interfaith dialogue in recent years, many of its members held to theological truths that were incompatible with other faith traditions. 'The strength of dialogue is that we acknowledge these differences and work for mutual understanding and tolerance.' While *Dominus Iesus* made no new theological claims for Roman Catholicism, some of the language used in the declaration was harsh and had caused offence to Jews and other faith communities as well as to other Christians. This was exacerbated by inaccuracies in translation from the Latin. The statement concluded that 'the task of those committed to dialogue is to ensure that such difficulties do not obscure the progress made and build on the more positive statements made over the last few decades on all sides'.

These were sentiments with which Sigi would undoubtedly have concurred. Taken from this perspective, the visit of Pope John Paul II to the Holy Land, which he had urged all those years earlier when he met the Pontiff for the first time, was a hugely positive landmark in the history of Catholic-Jewish relations. But in the interim period there had been an obstacle to these relations far greater than the unpopular beatification of Pius IX and the declaration *Dominus Iesus*, which had needed to be overcome.

7 The Auschwitz Convent Imbroglio

The name 'Auschwitz' still conjures memories of the greatest atrocity perpetrated in a century marked by unprecedented levels of violence, savagery and destruction. The extermination camp where some two million people, the vast majority of them Jews, were systematically gassed to death, Auschwitz is branded in the consciousness of most Jews as the horrific culmination of two millennia of persecution and martyrdom. Before the Wannsee conference of 1942, however, which put the finishing touches to Hitler's plans for the 'final solution to the Jewish problem', the concentration camp at Auschwitz had been earmarked by the Nazis for the incarceration and slaughter of Soviet prisoners of war and leaders of the Polish resistance. In 1979, the Polish government and the World Jewish Congress, a New York-based organization, agreed that Auschwitz should be placed on the UNESCO World Heritage List as a site of genocide.

On 1 August 1984, almost forty years after the camp was liberated, a group of some fifteen Carmelite nuns took over a building adjacent to the walls of the concentration camp. Known as 'the old theatre', the building had been used to store the Zyklon B gas utilized in the extermination chambers. At the request of Cardinal Franciszek Macharski, Archbishop of the Cracow diocese, the nuns had been granted a 99-year lease by the local authorities, and at the end of September a declaration was made by high-ranking members of the Polish Church voicing approval of the establishment of the convent at Auschwitz. The Church officials, including Macharski, had no inkling at the time of the tinderbox their decision had set alight.

On the contrary, viewed from a Catholic perspective, the desire of the nuns to pray for the expiation of the crimes committed in Auschwitz and to obtain by intercession the mercy of God seemed to reflect Christian goodwill and solidarity towards the suffering of the Jewish people. How were Catholics to know that in contrast to their own need to venerate and make sacred a site of martyrdom, Jewish tradition deems it fit to shun such a spot and leave it desolate? The fact that earlier, smaller scale initiatives to pray for the murdered and their oppressors had received a positive reaction from Polish Jews served to reinforce the Catholic position. And certainly, in the early days at least, the Carmelite convent at Auschwitz did not disturb the small Polish-Jewish community, as a prominent activist, Dr Stanislaw Krajewski, confirms. A member of the International Council of the Auschwitz-Birkenau Museum, Krajewski pointed out that the convent building was not part of the itinerary for visitors to Auschwitz: 'I saw that the convent was in an abandoned building just outside the camp base. I was and would have been satisfied with it had I been sure that it would-n't have grown.'

The convent came to the attention of the outside world in May the following year after the Belgian branch of an organiza-tion known as 'Aid to the Church in Need' issued a bulletin appealing for funds to help the nuns adapt and repair the convent building. Distributed shortly before Pope John Paul II was due to visit the Benelux countries, the bulletin spoke of the convent at Auschwitz as 'a gift for the Pope', who, it was later claimed, had proposed the idea for the convent when he was Archbishop of Cracow. The suggestion that the convent was to be 'a spiritual fortress' and 'a guarantee of the conversion of stray brothers' can be seen as particularly provocative.

While the latter sentiments might arguably have been directed at the numerous Poles who had embraced atheism under the Communist regime, the prayer for 'the conversion of the perfidious Jews' had long been a standard part of Catholic liturgy. The publication in 1965 of the Second Vatican Council document, *Nostra Aetate*, did, indeed, call for a radical review of Catholic perceptions of Jews and some of its tenets had been embraced by an enlightened Western Catholic elite. However, it is likely that the influence of *Nostra Aetate* would have been less far-reaching among the Catholic hierarchies of Eastern Europe.

The triumphalist tone of the Belgian bulletin and its notable omission of any reference to Auschwitz as a place where numerous European Jewish communities had been annihilated hardly endeared the cause it was promoting to the Jewish world. Reactions to the convent were first heard from Jewish organizations in the Francophone countries and shortly afterwards from other parts of Europe, Israel and the USA. Jews engaged in Christian-Jewish dialogue were, on the whole, muted in their response. Rabbi David Rosen, then the Anti-Defamation League's Director of Interfaith Relations in Israel, is one example: 'The ADL didn't want to make a thing of it. Their attitude was, it is not as if there are Jews there at the time who are involved in it and it's not as if it's actually on the property itself. By making a big thing, you're basically trying to go to war with the Catholic Church.'

During the latter months of 1985, however, the majority of Jewish voices, led by the influential World Jewish Congress (WJC), were raised in sharp objection. The hue and cry came as a surprise to Krajewski and other Polish Jews who remembered that there had been no protests at the way the Communist regime had virtually obliterated the role of the Jews as the principal victims of the extermination camp, putting Jews (*Zydow* in Polish) last on a list of twenty nationalities that had suffered at Auschwitz. Rosen sees the WJC's role as pivotal: 'To some extent the WJC did determine the tune. Their style created the atmosphere in which no public Jewish organization could avoid getting involved. Had the WJC not got involved, those issues might not have developed in the way they did.'

Forgetful, or perhaps ignorant of the fact that Poles saw Auschwitz as a focal point of their own suffering and martyrdom under the Nazis, Jewish protesters saw no justification for the presence of the Carmelites. They were affronted at what was perceived as an attempt, not merely to de-Judaise, but to 'Christianise' the vast Jewish graveyard that Auschwitz had become. Among the protesters were survivors of the Holocaust who, not surprisingly, were particularly offended. As Rosen points out: 'Once it had become a big issue, then you couldn't keep quiet any longer.'

Sigi, for his part, was initially indifferent to the presence of the nuns at Auschwitz. Since his appointment as Chairman of the Executive of the International Council of Christians and Jews in 1979, he had spent much of his time and energy assiduously cultivating improved relations with the Catholic world and was a firm believer in dialogue. While on a subliminal level he remained traumatized by the destruction of the bulk of Hungarian Jewry in a matter of months in 1944 when the allies were already aware of the implications of the 'final solution', he was always conscious of his own good fortune in having left Nazi Europe in time. On a gut level, then, the convent at Auschwitz was not offensive to him – 'it didn't bother me personally, it didn't bother me very much' – particularly as the building itself was outside the perimeters of the camp.

But if he had attuned himself to be sensitive to the feelings of his partners in dialogue, how much more so was he to the distress of his co-religionists who had survived the *Shoah*. 'The convent started bothering me when the survivors were upset by it. But I must be careful, I'm not in a position to judge because I've not been in the Holocaust. Obviously these people were outraged, people who were survivors. And if they felt bad about it, of course it started bothering me.'

Whether it was mere chance that Sigi's elevation to the Papal Knighthood that year coincided with circumstances which were threatening the goodwill that had been painstakingly built up between representatives of the two faith communities is open to question. The growth of trust between Jews and Catholics that had started gradually in the aftermath of the Second World War when a few farsighted clergymen felt the need to make amends for what was perceived as the Church's less than glorious role during the Holocaust, and had been accelerated by conciliatory voices and gestures at the Second Vatican Council set up by Pope John XXIII in the early 1960s, was now being threatened by the row simmering over the presence of the nuns at Auschwitz.

To defuse the controversy, fuelled by protests and demon-strations throughout the world, not only by Jews but also by sympathetic Christians, a Catholic-Jewish summit meeting took place in Geneva on 22 July 1986. Cardinal Macharski, accompa-nied by Fr Stanislaw Musial, Secretary of the Polish Church's Commission for Dialogue with Judaism, and Jerzy Turowicz, editor of the Catholic weekly *Tygodnik Powszechny*, joined three Western Cardinals, the Belgian Primate Cardinal Gottfried Danneels, Cardinal Albert Decourtray, Archbishop of Lyons and Chairman of the French Bishops' Conference and the Archbishop of Paris, Cardinal Jean-Marie Lustiger, a converted Jew. The Jewish delegation was led by Theo Klein, President of CRIF, the representative Council of Jewish Organisations in France. He was accompanied by his Belgian and Italian counter-parts, Markus Pardes and Tullia Zevi respectively, and by French Chief Rabbi René-Samuel Sirat and Professor Ady Steg.

At the meeting, which lasted one day, Macharski undertook to halt further construction of the convent while discussions continued. A joint communiqué was published recognizing 'the uncontested realities of the symbolic character of the extermina-tion camp of Auschwitz, monument and memory of the Holocaust' and pledging a continuation of dialogue. At the same time, the participants had drafted the Auschwitz Declaration, beginning with the Hebrew word *Zakhor* – Remember. The declaration recognized Auschwitz and Birkenau as symbols of the Final Solution but also remembered the others – Poles, Russians and Gypsies – who had been murdered in Auschwitz.

Seven months later, on 22 February 1987, a second meeting was held in Geneva when the original participants were joined by additional delegates from both sides. The most prominent addition to the Jewish delegation was Gerhart Riegner, the veteran co-chairman of the Governing Board of the WJC. Riegner had also received a Papal Knighthood in recognition of his many years of work in the field of Christian-Jewish relations.

After lengthy discussions, a communiqué was issued, reiter-ating the previous Geneva Declaration and proposing that a Centre for Information, Meetings, Dialogue, Education and Prayer should be built some 500 metres outside the Auschwitz-

Birkenau concentration camps. It was hoped that the centre would be used for conferences between Christians and Jews, as a resource to combat revisionism and disinformation about the Holocaust and to provide further information for visitors to the camp. Most significantly, the establishment of the new centre implied 'that the Carmelites' prayer initiative will find in this new context its rightful place, its confirmation and its true meaning'.

Essentially, then, the Geneva Accords of 1987 committed the Polish Church to relocating the Carmelites within the confines of the proposed new conference centre, well outside the camp. The deadline agreed was 22 February 1989, only two years away. While reactions to the accord were mixed, one less-than-enthusiastic voice stood out. This was the Polish Primate, Cardinal Jozef Glemp, who stated bluntly that 'the dialogue between the Jews and Catholics must continue. This matter is not terminated.' With hindsight it is easy to ask why Glemp's presence was not deemed indispensable to the Geneva deliberations.

This is certainly how Sigi sees the matter today. 'They should really have negotiated with Cardinal Glemp. He was the Primate of Poland.' It appears too, as Sigi learnt at a later stage, that Glemp resented having been left out of the discussions about the Carmelites. Sigi, in contrast, makes it clear that he had no interest in getting involved in the dispute at that stage. 'I left it to the others. Too many people were negotiating and I didn't believe they were going to get anywhere and I didn't want to get involved in their negotiations.' His scepticism was twofold. 'My belief is when too many people negotiate, usually nothing happens. The art is really to find the right person who can make decisions. They were not negotiating with the right person.'

Unsurprisingly, there was not much movement on the Polish front. No doubt the period prescribed by the Geneva Accords may have been unrealistic, given the time needed to prepare plans for the proposed centre and have them approved, let alone find funds for the project. As Archbishop Luigi Barbarito, the then Papal Nuncio in London pointed out, 'It was still the Communist government at the time. The church and the government didn't agree and the government had some interest in harassing the church and putting it on the spot.' The deadline of 22 February 1989 passed without any building works having commenced at the site of the centre. A new deadline for the departure of the nuns was set by the Catholic negotiators at Geneva for 22 July the same year.

The February date was marked in a very different way at the site of the convent at Auschwitz. It was, then, that a large wooden cross, some seven metres high, was erected in the centre of the lawn of the convent garden. As the French journal, *Libération*, reported five months later: 'On the 22 February, the fifteen Polish sisters, far from moving, were fitting out the place in a manner that was anything but provisional and were putting up, at the gate of the camp, a wooden cross seven metres high.' This was the cross which had been used for the mass John Paul II had said at Birkenau ten years earlier. The spot where it now stood marked the gravel ditch where all the Polish resistance fighters were shot at the beginning of the Second World War.

If the cross at Auschwitz can be seen to have tremendous significance for the Carmelites themselves and, by extension, for many Catholic Poles, it constituted an undeniable provocation to most Jews. In fact, as a report in *Le Monde* of 18 July pointed out, 'this new business of the cross puts the whole matter of the convent in second place'. Krajewski, too, found the cross unacceptable. 'To me it was certainly much more of a problem. It was and is much more of a problem than the convent itself because the cross is visible and it really tries to dominate the space over the camp and, in fact, it does.'

What is fascinating, however, is that both Krajewski and Waldemar Chrostowski of the Polish Academy of Catholic Theology date the erection of the cross as the *autumn* of 1989. Krajewski recalls that 'the cross came in the heat of the controversy in 1989, when the religious war was full on. It was at the peak of the religious war.' He stresses that it was put up *after* some controversial Jewish protests at the site of the convent that summer and *after* Cardinal Glemp had reacted to the protests with allegations that appeared to contain anti-Semitic stereotypes.

Chrostowski, in a document about the Auschwitz convent controversy, states that 'in Autumn 1989 a big cross was erected close by the Carmelitan nun's [sic] convent' and goes on to discuss the implications. While recognizing that, for many Jews, 'the appearance of the cross was a new manifestation of the 'christianization [sic] of Auschwitz', he points out that from the perspective of many Catholics, 'defence of the cross' became a priority and cites the words of Rev. Anastasy Gegotek: 'The departure of the nuns from this place would mean for them the renouncing of the Cross, that is the renouncing of their faith.'

1989 was the year the Iron Curtain was fast disappearing. Nevertheless, it was early enough in the new era for a process of disinformation to have continued, thereby causing both Krajewski and Chrostowski, who were based in Warsaw, to remain ignorant of a development that was widely and freely reported throughout the Western world. It is possible, of course, that Chrostowski's dating of the cross was part of the campaign of disinformation. The implications are obvious. For Poles, the cross was put up in defiant *reaction* to unseemly Jewish protests, whereas in fact it was one of the *causes* that fuelled those same protests. What the nuns at Auschwitz were defying in putting up the cross on 22 February 1989 was the original deadline of the Geneva Accord. Raising the cross was a declaration by the Carmelites vowed to silence that they were there to stay.

As the months passed, there was no reason to believe that the new July deadline would prove any more effective than the one it replaced. With the implementation of the Geneva Accords in jeopardy, hostile noises and threats of action were beginning to be heard from organizations throughout the Jewish world. Sensitive to the danger these rumblings posed to Catholic-Jewish relations, Sigi was advocating calm diplomacy. Speaking in June at a meeting at the Board of Deputies, he urged caution. 'Only the Catholic Church in Poland has the power to move the convent', he said. 'Wise, calm negotiations would be more effective than noisy protests.' In a private letter to an American-Jewish leader, he pointed out that it was point-less to assist 'those elements in the Church and elsewhere which are hostile to us by giving them a "cause" more attractive to and more comprehensible to the media than ours.' Sigi's warnings were not appreciated by the recipients of the letter. Even within Anglo-Jewry, a call was made by the Board of Deputies for prayers to be recited in synagogues for the removal of the convent.

It was at that point that Sigi decided to change tack and take a more proactive line. For some time, he had been in correspondence with the prioresses at two Carmelite monasteries in England who shared his concern that their sisters at Auschwitz were 'presenting a stumbling block' to relations between Jews and Christians but could offer no practical advice beyond faith in the power of prayer. With the July deadline imminent, he realized that a gesture from Poland was needed. Accordingly, on 10 July he wrote to the Polish ambassador in London, Dr Zbigniew Gertych, suggesting that the Polish government make an offer of temporary accommodation for the Auschwitz Carmelites pending the building of the new convent. The offer could be made in a statement or in an open letter to Sigi. At the same time, he declared himself willing to go to Poland to help negotiate the acquisition of interim premises, together with Rabbi Marc Tannenbaum, an American rabbi keenly involved in Christian-Jewish dialogue with whom he was in close touch.

It was too late, however, to calm the continuing frustration in some Jewish quarters which was fast simmering towards boiling point. The initiative was seized by a man whose course of action was diametrically opposed to anything Sigi would have prescribed. Rabbi Avi Weiss from Riverdale in the Bronx would seem an unlikely aggressor, as some have portrayed him. Clean-shaven and mild-mannered, he was a disciple of the 'hippy' rabbi, the late Shlomo Carlebach, and is happy playing the guitar and preaching peace and love. With quite a following among American Orthodox Jews, he is particularly admired by women for his attempts to include them as much as possible in Jewish ritual. An observer who attended a seminar given by him at the end of 1997 commented on the gentleness of his approach but could imagine that he was capable of great anger.

On 14 July 1989, a group of seven American Jews led by Weiss arrived at the gates of the convent. It was anger at what he perceived as an attempt to 'Christianise the Holocaust' that propelled Weiss to Auschwitz. The events that ensued, which have been interpreted in any number of ways, brought the convent imbroglio back to the headlines.

According to a notably objective Polish reporter, Anna Husarka, writing in the Solidarity newspaper *Gazeta Wyborcza*, the Jews rang the bell, wishing to explain to the sisters why they were there – although they could not speak Polish – and continued ringing and trying to attract the nuns' attention. Failing to receive any response, the seven men then scaled the fence and found themselves in the courtyard of the convent. They knocked on the wooden door of the convent but once again failed to get a response. It was Friday afternoon and they put on their prayer shawls, sat down, lit Shabbat candles, blew the *shofar* – rams' horn – and brought out their Bibles.

Another report, in *Le Monde*, mentions that the demonstrators brandished a banner inscribed in Polish: 'Sisters, do not pray for the Jewish martyrs. They were not Christian.' While his followers chanted prayers, Weiss read a declaration condemning the Holy See for authorizing the establishment of the convent to a group of journalists and onlookers standing in front of the convent. He then requested that the Polish ecclesiastical authorities at least remove the huge wooden cross, as an initial gesture of goodwill.

Reported this way, Weiss and his followers were engaged in nothing more than a peaceful, if hardly silent, demonstration. While such behaviour might have aroused little comment in America or the West in general, it was obviously perceived quite differently in an Eastern bloc country where free demonstrations were not run of the mill. Moreover, eyebrows may well be raised at the presence, in a courtyard of an enclosed convent of nuns vowed to silence, of seven strange men, whether they were engaged in non-violent verbal protest or in some sort of prayer with their heads covered. An outlandish way of going about things, no doubt. But violent it was not.

Before long, however, some Poles engaged in building works appeared at the windows of the convent, jeered at the Jews and demanded that they leave the convent. Then they drenched

Weiss and his followers with buckets of water mixed with cement, according to some French newspaper reports – or mixed with paint and urine, according to Weiss. Finally, they dragged the Jews out by force. Outside, while bystanders, including policemen and a priest looked on, the workers punched and kicked the Jews and shouted obscenities.

Two days later, according to *Le Monde*, Weiss and his followers tried in vain to issue a protest to Cardinal Macharski in Cracow; they were warned that if such a shameful incident should occur again, the Polish Church would report it to the international tribunal at The Hague. Undaunted, the Americans returned to the convent garden wearing the striped pyjamas of concentration camp inmates. They were joined by a group of thirty Canadian Jews who remained outside the convent.

The following Sunday, a large group of Belgian Jewish students demonstrated outside the convent and were succeeded the next day by a group of former camp inmates led by the former Chief Rabbi of France, René-Samuel Sirat. In Paris, representatives of Jewish youth organizations demonstrated outside the fence of the Apostolic Nuncio using the emotive slogan 'Pas de croix sur nos cendres' – 'No cross over our ashes'.

What Krajewski refers to as 'the religious wars' had begun. Even moderate voices in the Jewish world, particularly in America, were outraged at the treatment meted out to Weiss and his followers. While deploring the action Weiss had taken, Theo Klein, the leader of the Jewish delegation to the Geneva talks, called for a freeze in Catholic-Jewish relations. His successor as President of CRIF, Jean Khan, was more outspoken. 'The Carmelites' vow is to join in their prayers victims and executioners', he declared at a ceremony commemorating a notorious round-up of French Jews by the Nazis. 'This mixture in a place where the sky was silent while our people were being massacred is unacceptable to us.'

Ironically, as Anna Husarka made clear in an intriguing and insightful report for *The Washington Post*, one of the main problems with the Weiss initiative was 'a failure to understand'. 'Things went much better on the two occasions when the group's leader, Rabbi Avraham Weiss, was able to get round the language barrier and speak with the Poles', Husarka wrote. 'He had a courteous exchange with the secretary of the Cracow bishopric. The rabbi spoke Yiddish, the priest German.'

What was desperately needed to take the heat out of the situation was dialogue, as Sigi understood only too well. In his letter of 10 July to Dr Gertych he had warned that a breakdown of dialogue could result in a resurgence of anti-Semitism 'all over the world [and] especially in Poland, which would be extremely damaging to the country'. The Weiss escapade had intervened before there could be any reaction to his proposal of temporary accommodation for the Carmelites.

On 25 July, however, a statement was issued by the Polish government expressing interest in 'the initiation of peaceful and honest action for the implementation of the Geneva agreement as soon as possible'. The statement voiced concern at the recent protests at the convent and gave some details of approvals sought for the site of the centre proposed in the Geneva Accords, the earliest being in March 1989, the month after the original deadline for the nuns' move had expired. Since the centre had not been built, however, the convent had to remain on the present site.

Significantly, there was no mention of temporary accommodation, as Sigi pointed out in another letter to Dr Gertych, which he urged the ambassador to forward to General Jaruzelski, the Polish Prime Minister. He reiterated his suggestion that he and Tannenbaum be invited to Poland to speak personally to Jaruzelski.

Up to this point, Sigi had exploited his good relations with the Polish ambassador to push for some demonstration of goodwill from the Polish government. It was then that he received a prod from another quarter. Archbishop Luigi Barbarito, the Papal Nuncio in London, was worried by 'the deteriorating aspect of events', particularly after the Weiss incursion which in many newspapers was portrayed more as an 'assault'. 'To prevent this escalation from reaching a point of no return, I said to Sir Sigmund, "It's better that you deal directly with the Catholic hierarchy in Poland. When you can talk, dialogue and explain the reason and also if you can offer some help, this would be far more acceptable."'

Since Sigi was not acquainted with Cardinal Macharski and had only a nodding acquaintance with the Polish Primate, he was initially hesitant. But Barbarito, boosted by the fact that some months earlier the Primate had called at the *nunciatura* on his way to Ireland, was able to reassure him that he would write a letter of introduction. In it, the Nuncio asked the Polish cardinals to receive Sigi and Tannenbaum, together with Bishop Gerald Mahon from the Westminster Archdiocese, who was closely involved in dialogue.

Sigi was quick to put the letter to use. On 9 August, he sent a two-page telex to Macharski, reiterating the need for a 'temporary building' which would be purpose built. On a practical level, he indicated that finance for the building might be forthcoming from the Catholic Bishops' Conference in Bonn and suggested a meeting on the site with a group of key figures including the Mayor of Auschwitz, the engineer in charge of the proposed building works for the centre, an architect from Germany, a representative of the German Catholic Church and one of the Carmelite nuns. To add weight to his proposal he mentioned that he and other officers of the Council of Christians and Jews would be having an audience with the Pope the following month, coinciding with celebrations for the 80th birthday of Cardinal Johannes Willebrands, President of the Vatican Commission for Relations with Judaism, 'a joyous event … which should not be marred by anything that would detract from the occasion'.

This was combined with a warning. The European Jewish Congress, which Sigi would be attending, was to be held in London the following month and unless his proposals for settling the convent situation were heeded, a resolution would be drafted condemning those who were breaking the agreement. As a final twist to his arguments, he assured Macharski that in considering 'this unique proposition', the Cardinal would not be seen as having given in to pressure, since it was on record that Sigi and Tannenbaum had been discussing the matter well before the latest developments. 'At one stroke you will take the heat out of the situation and remove the tension', he concluded.

In taking his case to the highest echelons of the Polish Church, Sigi was laying his credentials as a Papal Knight on the line. Obviously, the Poles were smarting from the incidents of the previous month. Despite the high level of objectivity and neutrality with which these had been reported in the Polish press as a whole – more so, incidentally, than in the English press, which tended to portray Weiss and his associates as 'hotheads' or 'fanatics' who had 'physically assaulted' the Carmelites – the official Polish Press Agency and various church organs had used much more emotive language, describing the Jews as 'invading' the convent grounds with 'brutal shouting' and 'threatening behaviour' (see Emma Klein, *The Battle for Auschwitz* [London and Portland, OR: Vallentine Mitchell, 2001], pp.19–20).

In what appears to be an incredible coincidence of timing, Sigi's telex was pipped to the post by a statement issued by Macharski on 8 August. It was the first definitive Catholic counter-charge in the 'religious wars'. In essence, the Cardinal was backing down from the commitment he had made at Geneva to oversee the building of the Centre for Information, Meetings, Dialogue, Education and Prayer which was to incorporate a new home for the Auschwitz Carmelites, a project for which, he claimed, he had entertained the highest hopes. He justified his decision by excoriating the 'violent campaign of accusation and slander' the delay in the implementation of the 'unrealistic deadline' for the construction of the Centre had fomented in Western Jewish circles and the 'offensive aggression, which is not merely verbal' which had 'found an echo in Auschwitz'.

Amid the hostile reactions provoked by Macharski's statement was Sigi's three-page telex dated 14 August. It is possible he may not have been aware that the Cardinal's statement predated his earlier communication. Sigi professed himself 'devastated' by the stance Macharski had taken which implied, in effect, that the Carmelites would not move and warned that the consequences for Catholic-Jewish relations were 'unimaginable'. Taking issue with Macharski's allegation that the only voice calling for self-control was that of Jewish organizations in Poland, he produced a list of Jewish dignitaries and organizations, from the then Chief Rabbi Lord Jacobovits downwards, who deplored the demonstrations at Auschwitz and went on to cite a passage from a letter of support he had received from one of the English Carmelite prioresses. He reiterated his willingness to cut short his holiday and present the Cardinal with a plan which would solve the problem.

One section in Sigi's telex may be seen to be of particular significance: 'Since there is in Judaism no tradition of permanent contemplative prayer at any cemetery, we must reserve the right to ask that neither faith is permanently represented at the site which above all other places marks the graveyard of our people.' It was perhaps this appeal from the heart which prompted Macharski to respond personally with a short telex dated 22 August, in which he thanked Sigi for his 'serious approach to my pronouncement' and confessed that he made his decision 'with a heavy heart'. But his position remained unchanged. Sigi replied the same day, expressing his 'deep disappointment and considerable concern' and took the Cardinal to task for having 'chosen to see a demonstration by a small and totally unrepresentative group of individuals as typifying the response of Jews as a whole'.

Macharski's solidarity with the Jewish cause was one casualty of the 'religious wars'. He had, after all, been a signatory to the Geneva Accords and had worked in cooperation with his Western Catholic counterparts and a high level Jewish delegation. An indication of his concern for Jewish feelings about the convent at Auschwitz may be deduced from a letter he wrote in early June to Cardinal Decourtray, his colleague at Geneva, which Decourtray cited in a letter to Theo Klein, leader of the Jewish delegation. It was clear that Macharski empathized with Jewish impatience and suffering; nevertheless, he was only too aware and would have wanted to warn his 'Jewish brothers' that any demonstrations and actions in front of the theatre building against the presence of the Carmelites would only prove counterproductive and reinforce Polish public opinion in its 'blind defence' of the nuns.

The end of August was marked by two events in Poland of contrasting significance. On the political front, General Jaruzelski was replaced as prime minister by Tadeusz Mazowiecki, a Polish patriot and religious Christian who was deeply sympathetic to Jews and Judaism. The 'religious wars', on the other hand, gained momentum from the salvo fired by the Polish Primate, Cardinal Glemp, whose long silence over the Auschwitz convent dispute can be seen, with hindsight, as ominous.

Glemp's homily on 26 August at the shrine of Czestochowa in front of a congregation which included Prime Minister Mazowiecki was to ensure that his name hit the headlines of the world's newspapers. Focusing on Polish-German and Polish-Jewish relations among other issues of the day, he appeared, initially, to be decrying stereotypes and certainly parts of his sermon contain appeals for peace and dialogue. Nevertheless, his words were seized on, not without justification, as examples of classic anti-Semitic stereotyping. While conceding that there were 'Israelites' who gave their talents and their lives to Poland, he introduced 'Jew the innkeeper, who filled peasants with drink, and Jew the propagator of communism' as well as 'businessmen whose attitude to Poles was disrespectful and denigrating' and 'collaborators during the war who did not rise to the level of the heroic defenders of the Ghetto'.

In contrast to these negative depictions was a somewhat ambiguous statement that was equally unlikely to endear him to the Jewish world: 'Many Jews immersed themselves in Polish culture and in Christianity and the crosses on their graves do not nullify their love for their nation.' In view of the focus of the current controversy, this comment would appear quite insensitive. More offensive was his insinuation that Jews saw themselves as 'a nation elevated above all others' and his charge that Jews had the mass media at their disposal 'in many countries'.

But it was his interpretation of the Weiss fracas that was particularly sinister: 'Recently a squad of seven Jews from New

York attacked the convent at Auschwitz and although this did not lead to the killing of the sisters or to the destruction of the convent because the attackers were restrained, they should not be regarded as heroes.' Not surprisingly, Weiss, himself, used equally intemperate language, equating Glemp's statement to 'something out of the middle ages, a blood libel' and liable to incite a pogrom. Given the volatile mood in Poland as a result of the prolonged controversy over the Auschwitz convent, Weiss' reaction cannot be considered mere hyperbole.

While obviously winning himself support at home, Glemp's words enraged much of the Western world. Previously admired for his stance as a Polish patriot and courageous opponent of communism, the Primate suddenly found doors closing on him. A projected trip to the United States, where previously he may well have been fêted as a hero, was cancelled for fear of violent protest.

Among the almost universal condemnation was Sigi's relatively restrained telex of 29 August in which he expressed himself 'greatly shocked' at Glemp's reported statement on Jews and Poland and asserted firmly that 'Jews have fought and died for Poland over the centuries and Poland was the scene of the greatest Jewish tragedy'. Sigi concluded by assuming that Glemp was unaware of his earlier communications with Macharski and announced that he was sending copies of this telex to both Macharski and Mazowiecki.

There were signs that foreign reaction to the Glemp outburst was causing concern in Poland. On 6 September, Monseigneur Henryk Muszynski, President of the Polish Bishops' Commission for Dialogue with Judaism, published a communiqué in favour of proceeding with the establishment of the centre proposed in the Geneva Accords. This was sent to the Vatican. Two days later, the Polish Prime Minister wrote to Sigi, thanking him for the good wishes he had sent him in his capacity of convenor of the Religious Press Group. Mazowiecki declared himself 'deeply moved' by prayers for Poland and the Polish people spoken in synagogues in Britain and the United States, which he wished to reciprocate, and issued an open invitation to Sigi to visit Poland and meet with him.

Significantly, his letter spoke of 'the untold suffering of the Jewish people whose each and every member stands unequaled [sic] among all martirized [sic] nations' and of 'the tragedy and sacrifice of *shoah*' which 'defies any comparison'. These words were in contrast to Glemp's Czestochowa sermon which described 'Jews, Poles, Gypsies' as common victims of 'Hitler's strategy of extermination'.

By the middle of the third week of September, events were moving quickly. To compensate for the cancelled trip to America, Glemp decided to come to England. At the same time, the Vatican announced, through Cardinal Willebrands of the Commission for Religious Relations with Judaism, that it endorsed Monseigneur Muzynski's communiqué regarding the intention to proceed with the establishment of the much-discussed Centre for Information, Meetings, Dialogue, Education and Prayer outside Auschwitz. The Holy See was convinced that such a centre would contribute significantly to relations between Christians and Jews and that the proposed new convent 'at the heart of this centre' would play a decisive part in its success.

On releasing the announcement to the press on 19 September, the Vatican broke its silence on the contentious issue that had strained Catholic-Jewish relations for so long. No less significant was its decision to offer financial assistance to 'this important but costly project'. An Associated Press correspondent reported an immediate response from Jewish leaders in the United States who 'applauded the statement'. Cardinal Glemp, however, in Bristol for the consecration of a Polish Catholic church the same day, was unaware of the Vatican announcement.

In London, Sigi was busy polishing his Polish credentials. The day before Glemp's Bristol visit, he was at the Polish Embassy with the Deputy Director General of the Institute of Directors discussing the possibility of setting up joint ventures with Polish businesses, a subject close to the Polish ambassador's heart. Sigi had come armed with Prime Minister Mazowiecki's letter inviting him to Poland and suggested leading a delegation of British business leaders there. At the same time he was mooting a strategy to take advantage of Glemp's presence in England.

Sigi and Glemp had already rubbed shoulders at a meeting of the St Egidio, a group of forward-looking lay and religious Catholics who had important contacts with members of other faiths. Not surprisingly, then, the Cardinal was keen to meet with this Jewish Papal Knight, despite the less than enthusiastic letter he had received from Sigi a few weeks earlier. Sigi, however, had his own agenda. 'Glemp wanted to meet me at the airport and I wasn't going to meet him at the airport. I told the Polish ambassador that it was no good my meeting him. He must sign a letter that he was going to remove the convent. That was the only way I was going to meet him.'

In the event, a dinner meeting was arranged for the evening of 20 September at the Polish ambassador's spacious residence in Templewood Avenue, Hampstead. Sigi was due to come accompanied by Chief Rabbi Lord Jacobovits and Dr Lionel Kopelovitz, the President of the Board of Deputies. But a press conference Glemp gave in Bristol the day before put paid to their attendance.

At the press conference, Glemp, while paying lip service, as ever, to the need for dialogue, was in a less than conciliatory mood. After formulating a critique of what he called Jewish 'Shoah theology' which was none too sympathetic, he made vague noises of support for the prayer centre outside Auschwitz. While he hinted that the nuns might eventually consider moving there, he made it clear that they would receive his backing even if they refused to do so. The Geneva Accords were dismissed as 'wishful thinking'. When the Cardinal was eventually informed of the Vatican's newly-released announcement, his reaction was decidedly cool.

Glemp's clumsy handling of these sensitive issues was to prove his Achilles' heel. Initially, however, it was Sigi who was put on the spot. 'I was in great trouble because I promised him that he was going to meet the Chief Rabbi and the President of the Board of Deputies. Now, somebody else would have told him, "I'm sorry, I cannot bring you the Chief Rabbi and I cannot bring you the President of the Board of Deputies either, so therefore you must meet me on my own." Of course, that's not the way to operate.' Sigi was also under pressure not to attend himself. Jacobovits and Kopelovitz had advised him against it: 'Please don't meet him because this man will only humiliate you and you won't get anywhere with him.'

In the event, Sigi took Rabbi Tony Bayfield, Director of the Sternberg Centre for Judaism, and Professor Antony Polonsky, an expert on Polish affairs from the London School of Economics. Glemp came accompanied by 'a galaxy of priests' and they were all sitting down in the dining room of the ambassador's residence.

Underneath the facade of pleasantries, Sigi was very annoyed. 'I was in a corner in so far as no one wanted to come with me except Bayfield and Polonsky and when you're in a corner you act accordingly, then you fight.' This was something he had learnt in his business dealings. 'I'm a very peaceful person, I never start a row with anyone, except if someone puts me in a corner.'

It was Glemp's turn to face Sigi's well-honed negotiating tactics. Little was he to know that the paranoia he expressed at Czestochowa about Jews controlling the media was to be used against him. 'Glemp said Jews are very powerful people. When people say that, I say yes, the Jews are very powerful people, we're very clever and we're very powerful and we rule the world. Why should I tell them that we are just nothing. I know what stupid people we are but why should I tell the others?'

On a practical level, Sigi intended to telephone Clifford Longley, then Religious Affairs Editor at *The Times*, if things moved his way. He was perfectly aware that the beleaguered Cardinal might be vulnerable to such a display of 'media manipulation'. But he was none too confident himself. 'I was very concerned that this man was not going to sign anything. That was my greatest worry because I was told he was not going to sign anything and if he doesn't sign anything, then I look like a monkey.'

Sigi had rarely felt so exposed. Years earlier, when he had gone into prisons to involve inmates in metal recovery, he had run the risk, alone in a room full of prisoners, of being physically mauled. Now it was his reputation that was in danger of being mauled by recalcitrance on the part of the Cardinal. In a fax he had sent the Polish ambassador that morning, explaining that Jacobovits and Kopelovitz would not be attending the dinner, he had been quite candid. Unless the Cardinal signed a letter and press statement he had had prepared, he, Sigi, would lose all credibility with world Jewry. 'The Cardinal will have demolished the only link existing between world Jewry and the Vatican', he wrote, equally concerned that failure would damage the work in which he took such pride.

Knowing that he was taking 'a huge risk' in meeting Glemp in these circumstances, Sigi was as disarming as possible. With the greatest courtesy he explained to the Cardinal, 'You've put me in a very difficult situation coming and seeing you here.' But he sensed, at the same time, that he could do Glemp a favour. 'You must always give someone a fig leaf, to climb down, it's very important', he explains. And the fig leaf he was offering Glemp was the chance to repudiate what he had said in Bristol. 'You can say you have been misunderstood, misquoted and misunderstood. I want to ring *The Times* and you'll have a very nice leader in *The Times*.'

There are conflicting accounts of how long it took before Glemp actually signed. Clifford Longley remembers that he received a phone call at 9 p.m., just in time to change the unfavourable leader about Glemp he had prepared for the first edition of *The Times*. Many reports at the time gave the impression that Glemp, having found a sympathetic Jew who would listen to him, poured out his heart for several hours – and then he signed. Sigi insists today that the heart to heart was after the signing. 'He signed first because I told him, "We know exactly why we are here. You've got to sign this letter, it's very important this letter." And then I phoned *The Times* and then he signed the letter and later he said he didn't realize that there are such nice people, that Jews are such nice, understanding people.'

In the famous letter, theoretically in response to Sigi's telex to him, Glemp affirmed his intention of implementing the Geneva Accords of 1987. He cited both the sympathetic awareness of

Jewish suffering in Prime Minister Mazowiecki's letter to Sigi, which he claimed to have seen, and the Pope's reference to the 'immense suffering of the Jews in Poland' and welcomed the opportunity to meet Sigi in Poland. He was glad, too, to learn that 'some of the shrill voices do not reflect the feelings of world Jewry and aggression is not part of Jewish philosophy'. As Longley's leader in the second edition of *The Times* put it: 'Cardinal Glemp ... unexpectedly accepted an olive branch offered to him at the last minute by a group of British Jewish leaders, and responded generously'.

Congratulations were now the order of the day. One of the first of many dignitaries to express gratification for the new beginning was Lord Jacobovits who, in a letter to Glemp, praised the Cardinal for helping 'to do much to restore the mutual respect between our two great faiths, building on the goodwill and understanding initiated by the late lamented Pope John XXIII'. Sigi, too, was flooded with messages acclaiming his 'constructive role' in resolving the conflict. Not least was a cordial telex dated 29 September from Cardinal Glemp himself, expressing his appreciation of Sigi's 'opennes [sic] to solve a difficult problems [sic] and the understanding of others'. Glemp also welcomed the invitation Sigi had extended to visit the Sternberg Centre and hoped to be able to do so in the future.

How widely the events of 20 September were reported in Europe is another matter. The Polish left-wing daily, *Trybuna Ludu*, of 23–24 September did indeed have an account and quoted Sigi, described as an 'eminent Jewish spokesman', as being 'delighted' with the positive development: 'Cardinal Glemp has seen that we Jews are sensible people and this is a victory for common sense.' On the other hand, in a letter of 2 October faxed to Rabbi Marc Tannenbaum, Sigi refers to the Munich daily *Suddeutsche Zeitung*, cited in the *International Herald Tribune*, and comments: 'I have heard that it is not we who solved the problem but it was solved by other methods. This lie will have to be countered.'

In November Sigi visited Poland to re-launch the Rotary Club in Warsaw. Together with Professor Polonsky, who had accompanied him to the crucial dinner, he called on Cardinal

Glemp. By this time, Glemp was telling them, together with a delegation of the American Jewish Congress, of his wish to concentrate his efforts on the promotion of Catholic-Jewish understanding, particularly at the popular level where 'ignorance of Jews and Judaism is widespread'.

Feeling his trip to Poland would not be complete without a journey to Auschwitz to see the scene of the five-year controversy, Sigi duly turned up at the convent and knocked on the door. The story has it that a nun looked through the grille and was astonished to see the strange man waiting outside. Sigi then pushed a crumpled photograph of himself in Papal Knight's regalia together with Pope John Paul II through the opening. It turned out to be the 'open Sesame' Weiss had lacked!

Building work started a few months later at the end of February 1990 when, as reported in some Western newspapers, 'a Roman Catholic Cardinal and a Polish government minister dug the first spadefuls of earth to build the interfaith centre'. The Cardinal in question was Macharski. Before that Sigi had tried to quell the impatience of some Jewish organizations in Israel which had placed a full-page advertisement in the *Jerusalem Post*'s international edition announcing a campaign to collect support and signatures against the delay in the implementation of the Geneva Accords. The advertisement was signed by the Chief Rabbis of Israel, mayors, other rabbis and various personalities. Sigi was also anxious to discourage a libel suit Weiss was intending to pursue against Cardinal Glemp, for which he had engaged Alan Dershowitz, a well-known American trial lawyer, fearing that this might disturb the delicate new status quo.

The prayer centre was finally built with the new convent nearby. But the erection of the infrastructure prescribed by the Geneva Accords was insufficient to move the reluctant Carmelites, cosily ensconced in the revamped 'old theatre' building. Many Poles supported the nuns in their opposition to the move. It appears that the Mother Superior was determined to stay and her attitude influenced the younger sisters who would have been more compliant and ready to compromise. In the end, it was the Pope himself who ordered the Carmelites to vacate the premises. While most of the sisters moved to the new convent near the prayer centre, the Mother Superior and one or two others went elsewhere.

Unfortunately, the centre has become something of a white elephant and is rarely used. And the seven metre cross, which provoked such anger and anguish, did not move with the sisters but remained in place. Only in Spring 1998 was some agreement reached for the removal of the cross.

Looking back, Sigi can say in one breath that 'it shouldn't have happened at all. It would have been better if they had left the nuns there. So much bad blood and so much energy was wasted – but it happened.' This is one side of the picture. But being a creature of contradictions, like so many of us, he is perfectly capable in the next breath of taking an opposing point of view, in a far more emotional tone: 'Nuns should not pray for Jews who perished in the camp. We don't want it, it's not their job. The Jewish attitude is "This is a Jewish cemetery and in a Jewish cemetery you don't want a convent." This is quite straightforward. It's the largest Jewish cemetery and we don't want a convent.' He does not appear to be conscious of coming across as two different people, on the one hand the universalist, the champion of dialogue, and on the other hand the human being, the Jew, who is allowed to have feelings even if they are not politically correct.

But it was as the universalist and the skilful exponent of quiet diplomacy that Sigi succeeded in cooling tempers. By winning the friendship of Cardinal Glemp and changing his perception of Jews, he made a valuable contribution, together with the Vatican, towards ending the 'religious wars'.

8 From Tension to Triumph: The Templeton Prize

Sadly, that was not the end of the 'religious wars'. Despite a warm letter of greetings for Christmas and the New Year that Sigi had received from Cardinal Glemp, the agreement about the removal of the Papal cross in Spring 1998 was to provoke an unforeseen backlash.

In Poland, intimations that the cross was to be relocated led to a series of acts of protest by a group of militant Catholics, who called themselves 'the defenders of the cross'. Their leader, Kasimierz Switon, a former trade union activist, enlisted the support of the chairman of the Polish War Victims Association, who was leasing the former convent building, and was given a key to the property. In mid June, as tensions over the future of the cross continued to rise, he began a 42-day fast 'in defence of the cross', ending it only at the request of an archbishop. In a statement announcing that he had ended his fast, Switon appealed to the Polish public to bring small crosses to erect around the large Papal cross and by the end of the day fifty small crosses had been erected. The climate of protest is also likely to have contributed to the desecration of some fifty graves of Jews executed by the Nazis in Palmiry, near Warsaw.

Not surprisingly, opinion in the Jewish world was enflamed and in August Rabbi Avi Weiss announced that he would travel to Poland to protest against the crosses. Israeli authorities, too, issued a complaint to the government of Poland, demanding that the crosses, 'an affront to the Jewish victims of the Holocaust', be removed.

Cardinal Glemp also intervened, saying that the crosses should remain in place to mark the deaths of the many

Christians who had perished in the camps. He also intimated that 'the defenders of the cross' came into being as a result of Jewish harassment regarding the removal of the crosses. He was obliged to take back his words the following week, however, further to representations made to the Vatican by interfaith activists, including Sigi, who argued that dialogue and consultation were the only means to resolve the dispute. At that point, Glemp appealed to the militants to stop erecting any more crosses.

Despite interventions by the Polish government, other senior representatives of the Polish church and the regional council of Oświęcim, all favouring the removal of the crosses, Switon and his followers remained unmoved and by August over 100 crosses had been erected. By now the independent Catholic radio station, Radio Maryja, was urging Catholics abroad to support the erection of crosses as part of 'a holy war against alleged Jewish conspiracies, the government, the West' and anyone who disagreed with the militant Catholics' view of 'God's word'.

At this point Sigi organized a special emergency session on the situation during the annual consultation of the International Council of Christians and Jews that was taking place at Erlbach in Germany. Among the speakers were Stanislaw Krajewski, Father John Pawlikowski, Cardinal Cassidy and Sigi himself. It was agreed that the crisis should be handled by the Polish government and the Catholic bishops without outside interference. If they failed to reach a satisfactory resolution, the Vatican should then intercede.

By late October, there were 238 'Switon' crosses surrounding the Papal cross. On a visit to Warsaw at the invitation of President Kwasniewski, Sigi was apprised of the Polish government's discomfiture concerning the negative impact the Auschwitz cross controversy was having on Poland's image abroad. Sigi suggested that such situations might be avoided in the future if a task force were established consisting of a member of the government and representatives from the Jewish and Catholic communities.

In an address at Warsaw University, he declared that

Auschwitz was not a place for a war of religion, 'of Cross against Star of David, of rabbi against priest, of Christian against Jew ... Auschwitz does not need a "selection process" that suggests that one religion's dead are more worthy than another.' He was in favour of 'a simple monument which would record the men, women and children who died there as martyrs'.

The year ended with no solution to the Auschwitz cross controversy in sight, while Catholic-Jewish relations were further ruffled in the latter part of the year by a beatification and a canonization, which proved to be contentious. During a visit to Croatia in early October, Pope John Paul II carried out the beatification of Cardinal Alojzije Stepinac who, according to Jewish leaders, turned a blind eye to the behaviour of the Croatian government during the Second World War. The Cardinal's defenders claimed that once he became aware of the atrocities being committed he saved many Jewish lives, and a representative of the Jewish community acknowledged that while he should have protested earlier, he was a brave man. Far more provocative was the canonization in Rome of Edith Stein, born an orthodox Jew, who later converted to Catholicism and entered the Carmelite order as Teresa Benedicta of the Cross. In 1942 she was deported, together with her sister and other Jews who had converted to Catholicism, to Auschwitz, where they were all gassed. 'Teresa' had already been beatified in 1987, amid considerable controversy.

While the Pontiff claimed that declaring Stein a saint 'serves to make an ever stronger bridge in the reciprocal comprehension between Jews and Christians', his sentiments, on this occasion, failed to resonate with Jews in the way he may have wished. Amos Luzzato, President of the Union of Italian Jewish Communities, disputed the Pope's claim that the canonization could be considered a 'bridge' between Catholics and Jews. Stein, he said, died because she was a Jew, not because she was a Jew who had converted to Catholicism. 'If she is a martyr because she died in the Holocaust, then six million Jews should also be considered martyrs.' Others called the canonization 'outrageous' and said it would 'inflict a fresh wound on the hearts of the descendants of the victims of the Holocaust'.

Sigi, usually so circumspect regarding matters of dispute, felt obliged to intervene. 'I am not one to rush to the media with statements of regret and concern', he wrote to the Apostolic Nuncio in Great Britain, Archbishop Pablo Puente. Sigi continued, in an unusually impassioned letter:

> It is with sadness that I have to say that my task, and that of others who speak to and for the Jewish people on interfaith issues, has been placed under a heavy shadow by the manner in which Sister Teresa Benedicta of the Cross, better known to the world as Edith Stein, has been canonized … In proclaiming Edith Stein a Christian martyr, many Jews suspect an attempt to bleach out the fact that the mass slaughter of their people took place in the midst of Christian Europe.
>
> What complicates the canonisation of Edith Stein for me is the fact that, although her only connection with Auschwitz was her incarceration and killing, she had been appropriated as a symbol by those Polish nationalists and anti-Semites who are responsible for the field of crosses thrown up on the Auschwitz perimeter as a deliberate provocation to the Jews. It is not without some significance that a wreath with the name 'Edith Stein' and not Sister Benedicta has been displayed in the vicinity of the crosses by those responsible for the planting of the crosses.

While Sigi recognized that the canonization could not be reversed, he hoped some action could be taken to 'ease the impact' and proposed the removal of the crosses from Auschwitz as one positive gesture, as well as the widening of access to wartime Vatican archives.

Sigi concluded by asking the archbishop if he could enlighten him as to what might have influenced the Pope to choose this particular candidate for canonization at that time, so that he might be able to explain this to others. 'It would be desperately sad indeed if all that has been achieved this last twenty and more years by Christian-Jewish dialogue were now to be slowed down, even petrified, by what happened in Rome', he added. At a later date, the archbishop sent him a paper on how the canonization of Edith Stein might affect Catholic-Jewish relations prepared by Cardinal William Keeler, the Episcopal Moderator for Catholic-Jewish Relations on the National Conference of Catholic Bishops in America. In the paper, Cardinal Keeler attempted to address Jewish concerns that the canonization might imply that there was a new movement aimed at proselytizing and converting Jews and also that it might suggest that the Church was 'appropriating' the Holocaust itself.

Cardinal Keeler was of the view that 'in honouring Edith Stein, the church wishes to honour all the millions of Jewish victims of the Shoah'. As was the Rev. Remi Hoeckman, secretary of the Vatican's commission for relations with the Jews who said of the canonization: 'It in no way lessens, but in reality strengthens, our need to honour the six million Jews who died in the *Shoah.*' However, in his letter to Archbishop Puente, Sigi made another important point that these responses, however well-intended, could not answer. As he put it: 'What rankles above all else is that Sister Benedicta's last will and testament said that she offered herself to God "for the atonement of the unbelief of the Jewish people." That of the many Christian martyrs from the Holocaust period, the Church should choose the one who rejected her own people but nevertheless died as one has enabled observers to find disturbing mixed messages in her canonization.' The controversy was unlikely to die down quickly.

Despite what might be seen as setbacks in Catholic-Jewish relations in the latter part of 1998, for Sigi, himself, the year had been a memorable one. The announcement that he was to be awarded the Templeton Prize for Progress in Religion, which was made early in March, earned him a stream of congratulations from many distinguished people which was to continue throughout the year. One of the first to congratulate him was Archbishop Luigi Barbarito, formerly the Papal Nuncio to Great Britain, who sent a letter from Rome, having read about the award in *The Tablet*, the Catholic weekly. 'I feel confident that the friendly dialogue [between Christians and Jews] will develop further and enrich both communities who share the spiritual inheritance of Abraham, of the Law and of the Prophets', he wrote. Not long after that Sigi received a letter from Judge Richard Goldstone, author of the 2009 United Nations report into Israel's actions in Gaza, and at that time a Justice of South Africa's Constitutional Court, congratulating him on his 'very well deserved award'. Stuart Eizenstat, then American Under Secretary of State for Economic, Business and Agricultural Affairs, also wrote to congratulate him later in the year. 'Your promotion of greater understanding between Christians and Jews is inspiring', he said. And in his letter, Lord Frank Judd, a Labour peer and member of the Joint Committee on Human Rights put it this way: 'It is hard to think of anyone who could deserve it more or who would put it to better use.'

Sir John Templeton, the founder of the prize, was an American-born British businessman, investor and philanthropist, who, in 1987, established the Templeton Foundation. The Templeton Prize, first awarded in 1973, was designed to reward 'a living person who has made an exceptional contribution to affirming life's spiritual dimension, whether through insight, discovery or practical works'.

Sigi had been involved with the Templeton Foundation for some ten years, since the prize was won in 1988 by Dr Inamullah Khan, at that time the Secretary-General of the World Muslim Congress who had been active in promoting peaceful relations between Muslims, Christians and Jews. The Anti-Defamation League (ADL) in America, however, had criticized the Templeton Foundation for awarding Khan the prize, charging that he had supported anti-Semitism and that the newsletter of the World Muslim Congress had supported anti-Semitic propaganda such as *The Protocols of the Elders of Zion*. It was therefore inferred that the Templeton Foundation itself was in some ways anti-Semitic.

Sigi made a statement to the contrary and issued a press-release that was sent to the ADL. He asserted that Sir John Templeton, the founder of the prize, was in no way an anti-Semite. He was later invited to meet Sir John, who suggested that he might like to become one of the judges of the prestigious annual award. Sigi considered Sir John's proposal and finally assented, giving, as a condition, that the prize, which had been given annually for fifteen years, should, at some stage, be awarded to a Jew. The fact that three years later the winner was announced to be retiring Chief Rabbi, Lord Immanuel Jacobovits, was, naturally, gratifying to Sigi, whose influence might have made some contribution to the decision of his fellow judges.

Sigi learned early in 1998 that he was to receive the Templeton Prize but was obliged to keep this confidential until the formal announcement in New York on 4 March, which was made at a news conference in the Church Centre at the United Nations. In a letter to Sir John, he stated that despite the many awards he had received,

> nothing that has gone before prepared me for the ultimate accolade: the Templeton Prize for Progress in Religion. I am indeed most humbled by the fact that the judges have chosen me from amongst what I am sure was a rich mix of worthy candidates to receive this most celebrated of awards. I also appreciate the opportunities which are provided by the ceremonies associated with the Templeton Prize to proclaim my absolute commitment to dialogue designed to eradicate religious prejudice and to create a climate in which we can live together in justice and integrity.

He added that the cash award would enable him to expand his support for interfaith activities, and in a handwritten postscript, Hazel, his wife, added that they were looking forward to using their augmented funds to further the work they had already undertaken.

For his part, Sir John paid tribute to Sigi's pioneering interfaith endeavours in his speech nominating him for the award: 'Some of the deepest suspicions, resentments and divisions of this century and of human history have lain between adherents of different religions. Sir Sigmund has pioneered and proved inter-religious dialogue as a new force for reconciliation and the understanding of God.'

Sigi and Hazel's trip to New York to be present at the announcement was certainly busy. There were, of course, several meetings with key personnel of the Templeton Foundation: Sir John himself, his son, John Templeton Junior, known as 'Jack' and Wilbert Forker, the Executive Vice-President of the Templeton Foundation. A Methodist clergyman of Irish origin, Forker became the chief press officer for the World Council of Churches in Geneva where he met Sir John Templeton. Sir John then invited him to help establish the Templeton Prize. Forker was in frequent contact with Sigi with regard to the complex arrangements concerning the award. Their faxed correspondence even included suggestions for refreshments for the cocktail reception following the formal ceremony at the United Nations in June. Sigi, of course, had to veto any hors d'oeuvre containing meat or shellfish and proposed, since there would also be Muslim guests, that only dairy and vegetarian products should be served. Sigi was also in contact with Donald Lehr of the Nolan/Lehr Group, who was in charge of the publicity surrounding the Templeton Prize and acknowledged how much he had enjoyed working with him.

Sigi's first meeting on 2 March, the day after his arrival, was with Rabbi Leon Klenicki, the director of interfaith affairs for the ADL and its co-liaison to the Vatican. He was also the first Hugo Gryn Fellow at the Centre for the Study of Jewish-Christian Relations at the Woolf Institute of Abrahamic Faiths. Two years before his death in 2009, Rabbi Klenicki was named a Papal Knight of the Order of St Gregory the Great by Pope Benedict XVI.

Another meeting was with Rabbi Mark Winer, Chairman of the International Interfaith Taskforce for the World Union for Progressive Judaism, who had also been involved in negotiations concerning the convent at Auschwitz. Later that year, Rabbi Winer was to take over the post of Senior Rabbi at West London Synagogue as the long-awaited successor to the much-loved late Rabbi Hugo Gryn. One significant event during Rabbi Winer's first High Holy Day season at West

London Synagogue later that year was to host a special Succot service attended by several ambassadors whom Sigi had invited.

Naturally, Sigi was obliged to give numerous interviews either in person or on the telephone and before he left New York, he and Hazel were taken on a satellite television tour. It appears that the media tour was a great success, as Wilbert Forker informed Sigi on his return to London. The highlight of the trip was, of course, the news conference at the UN Church Centre, televised coast-to-coast and also on CNN, followed by a private lunch with Sir John, Jack and the Templeton Prize judges at the UN Plaza Hotel. In his speech at the news conference, Sigi said how greatly he felt humbled by the award:

> This is an astonishingly humbling day for me. I have myself been a judge in past years for the Templeton Prize. I know the calibre of people who have been nominated and those who have been selected. They range from near saints such as Mother Theresa through some of the leading religious thinkers and theologians of our time to top names in the scientific world and academia. I qualify in none of these categories. I am a simple soul, a businessman, who, in a modest way, has been smiled on by fortune – fortune which I believe to be divinely inspired – and who has tried to repay the blessings which have been bestowed on me by opening to others a sense of the goodness which lies in us all, regardless of our faith, or, indeed, whether we have religious faith at all.

Sigi went on to speak of his 'unrequited passion' to form a partnership with thousands of people across the globe who could contribute to global healing. 'It is time for religion to come out of the church, the synagogue, the mosque, the temple and to create bonds between people which ... if harnessed, could contribute to the creation of caring societies.'

Sigi was the first businessman to be awarded the Templeton Prize. In an article published in the *Financial Times* on Saturday 7 March, he wrote of the immense satisfaction he had derived through his involvement in Jewish-Christian dialogue from seeing the 'tremendous reduction in the tensions and suspicions which once characterized relations between these faith communities'. He also spoke of his desire for Christians and Jews to reach out to members of the third Abrahamic faith, Islam, to which end he and other like-minded Christians and Jews had set up the Three Faiths Forum, together with Sheikh Zaki Badawi, then head of the British Council of Imams and Mosques. The main purpose of the article, however, was to urge businessmen to become more involved in interfaith activity. His aspiration was 'to see a great assembly of businessmen and women, a sort of Davos convocation of the soul, seeking together for a set of beliefs which would bind them in a fellowship of the spirit capable of leaping over every border, political and physical'. He also pointed out that he was 'earmarking' a large part of the million dollar Templeton Prize for the furtherance of inter-religious dialogue.

In an interview with *The Christian Science Monitor* published two days earlier in the wake of the prize announcement, Sigi again spoke of interfaith work from a businessman's perspective: 'I'm someone who believes this interfaith work is a good investment because people come together, they have dialogue, get to know each other and usually want to live in harmony and peace. The alternative is violence.'

In New York, Sigi had met a prominent lawyer, Roger M. Deitz, whom he had invited to join him at the London Rotary Club. With a letter saying how much he had enjoyed meeting him and hearing him speak, Deitz enclosed an article from *The New York Times* about the Pope's longstanding friendship with a Jew, Jerzy Kluger, which dated back to their boyhood days in Wadowice, and how Kluger had helped him forge relations between the Vatican and the State of Israel.

The visit to New York in March was just the first of what could be seen as a process in three stages. Sigi was to be formally awarded the prize by the Duke of Edinburgh at Buckingham Palace on 13 May, and on 26 June there was to be another formal ceremony at the United Nations in New York.

Back in London, Sigi was soon putting his new award to good use. The Social Column of *The Times* reported on a discussion dinner of the Three Faiths Forum at the Reform Club the previous evening, hosted by 'Sir Sigmund Sternberg, recipient of the Templeton Prize for Progress in Religion', at which the Commonwealth Secretary-General, Chief Emeka Anyaoku, was the guest speaker.

Sigi had also been making arrangements relating to the Buckingham Palace ceremony and events linked to this very special occasion. In a letter to Brigadier Miles Hunt-Davis, Private Secretary to the Duke of Edinburgh, he said how honoured he felt that he would be receiving the prize 'from the hands of the Duke'. 'It will be a Red Letter Day not just in the life of my family and myself, but of all those who have involved themselves in interfaith dialogue and the search for understanding and respect between religions.' 'With considerable diffidence' he pointed out that unlike in previous instances, there would be no service and reception at Westminster Abbey and, in view of this, he wondered whether it might be possible for the ceremony at the Palace to be 'enlarged to allow a larger audience than is usual'. Sigi had in mind some fifty extra guests, 'representatives of the Christian, Muslim and Jewish communities ... as well as leaders of other faith communities, some ambassadors whose countries have branches of the International Council of Christians and Jews and the President of the London Rotary Club'. A few days later, Sigi received a personal, handwritten letter from Hunt-Davis, saying how delighted he was to learn of the award: 'I know you have received many honours and awards but I feel that Sir John's prize is such a true recognition of the work you have done over the years in a field that has not, perhaps, always been very easy.' Sigi learnt from an Equerry to the Duke of Edinburgh that his request for an increase in numbers had been accepted 'in principle' and a suitable room for the occasion was being investigated.

Sigi had also written to the German ambassador, suggesting that a reception might be held at the German Embassy on 12 May, the day before the Palace ceremony. The reception took place as Sigi had planned and many distinguished guests attended. He had written, too, to the Archbishop of

Canterbury, Dr George Carey, informing him that he would be receiving an invitation from the Templeton Foundation to lunch at Claridges on 13 May and also to a Reception at the Oxford and Cambridge University Club two days earlier. The Archbishop and his wife, however, were to be out of the country at the time. Sigi's 'own' rabbi, Dr Tony Bayfield, who was invited to the award ceremony at Buckingham Palace, wrote to say how proud he was to be associated with his work and how much he was looking forward to 13 May. Sigi also invited the leader of the Jewish community in Germany, Ignatz Bubis, to the Palace ceremony and other events but it appears that Bubis was unable to attend. However, Sigi and Bubis were in touch with each other in September, when Sigi was in Berlin to attend the presentation of the German Medal of Honour to the film-maker Steven Spielberg. Bubis also wrote to congratulate Sigi on receiving the first Community Service Award from the Board of Deputies of British Jews for his 'outstanding service to interfaith work'.

One particularly important guest at the Palace presentation was Cardinal Edward Cassidy, President of the Vatican's Commission for Religious Relations with the Jews, who was a key figure in bringing out the Vatican statement: *We Remember: A Reflection on the Shoah*. Sigi had contacted the Board of Deputies in order to co-host a lunch at the Board in the Cardinal's honour and also arranged a press conference with the religious press group. As it happened, the timing of the award ceremony in May coincided with the closing days of a Special Synod for Asia of the Synod of Bishops in Rome, and the Cardinal had hoped to be in Rome when the final voting was to take place before leaving on a pre-arranged trip to Washington DC. Indeed, as he put it in a letter to Sigi: 'It is only because of my great respect for you that I am even thinking of leaving the Synod in order to be with you on May 13th'. Sigi had also invited Israel's ambassador to the Vatican, Aharon Lopez.

Sigi had hoped that Prime Minister Tony Blair might be able to meet Sir John Templeton on one of the ceremonial occasions. He was very impressed with Blair and greatly optimistic about the 'New Labour' project. In a letter to the *International Herald Tribune* in July, he 'took issue' with the newspaper's inference that there was anything 'improper' about the Prime Minister's links with business.

> As one of the few businessmen close to the last Labour government of Harold Wilson, I am delighted that this administration has gone out to listen to the views of the business community and to include leading members of that community in senior government posts. It is New Labour's fusion of social democratic principles with enlightened business practice that distinguishes this administration from all that has gone before and is already creating a new beginning for Britain.

Sigi also praised Blair's approach to Britain's minority communities. In a letter to the Speaker, Betty Boothroyd, with whom he enjoyed a personal friendship, he wrote that 'the Indian, Muslim, Hindu and Jewish communities are very joyous at the support they are receiving from the Blairs, who have done more for the minorities in this country than any other prime minister'. Boothroyd, who was a patron of the recently formed Three Faiths Forum, had entertained Sigi and Hazel at Speaker's House, and had congratulated Sigi in a handwritten letter on his 'splendid' speech on accepting an Honorary Doctorate from the Open University, in the wake of the Templeton award.

Prime Minister Blair, however, was not available to meet Sir John, and on learning that the hoped for get-together was not possible, Sigi wanted to arrange a meeting between Templeton and Peter Mandelson, as he mentioned in a letter to the Labour peer, Lord Michael Montague. Mandelson was invited to a private dinner at the Athenaeum on 11 May, to be hosted by Sir John's son, Jack, but was not able to attend. Nonetheless, Foreign Secretary Robin Cook was present at the reception at the German Embassy together with his wife, as was Margaret Beckett, President of the Board of Trade, while Jack Straw, the Home Secretary, also attended one of the celebratory events.

If Sigi was disappointed at Blair's absence from the

Templeton Prize celebrations in London, he received, as it were 'in compensation', a fulsome letter of congratulation from the prime minister which was read out at the Palace ceremony. Tony Blair spoke of him as 'one of those rare individuals whose personal efforts have made a difference' and wished him continued strength and success in 'devoting his considerable energy to furthering his accomplishments'. A few days earlier, Sigi had received a message of congratulations from German President Roman Herzog: 'Through your many years of committed work for increased dialogue between Christians and Jews and as a co-founder of a forum for discussion between Christians, Muslims and Jews, you have made an outstanding contribution to greater understanding between the world religions.' In particular, Herzog praised Sigi's initiative 'in setting up local dialogue groups and arranging intensive talks between members of different religious persuasions in cities and local communities', which, he believed, showed 'a way forward' that he hoped others would emulate.

Moreover, further to the announcement of the award in March, Labour MP Dr Rudi Vis had raised an Early Day Motion in the House of Commons in order to publicize the award and enable other members of parliament to express their congratulations to Sigi. Nearly fifty members, including well-known figures such as Martin Bell, Ken Livingstone, Gwyneth Dunwoody and Tony McNulty, gave their support to the motion. And shortly afterwards, *The Jewish Chronicle* carried a large congratulatory announcement endorsed by numerous organizations both in Great Britain and throughout the world including Charter 88, AFASIC, the Imperial War Museum, the Fabian Society, Mind and the Institute of Archaeology among many others. As well as former Chief Rabbi Lord Jacobovits, the Archbishop of Canterbury, the Cardinal Archbishop of Westminster and Archbishop Gregorios of Thyateria and Great Britain were all among the signatories.

An early message of congratulation had come from the recently appointed Japanese ambassador, Sadayuki Hayashi. On learning that Hayashi was keen on reconciliation Sigi had written to him, inviting him to the award ceremony at Buckingham Palace. He had also sent the ambassador a video of the presentation of the Interfaith Gold Medallion to President Niwano of the Rissho Kosei-Kai organization, which had made a contribution to reconciliation between the Japanese and the British people. In the letter, Sigi pointed out that Niwano was the only Japanese person to have received the Templeton Prize. Sigi also hoped that the Emperor of Japan, who was due to visit London in May, might be able to meet people in the interfaith movement to talk about the meaning of reconciliation. He put forward the suggestion, too, that a small delegation from the Board of Deputies of British Jews might be able to call on the Emperor during his visit to pay tribute to his dedication to the principles of peace and reconciliation and to voice their appreciation of two individual Japanese diplomats who helped save the lives of many thousands of Jews during the Second World War.

Sigi had also received messages from various individuals who felt his experiences impacted on their lives. One was from a distant relative, Pier Marton, who wrote that Sigi's recent accomplishments and entire career reminded him of the life of Hillel, the great sage of the Second Temple period, renowned for his love of peace and love of his fellow man. And among the most unusual was one from Dr Fiorenza Di France, Professor of Drama at John Cabot University in Rome. She was, she wrote, the daughter of an Italian father and a Hungarian Jewish mother. Her father, a diplomat at the Italian Embassy in Budapest, had been arrested by the Gestapo shortly after the start of the Nazi occupation of Hungary in March 1944. He was sent to Mauthausen for having saved the lives of relatives of his wife and other Jews but almost never spoke of his experiences for fear of harming his family. Dr Di France, who had found out about her father's life in Mauthausen after his death from the book of a fellow inmate, was in the process of finishing her own book on her family's and her own experiences during the war when the Vatican statement, *We Remember: A Reflection on the Shoah*, was issued. As well as quoting from these documents, she was collecting reactions to the Vatican Statement from various Jewish communities. She appealed to Sigi: 'Who better than you, founder of the Three Faiths Forum, can share my views? I hope you will answer me with your view on the ongoing dialogue between Catholics and Jews, giving me permission to quote you in my book, which I write because I firmly believe that the Holocaust cannot be forgotten.'

Sigi had, indeed, prepared a statement in response to the Vatican pronouncement: 'I am sure that Jews everywhere will share the Pope's hope that today's Vatican document will help heal "the wounds of past misunderstandings and injustices"', he began. He went on to commend the Pope, himself, for his contribution to the healing process and also 'those French and German bishops who apologised to the Jewish people in forthright terms for the Church's failure to respond in an appropriate way to the deportation and murder of innocent men, women and children'. Sigi had special praise for 'those Christians in a Europe bathed in blood who held out a hand in succour to Jews seeking refuge from the Nazi killing machine'. While their memories would be blessed, it was important not to forget the silence of those in the Church who knew what was happening to the Jews 'and raised neither their voices nor their hands in aid or comfort'.

Sigi had sent Brigadier Miles Hunt-Davis a draft copy of the speech he proposed to give at the presentation ceremony at Buckingham Palace. Hunt-Davis made one or two suggestions for minor changes but said the speech was 'quite excellent'. On the day itself, Sigi began his address with two traditional Jewish blessings, joking that Chief Rabbi Jonathan Sacks, who was one of the guests, would allow him 'to poach a little on his territory'. He went on to explain that he had been present at the Palace at several previous Templeton prize-givings, 'always the bridesmaid, never the bride' but never believed that he, himself, would be a recipient of the prestigious award. 'A knighthood, the Templeton Prize, good friends – how much more can I ask of life?'

Sigi also paid tribute to Prince Philip, who was his contemporary, both having been born in 1921, and recalled sharing some special occasions with him. 'Most memorable for me was that day in 1994 when he spoke so movingly in Jerusalem at the ceremony in which his late mother was honoured with Yad Vashem's award of "Righteous Among the Gentiles" for saving Jewish lives at the risk of her own life.' He was also particularly impressed with Prince Philip's work in drawing together experts of all faiths to formulate a set of business ethics and said he planned to use some of the Templeton Prize money to bring together international businessmen 'to embrace and promote such an ethical programme'.

He reiterated this aim in a letter to Sir John:

> I intend pressing on with my notion of a convocation of world businessmen and women drawn from all the faith communities who are willing to commit to the search for a unifying ethic. There is a need for moral theologians and business people to reflect together on some of the complex issues of the day, from simple business practice and employer-worker relationships to the role of commerce in safeguarding the environment.

Sigi also expressed the hope that Sir John would join him in this endeavour, 'if only in a token manner', since 'the very knowledge of your support would act as an inducement to others to rally to the cause'. Sir John, however, felt obliged to decline, citing his age – he was nearly 86 and his body was saying 'slow down' – but wished Sigi 'every success in your new endeavour. It is a daunting task but one that with your energy and network of friends may help the world to be better off as a result of your vision and dedication.'

Sigi had also asked Wilbert Forker, who had been appointed to the Advisory Council of the ICCJ, whether he would consider assisting him in the work of the Sternberg Foundation after he had retired from the Templeton Foundation. So eager was he for 'new blood' to add impetus to his endeavours that he even approached Senator John Glenn, the first American space-traveller, who was taking off on his second journey into orbit in October that year. Wishing him 'bon voyage' on his return journey, Sigi also referred to the fact that they had both reached 'the blessed age of 77', and asked the senator whether he might consider lending 'moral support' to his new initiative of uniting business men and women of all faiths behind a global ethic, which was to hold its founding meeting at the Windsor Castle conference centre the following year.

The timetable of events in London included a reception at the Royal Society of Medicine co-hosted by Sigi on the afternoon following the Palace presentation to mark the publication of Sir John's book, *Worldwide Laws of Life,* and ended with a reception at the Sternberg Centre. It had been, as Sigi told Sir John, 'an incredible week' for him and his family, several of whom had shared the occasion with him. Michael, his son, had been at the Palace with his wife Janine and their daughter Rachel, as had Sigi's step-daughter Ruth, with her husband Noam and their daughter Elinor. Suzanne, his sister, was also there. However, Frances, his daughter, who had become a distinguished artist, was on an art scholarship programme in California and was therefore unable to attend.

Frances had flown out to California on 21 April. She had been awarded a scholarship on the Djerassi Resident Artists Programme, founded by the celebrated chemist, Karl Djerassi, who had invented the oral contraceptive, in memory of his artist daughter who had committed suicide. Djerassi, a Jew of central European origin, also knew of Sigi. For the first three weeks of her stay in America, Frances was flown round the country in the company of a minder, visiting art collections from one city to another. For the final weeks of the programme she was based in California. She returned to London in early June, in time for an exhibition of her own work. Because she was busy with interviews and meeting many people in the art world and because she had been flying so frequently in recent weeks, she and Sigi decided that she should not fly out, once again, to New York for the Templeton ceremony on June 26.

For any individual, the award of such a prestigious prize and the events surrounding it would surely have been all-consuming. Sigi, as ever, was the exception to the rule. Barely a week before the London celebrations he had been in Lisbon, on the occasion of his installation as a Visiting Professor in Jewish Studies at the Universidade Moderna and used this opportunity to win support for the establishment of a Council of Christians and Jews in Portugal. In his address, Sigi outlined the tragic history of the Jews in Portugal under the Inquisition but saw his installation as 'a significant step towards the reconciliation of the sovereign state of Portugal and the Jewish people'. He paid tribute to the memory of Aristides Sousa Mendes, the Portuguese consul in France during the Second World War, who had risked his life to help Jews escape from the Nazis, and also invited Portuguese businessmen to join him in his planned convocation of world business leaders to find a globally unifying ethic. And between the ceremonies in London and New York, he was as active as ever in furthering his many causes, one of which was reconciliation in the Holy Land. To this end he gave an address in early June to members of the Equestrian Order of the Holy Sepulchre of Jerusalem, in which he, of course, spoke of the importance of dialogue but also introduced the question of building up the means of livelihood for the peoples of the Holy Land in tandem with the business community.

Sigi and Hazel arrived in New York on 24 June to be faced with another full programme of events. They lunched the following day with Dr Georgette Bennett, President of the Tanenbaum Centre for Interreligious Understanding, and held two further meetings that afternoon with people Dr Bennett believed would be interested in Sigi's work. One of the meetings was with Douglas Makepeace, who was willing to further Sigi's aspiration to set up a business leaders' conference on spirituality with a personal donation of $100,000. In the same vein, Sigi had contacted Dr Bennett regarding the possibility of her speaking with Rabbi Sidney Brichto, on his recent trip to Washington, to discuss Brichto's idea of setting up a forum with business people willing to be involved in the application of interfaith work to the realm of commerce and industry. Sigi had also arranged for an announcement in the Social Column of the London *Times* to present his new initiative, Faith in

Business, which he would be outlining in his acceptance speech at the UN.

That evening, Peter Gruber of the Globalvest Management Company hosted a reception in Sigi's honour at his home, which he hoped would be 'a small gathering of like-minded people who are interested in your efforts'. The guests included Cardinal John Connor, Jack Templeton and his family, Sigi's sister Suzanne, and her New York-based son Louis, who was hosting a dinner at his home the following evening after the ceremony at the United Nations. Georgette Bennett was at the Friday night dinner, as were Sanford Cloud Jr and Karl Berolzeimer of the National Conference for Community and Justice, together with their wives. Among the guests who had come to New York specially to attend the prize ceremony was Lillian Hyatt, widow of David Hyatt, a former president of the National Conference of Christians and Jews. Richard B. Sainberg, President of the Rotary Club of New York, also attended.

The Templeton Prize Ceremony was, of course, the major event, where Sigi was praised as a most worthy recipient by the cast of distinguished speakers. In his introduction to the ceremony, the Chairman highlighted several of the landmarks in Sigi's pursuit of interfaith understanding, notably receiving the Papal Knighthood, accompanying the Pope to the Rome Synagogue and being present at the ceremony marking the signing of the agreement to establish diplomatic relations between the Vatican and Israel, during which a message was received from the Papal Knights' Association of Great Britain, which included congratulations to Sigi 'for all he has done to contribute to this breakthrough'. 'He is bringing his vision of "shalom" to make religion not a constraint but a liberating and reconciling force', the Chairman concluded. The theme of liberation was taken up by Dr John Templeton Jr in his address. Sigi, he said, 'has not been bound by religion but has been empowered by his faith to liberate himself and others from the bonds of discrimination and prejudice'. This theme was also present in the message from UN Secretary-General Kofi Annan, delivered by his deputy, Gillian Sorensen: 'In an era in which identity politics based on religion and ethnicity have intensified and in which intolerance still finds its way into textbooks and official pronouncements, it is remarkable individuals such as Sir Sigmund Sternberg who represent the countervailing trend who give us hope for the future.'

The theme of hope was taken up by Sigi in his address upon receiving the Prize. He praised Sir John Templeton for his belief that the rate of progress in human endeavour was 'speeding up' and would spread across 'countless areas in coming decades'. 'I share Sir John's optimism', Sigi declared. 'I share it despite the Shoah, despite My-Lai, despite Rwanda, despite the many horrors God's creatures have visited upon each other in His name. I share it because ... we have lived through the century in which freedom beat back the two totalitarian alternatives that rose to challenge it, Fascism and Communism.' He regretted that it was so rare for a businessman to receive the Templeton Prize and reiterated his aspiration for 'a sort of Davos convocation of the soul' that he had first raised in March following the Templeton Prize announcement news conference. Another aspiration he voiced was for the Declaration of a Global Ethic, similar to the set of ethical values devised by the distinguished theologian, Professor Hans Kung, which he saw as complementing in several respects the UN Declaration of Human Rights. 'If we can but agree on a global ethic acceptable to all men and women of religion, if we can but create an emblem that says "I share your values and I care", then the Buddhist, the Christian, the Hindu, Jain, Muslim, Sikh, the Taoist – no matter what religion – the adherents of faith can meet the other anywhere on this globe and raise a hand in a gesture of Shalom, a gesture of peace.'

Sigi had written to Hans Kung in April, saying that he was hoping to refer to his work in his speech at the UN. He was on friendly terms with Kung and had tried to arrange a meeting between the theologian and Prime Minister Blair, as Kung had requested, during a visit Kung had proposed to make to the UK in January or February that year. In the event, Blair was unable to meet Kung, so Sigi suggested that a meeting might be arranged with Peter Mandelson. Mandelson at the time was in charge of the Millennium Dome project and had put forward the idea in an interview with a journalist on *The Daily Telegraph* that the Dome should be a 'spiritual beacon'. However, Kung had read a less flattering account of the Dome project and Mandelson's involvement in it in an article in *The Economist* and explained to Sigi that he felt it would be unwise for a foreigner to be embroiled in the discussion. He decided to postpone his visit to a later date.

In the event, the visit took place during three packed days in October. As well as attending a number of meetings and giving several press interviews, Professor Kung was guest of honour at a dinner hosted by Sigi at the Sternberg Centre, where he was presented with the Interfaith Gold Medallion of the International Council of Christians and Jews by Lord Yehudi Menuhin. A breakfast was also held in Professor Kung's honour at the German Embassy and a reception hosted by his publishers, SCM Press, and Sigi took place in the Jerusalem Chamber at Westminster Abbey to celebrate his 70th birthday and the publication of his book on global ethics and a book about him and his work entitled *Hans Kung: Breaking Through*.

In his introductory remarks at the dinner at the Sternberg Centre, Sigi spoke of 'the huge personal influence' Hans Kung had had over his 'thinking about the nature of the world we are preparing for our children and grandchildren'. Kung, he said, was 'a man who, more than any other single individual, has touched the consciousness of the world with his insistence that, as we enter the twenty-first century, we take with us more than the baggage that has weighed us down as we journeyed through this century'. Sigi acknowledged that Kung could be controversial 'but he engages in the kind of controversy that we in Judaism dignify with the description, *b'shem shamayim* – in the name of heaven'. In his own speech Professor Kung put forward 'A Vision of Hope'. Despite his familiarity 'after forty years of study and experience' with the 'weaknesses and dark sides' of the world religions, he did not find it useful to propagate a new global political paradigm of the clash of civilizations, as put forward by Samuel

Huntington. He had never abandoned hope that peace between the religions was possible and saw it as a requisite for peace among the nations of the world.

After the visit, Sigi received a letter of appreciation from Dr John Bowden, Managing Director of SCM Press, commending him for the major part he played in making Kung's visit 'a triumphant success'. Lord Menuhin's secretary also wrote to say how much Lord Menuhin had enjoyed being at the Sternberg Centre dinner and having the opportunity to present the Interfaith Gold Medallion to Hans Kung.

Another commitment Sigi was keen to fulfil fell in November, when he travelled to Argentina to unveil a statue of Raoul Wallenberg, the Swedish humanitarian working in Budapest who had saved thousands of Jewish lives during the Holocaust and who was captured by the Soviets at the end of the war. Exactly when and how he died has remained something of a mystery. Many distinguished visitors, including American Under Secretary of State for Economics, Business and Agricultural Affairs, Stuart Eizenstat, attended the unveiling ceremony in Buenos Aires. Sigi had long been involved in efforts to honour Wallenberg and played a key role in having a memorial erected in Great Cumberland Place in London, outside the Western Marble Arch Synagogue. This was unveiled by the Queen in February 1997 and has since been visited by the Prince of Wales. Sigi was also instrumental in setting up memorials honouring Wallenberg in other countries, including a plaque in Slovakia, a sculpture in Chile and a street bearing his name in Uruguay.

The London unveiling ceremony was also brought up in the message delivered by Gillian Sorensen on behalf of UN Secretary-General, Kofi Annan, at the Templeton Ceremony in New York in June the following year:

> I had the good fortune to join Sir Sigmund in London for the unveiling of a monument dedicated to Raoul Wallenberg, my wife's uncle. The monument was commissioned by Sir Sigmund's organization, the International Council of Christians and Jews, as part of the Council's long-standing efforts to promote interfaith dialogue and

understanding. I was extremely grateful to Sir Sigmund for this initiative – for this important act of remembrance – and I was impressed by his strong belief in the dignity and worth of every human being. The ceremony itself was not easy … it forced me to dwell on difficult questions – matters involving atrocious violence, injustice and the dark side of human history. And then I realized that this is precisely what Sir Sigmund has been doing so well for so many years: looking forthrightly at some of the most vexing issues facing mankind and finding solutions that bring people together in common cause.

Sigi was eager for other courageous gentiles who had rescued Jews during the Nazi era to have recognition and had written to a Swiss newspaper at the time of the London unveiling ceremony urging that Switzerland should create a monument commemorating the bravery of Carl Lutz, the Swiss vice-consul in Budapest during the 1940s, who helped save the lives of tens of thousands of Jews from deportation to the extermination camps, as well as other Swiss nationals who had made efforts to save the lives of Jews. And a few years later, in November 2003, when he received the Madara Horseman Order from the government of Bulgaria, he pointed out in his acceptance speech that 'Bulgaria was the only nation at the heart of Europe from which not one of its Jewish citizens was deported to a Nazi death camp. The saving of 50,000 lives is an amazing and heart-warming fact of history of which Bulgaria can be immensely proud.' More recently, he was particularly influential in having a plaque, a bronze relief by the sculptor Philip Jackson, honouring British diplomats who had helped Jews and other victims of Nazi persecution, installed at the Foreign Office in London. The plaque was unveiled by the Foreign Secretary, David Miliband, in November 2008. In a pamphlet issued on the occasion of the unveiling ceremony, Sigi was commended for his initiative in instigating the creation and unveiling of the plaque.

In the list of Templeton Prize laureates, Sigi is styled 'philanthropist'. Indeed, he donated much of the substantial prize money to the Sternberg Centre to further its interfaith work.

Other beneficiaries included the Leo Baeck College, the One World Action organization, the Friars of Atonement and the Assisi earthquake appeal. But these beneficiaries were by no means the only instances of his contributions to charitable causes that year. In April, for example, he had hosted a meeting about the Immigration Advisory Service which was addressed by the Home Secretary, Jack Straw, and had made a large donation to help sponsor their projects. Among the guests at the meeting were two of the Hinduja brothers, who hoped to cooperate with Sigi on the good causes to which both he and they were committed.

Sigi had also hosted a dinner at the Royal Overseas League in July, shortly after returning from New York, to launch the Centre for the Study of Jewish-Christian Relations at Cambridge University. One important guest was the Bishop of London, Richard Chartres, who was particularly impressed with Edward Kessler, the founder-director of the new centre.

Among the many other bids for funding Sigi had received that year was a request from Dr Stefan Reif for a modest donation in support of the Cambridge University Geniza Research Unit and another relatively modest request from the East European Jewish Heritage Project for finance to prepare trips for Jewish and Christian schoolchildren to visit centres of Jewish life in Eastern Europe and actively participate in the process of Jewish cultural renewal and reintegration. A far more substantial donation was requested by the Institute for Jewish Medical Ethics at the Hebrew Academy of San Francisco to help set up the 'Lord Jacobovits Prize for Jewish Medical Ethics'. And, from Israel, the Jerusalem Foundation was looking for donations to renovate the YMCA to provide the venue for an interfaith centre. The World Jewish Congress had shown interest in the project but appeared to be reluctant to make a commitment. Sigi made a donation and indicated that he was willing 'to start the fundraising ball rolling' with his name. In another vein, he had agreed to support the Honours Nomination for Ben Helfgott, a prominent Holocaust survivor and champion weightlifter. Helfgott was later awarded an MBE. And of his own volition, Sigi wrote to the

Apostolic Nuncio, Archbishop Puente, commending the conferment of a Papal Knighthood on Sir John Templeton.

The year ended with plans for Sigi to travel to Rome again with a group of eight leading Reform rabbis to see the Pope. He was also due to attend a meeting of the ICCJ in Heppenheim in January, where he looked forward to meeting the Archbishop of Milan, Cardinal Carlo Maria Martini, whom he hoped would accept the Interfaith Gold Medallion 'Peace through Dialogue' in recognition of his work in the field of Christian/Jewish dialogue. The Cardinal agreed and was presented by Sigi with the award at the Martin Buber House in Heppenheim. Others at the award ceremony included Pastor Friedhelm Pieper, the ICCJ's General Secretary, ICCJ President Rabbi David Rosen, Ignatz Bubis, the leader of Germany's Jewish community and Sheikh Zaki Badawi, one of the founders of the Three Faiths Forum.

'The award is an expression of our grateful recognition of your decades-long efforts to promote understanding between Jews and Christians and understanding for other faith communities', Sigi told the Cardinal. He added that the ICCJ was proud that Cardinal Martini had declared himself ready, several years earlier, to take up the honorary presidency of the ICCJ, together with Cardinal Edward Cassidy, the only other holder of this distinction from Vatican circles. Sigi had 'held important discussions' with Cardinal Cassidy on his recent visit to Rome and had learnt from him of Cardinal Martini's deep feeling for the holy city of Jerusalem. 'With this award', Sigi concluded, 'I would like to stress not only our recognition of your work but especially our friendship and our common struggle for justice and peace. Let us hope that this common struggle will be blessed.'

9 Remembering Raoul Wallenberg

In 1944, armed only with determination and courage, Raoul Wallenberg, the son of a well-known Swedish industrialist family, arrived in Budapest as a member of the neutral Swedish legation and set about rescuing the 230,000 Jews who remained. He commanded the removal of others from trains departing to the gas chambers at Auschwitz. He placed tens of thousands under the protection of the Swedish crown by issuing them with false passports, 'Schutz-passes', sheltering them in safe houses from which he flew the Swedish flag.

Wallenberg's courage and bravery helped save the lives of as many as 100,000 men, women and children destined for the death camps only because they were Jews. When, in January 1945, Budapest fell to the Soviet army, Wallenberg was taken under guard to Moscow where he vanished into the Soviet prison system. The last resting place of this selfless hero is unknown.

The 20th Century spawned two of history's vilest tyrannies. Raoul Wallenberg outwitted the first but was swallowed up by the second. His triumph over Nazi genocide reminds us that the courageous and committed individual can prevail even against the cruellest state machine. The fate of the six million he was unable to rescue reminds us of the evils to which racist ideas can drive whole nations. Finally, his imprisonment reminds us not only of Soviet brutality but also of the ignorance and indifference which led the free world to abandon him. We must never forget these lessons.

These words, inscribed on the memorial to Raoul Wallenberg in London, outside the Western Marble Arch Synagogue in Great Cumberland Place and very near the Swedish Embassy in neighbouring Montagu Place, encapsulate the nobility of this 'unsung hero' of the Second World War, who so greatly impressed Sigi. While there was some dispute over the wording which read 'Budapest fell to the Soviet army' rather than 'Budapest was liberated by the Russian army', there could be no dispute over Wallenberg's courage and commitment.

Wallenberg was barely 32 years old when he arrived in Budapest on 9 July 1944. Since April that year, some 400,000 Jews from the Hungarian provinces had been deported to Auschwitz. About 200,000 Jews still remained in Budapest. The 'Schutz-pass' Wallenberg created, decked out in the Swedish national colours, bearing the coat of arms of the Swedish royal family and signed by the Swedish ambassador, was designed to impress the German occupiers. He was given permission to issue 5,000 but distributed many thousands more. He was tireless in his efforts to hand out the passes, at the railway station or on the roads, in exchange for anything the Germans could not read, be it a driving licence or a library card, to make it look as if this was a formal exchange of identity papers. He snatched people from the cattle trucks destined for Auschwitz and pulled them out of the thousands on forced starvation marches. Sandor Ardai, a driver sent by the Jewish underground to work for him, recalled one specific incident:

> [H]e climbed up on the roof of the train and began handing in protective passes through the doors which were not yet sealed. He ignored orders from the Germans for him to get down, then the Arrow Cross men began shooting and shouting at him to go away. He ignored them and calmly continued handing out passports to the hands that were reaching out for them. I believe the Arrow Cross men deliberately aimed over his head, as not one shot hit him, which would have been impossible otherwise. I think this is what they did

because they were so impressed by his courage. After Wallenberg had handed over the last of the passports, he ordered all those who had one to leave the train and walk to the caravan of cars parked nearby, all marked in Swedish colours. I don't remember exactly how many, but he saved dozens off that train, and the Germans and Arrow Cross were so dumbfounded they let him get away with it.

Per Anger, a Swedish career diplomat serving in Budapest at the time, recalls asking Wallenberg why he took such risks. Wallenberg replied that for him, there was no other choice. 'I could never return to Stockholm without the knowledge that I'd done everything in human power to save as many Jews as possible.'

Towards the end of the war, when the German commanders were about to get rid of those Jews still remaining in Budapest, Wallenberg warned them that the Russian guns were at the gates of the city and that he, personally, would see that they were hanged as war criminals if they proceeded with their murderous task.

The Wallenberg Appeal, to fund a permanent memorial in London, was a project of the International Council of Christians and Jews in conjunction with the Holocaust Education Trust. Sigi was chairman of the committee, which included several distinguished figures, among them Chief Rabbi Jonathan Sacks, Lord Weidenfeld, Geoffrey Paul, a former editor of *The Jewish Chronicle*, David Amess MP, as well as other Members of Parliament and of the House of Lords and prominent members of the Anglo-Jewish community, including Jonathan Djanogly.

Raising the finance for the memorial was, of course, an onerous task which Sigi was obliged to undertake, as soon as he had been approached to head the Appeal committee. Once it was decided that the distinguished sculptor, Philip Jackson, should be commissioned to create the memorial, it was clear that the project would involve considerable expense. The fee paid to Jackson was some £47,000. About a year before the memorial sculpture was unveiled, it became apparent that the fund-raising process was undergoing difficulties. One donor wondered whether there might be a 'fall back plan' in case sufficient funds proved to be unavailable and suggested 'a large, readable bronze plaque' on the Swedish embassy building.

In the event, considerable funds were raised, of which Sigi donated some £20,000, so the commissioned sculpture took shape. While there is likely to have been a shortfall, owing to additional costs which may not have been accounted for, the fact that the memorial exists at all as a testimony to Wallenberg's selfless achievement is due to the hard work and commitment of the Appeal committee.

The unveiling of the memorial by Her Majesty the Queen on 26 February 1997 was, as Sigi put it in a letter to committee members the following year, a 'unique' occasion. That the Queen, with her extremely busy schedule, would agree to lead a ceremony honouring a Swedish diplomat who had saved Hungarian Jews, in which there was no British involvement whatsoever, was virtually unprecedented. The Queen and the Duke of Edinburgh were accompanied by Ezer Weizman, the President of Israel, and his wife and Kofi Annan, Secretary-General of the United Nations, and his wife, herself a relative of Raoul Wallenberg. Also accompanying them were Princess Christina of Sweden, representing the Swedish Royal Family, and a Cabinet Minister representing the President of Hungary. The dignitaries were joined by Holocaust survivors, many diplomats, parliamentarians and local government officials and religious leaders of all faiths, including Chief Rabbi Jonathan Sacks and the Chief Rabbi of Hungary. The unveiling ceremony was followed by a reception hosted by the officers of Western Marble Arch Synagogue and by the President of the United Synagogue.

As Sigi pointed out in his letter to the committee, the event required security and organization 'of the highest order'. The Metropolitan Police and Special Branch were joined by Diplomatic Defence Personnel, Security Officials from the Israeli Embassy and Royal Bodyguards and, on the day, over 400 police officers and helicopters were involved. He praised, too, the 'splendid example of teamwork' by the foundry and the creative work of sculptor Philip Jackson in the complex operation of researching, designing, manufacturing and installing the monument. He paid special tribute to David Amess, 'who strove for over ten years to bring Wallenberg's humanitarian deeds into the public domain in this country', and also expressed his gratitude to his colleagues on the committee, Maurice Djanogly and Lionel Altman, who, he asserted 'have shouldered the major part of our efforts'.

On the day, the gathering was addressed by Kofi Annan, who made a link between Wallenberg's deeds and the work of the United Nations.

> You will understand, I am sure, if I perceive a direct link between the person of Raoul Wallenberg whose noble spirit we have honoured here today, and the United Nations, which I have the privilege of serving as Secretary-General.
>
> It was in the spirit of Raoul Wallenberg's struggle against inhumanity, injustice and barbarism that, immediately upon the conclusion of the Second World War, the leaders of forty-five nations met in San Francisco and, in the Preamble of the Charter of the United Nations, reaffirmed their faith in fundamental human rights, in the dignity and worth of the human person, in the equal rights of men and women and of nations, large and small.

The Secretary-General made it clear that he believed that 'assisting the oppressed remains the primary challenge to the United Nations'. While the UN had no intention of interfering in the internal affairs of all its member states,

> in those situations where ... there are compelling humanitarian reasons or that a leader is unreasonably brutalizing his or her population, the (Security) Council will intervene ... Had this been the sense of the international community in the 1930s, we might not have been gathered here today and Raoul Wallenberg might have been peacefully living out his life as an octogenarian in his home country.

Kofi Annan concluded:

> This has been for me, as I am sure it has been for all of you, a most memorable day. In a world more given to memorializing its generals than its men of peace, we have saluted a noble son of Sweden who, by his selflessness in helping the oppressed, his refusal to turn his back on evil and his determination to uphold justice, lit a bright torch in a dark world, one whose beam still beckons to us.
>
> To you, Sir Sigmund, to the members and supporters of the Wallenberg Appeal Committee and to the International Council of Christians and Jews, I give my grateful thanks for inviting my wife and I to join you on this very special day. It is not one we will ever forget.

Sigi later received, on behalf of the Appeal committee, numerous letters of congratulation, including one from Buckingham Palace and one from Kofi Annan. The late Lord Coggan, the former Archbishop of Canterbury, was also very impressed: 'I was impressed that when he had taken on a cause, nothing would stop him. He pursued the cause and it was his pursuit and driving to a conclusion that made this memorable event possible. And enlisting people of financial means and making the thing go.' A few months later, Sigi unveiled a plaque on the wall of the Bet HaMidrash in Nove Zamky in Slovakia, erected in memory of Wallenberg by the Slovak Council of Christians and Jews.

Not one to remain satisfied after an outstanding achievement, within weeks of the momentous event in London Sigi was trying to urge Christians and Jews in Switzerland to press for a monument to be erected to those Swiss citizens who were involved in rescuing Jews during the Nazi era. In a letter sent through the offices of the ICCJ, he wrote:

> One of the most impressive events in London this spring was the unveiling by Queen Elizabeth, in the presence of President Weizman of Israel and the UN Secretary-General, Kofi Annan, of a statue commemorating Raoul Wallenberg, a hero of the wartime rescue of Jews from the Nazis in Hungary.

I hope that the people of Switzerland will just as enthusiastically embrace a project to erect a monument to those Swiss citizens who were also involved in this rescue operation and whose contribution has been overlooked, people like Consul Lutz, Friedrich Born of the International Committee of the Red Cross and Dr Schirmer, who helped him …

These men were heroes with stories every bit as remarkable as Raoul Wallenberg and equally worthy of commemoration. I hope that at this time of sensitivity in Swiss relations with the Jewish world, Christians and Jews in Switzerland … will take it on themselves to create a lasting monument to their endeavours.

However, whereas Wallenberg has become a national hero in his own country, it would seem that Lutz, Born and Schirmer have not been honoured in the same way. Indeed, King Carl Gustav of Sweden, himself, was another prominent visitor who came to pay tribute to his noble fellow country-man that year. On 13 November 1997, accompanied by the Swedish ambassador, Mats Bergquist, Count Bertil Bernadotte, the son of the assassinated United Nations media-tor and Sigi, he visited the memorial monument in Great Cumberland Place. Maurice Djanogly and Lionel Altman were also present, as were the president and vice-president of the Western Marble Arch Synagogue. The King praised the initiative and work of the Wallenberg Appeal Committee and signed the synagogue's visitors' book.

In the wake of the royal visit, Sigi was informed that he was to be created a Commander of the Royal Swedish Order of the Polar Star, an award that is made very rarely, 'in recog-nition of his personal services to Sweden'.

Sigi's determination to ensure that Wallenberg's memory was preserved and honoured took him to Latin America on two occasions in the following two years. In November 1998, a replica of Philip Jackson's monument in Great Cumberland Place was erected in the Avenue del Liberator in Buenos Aires. The unveiling of the bronze statue took place during a three-day conference organized by a government-sponsored commission created the previous year to monitor Nazi activity, which examined the effect on Argentina of the thousands of Nazis who sought refuge there after the Second World War. Sigi told the conference that nearly 150 Nazi war criminals were still alive in Argentina.

A year later, an intensive three-country trip brought Sigi back to Buenos Aires. But before arriving there to receive the 'Order de Mayo al Merito en el Grado de Gran Oficial' from the Argentine Foreign Minister Guido di Tella and to attend a session of the local CCJ branch on 'Advances and setbacks on prejudice in Argentina', he and Hazel had made a whirlwind visit to Uruguay and Chile, where they took part in ceremonies honouring Wallenberg.

In Montevideo, where Sigi was presented by the mayor with the Freedom of the City, they attended the unveiling of a plaque in Wallenberg's honour. In a speech, Sigi expressed his pleasure at being present at the ceremony and praised Uruguay for its relations with the Jewish people.

> It seems absolutely fitting to me that this country which gave refuge to a large number of Hungarian Jews at the end of the Second World War and which has always been welcoming to newcomers of the Jewish faith should commemorate this hero of our time. Raoul Wallenberg, in his person, symbolized that sense of justice, human dignity and freedom from persecution which characterizes the outlook of Uruguay. They were considerations such as these which prompted Uruguay to be the first country in South America to recognize the State of Israel. And it was here that the first Israeli embassy on the continent was opened exactly fifty-one years ago. These relations have withstood the test of time and Uruguay remains at the top of the list of Israel's best world friends.

Sigi went on to say how much he looked forward to returning to Uruguay in 2001 to attend the first ICCJ conference in Latin America.

From Montevideo Sigi and Hazel went on to Santiago, where their programme was particularly hectic. On 8

November, they took part in a memorial of Kristallnacht at the Hebrew Day School, attended also by the German ambassador and students from the Deutsche School. They lunched with the Papal Nuncio at the home of Rabbi Angel Kreiman, the Chief Rabbi of Chile, and dined at the UK Embassy with the Catholic Archbishop of Santiago and the local Anglican Bishop.

Rabbi Kreiman was President of the Homage to Raoul Wallenberg Co-ordinating Committee in Chile and had expressed his appreciation for the support he had received for furthering the committee's project to honour Wallenberg:

> Dedicating a sculpture to someone who saved thousands of lives is, in itself, an act of justice. Doing it in Chile, to pay homage to a gentile who saved thousands of Jews, is an honour for the Chilean Jewish community. The fact that the organizing committee is integrated by officials from the Chilean Foreign Ministry and the Swedish Embassy shows the universal character of our purpose. To have chosen the 9th of November for placing the monument is one of the best ways of remembering the tragic Crystal Night. The fact that the sculptors involved in the project are renowned artists is significant to this piece of work. The importance of the location of the statue in the area of Vitacura shows how much Chile is involved in educating future generations about the fearlessness and courage of those who do not discriminate against religion and spare no effort to save the life of man created by Divine likeness and resemblance.

For Sigi and Hazel the 9th of November began with an interreligious service at Santiago College, dedicated to the ICCJ, Kristallnacht and Wallenberg. This was followed at midday by the unveiling of the monument dedicated to Wallenberg. The President of Chile, Eduardo Frei, made a moving speech at the unveiling ceremony. He paid tribute to those who had risked their lives to 'save people who bore no connection to them at all' from the devastation of Nazi totalitarianism:

Among the people who exceeded their own interests and fears is Raoul Wallenberg, a Swedish diplomat to whom we testify our gratitude today. His human qualities turned him into an active defender of the peoples subjected and tormented by Nazism, especially the Jewish people. So he rescued thousands of families whose lives were in danger, in Hungary.

Ingeniously and courageously, many times using unconventional but necessary methods, Wallenberg played a key role in helping these people escape the Holocaust. This is why we consider him today as one of those who fearlessly confronted what was one of the most important challenges in the history of humanity.

His strange disappearance has not made us forget his work. On the contrary, it has presented us with his legacy in an even greater luminosity and strength. Wallenberg's example impels us to collect the teachings emerging from the painful facts he had to face.

The main lesson, President Frei explained, had been an awareness of the senselessness of those responsible for the horrendous persecution and devastation, as well as the inspiration the community of nations had derived from an exceptionally traumatic experience which led them to assume that the acceptance of fundamental and unquestionable respect for life and human rights was crucial to the future of humanity.

The people of Chile, especially those who one way or another are connected to the memory of this sombre period, pay a deserved homage to Raoul Wallenberg. His name is not a motionless presence among us. It summons us to pose the ever disturbing biblical question: 'What have we done to our brothers?' and it invites us to become architects of a respectful community which is welcoming to those who are different from us, projecting itself into a future in which everybody has a dignified place from where they are able to continue building their country.

The dedication ceremony was followed by a reception at

the Swedish Embassy and that night Sigi and Hazel attended a dinner hosted by the Chilean Council of Christians and Jews in honour of the guests who had come to Santiago for the Wallenberg memorial. Before leaving for Argentina the following afternoon, Sigi presented President Frei with the Interfaith Gold Medallion, attended a lunch of Rotarians in his honour and then met with the emeritus Chief Rabbi of Sweden, Rabbi Morton Narrowe, Gunnel Borgegaard and members of the English Speaking Community Church.

Sigi and Hazel's final day in Buenos Aires before their departure for London was spent in various activities involving the Argentine Jewish community. They held a lunchtime meeting with executives of DAIA, the umbrella organization of the community, and attended a *Kabbalat Shabbat* at the Bet El synagogue, affiliated to the Masorti movement, before dining with the rabbi, Daniel Goldman. Their ten-day trip to three Latin American countries was yet another triumph for Sigi's global networking skills and achieved his core aim of ensuring that Wallenberg's memory would always be honoured.

The task Sigi and his colleagues on the Wallenberg Appeal Committee had set for themselves was not an easy one and had demanded a considerable amount of time, hard work, financial commitment and patience. Some of their aspirations had failed to materialize, such as, for example, the application made by one of their members, Councillor Cyril Nemeth, for the part of Great Cumberland Place adjacent to the Wallenberg statue to be renamed 'Wallenberg Place'. And, on a deeper level, they lacked, of course, the power to pressurize Western governments into forcing the Russian government to make known the true details of Wallenberg's fate. Nevertheless, a testimony to their success in raising Wallenberg's profile could be seen in a statement sent from 10 Downing Street by Prime Minister Tony Blair in November 1998:

> Raoul Wallenberg is one of my twentieth century heroes. There can be few examples of where one man's personal courage can truly claim to have saved so many innocent

lives. His was a heroism of the highest order at the darkest hour in modern European history.

As we approach the millennium, we must never forget the horrors of the twentieth century. We must continue to commemorate the humanitarian spirit and outstanding bravery of those like Wallenberg who rose to the moment of that appalling episode in Europe's history.

Not content with what he had already achieved in honouring Wallenberg's memory, Sigi was determined to see monuments dedicated to this hero ever further afield. And six years later, in November 2004, a striking memorial was unveiled in the Slovak capital, Bratislava. Sigi, as Patron of the ICCJ, had initiated the project and sent a message saluting the Association of Christians and Jews in Slovakia 'for bringing this project to so fine a conclusion'. And to quote an announcement made on the day of the unveiling ceremony: 'This strikingly imaginative monument will forever serve as an eloquent tribute to remind all those who contemplate it that what Raoul Wallenberg did was to save the conscience of the whole world.'

10 The Three Faiths Forum

For several years Sigi had tried to impress on his colleagues in the Council of Christians and Jews that interfaith dialogue should be extended to include members of the Muslim faith. The responses he received, however, indicated that there was little desire or likelihood of establishing a Council of Christians, Jews and Muslims. The ICCJ did, however, set up an Abrahamic Forum.

One note of caution was sounded by the late Lord Coggan, the former Archbishop of Canterbury. While having no objection to furthering relations with Muslims, Coggan felt there was so much work still to be done in the field of Christian-Jewish relations, that nothing should obstruct that:

> There is always the danger of the upsurge of anti-Semitism, there is an appalling ignorance among our Christians about Judaism – there is an appalling ignorance among Jews about Christianity – many responsible people have never entered a synagogue and many Jews have never entered a church and so the work to be done with the rising generations and the present generation is enormous and I don't want that interest dissipated at all.

Sigi's own perception was shared by a fellow Jewish colleague on the CCJ executive, Sidney Shipton, who was also a prominent Zionist activist. Like Sigi, Shipton had come to recognize that a bilateral approach to interfaith relations was no longer adequate in a Britain approaching the end of the millennium and began advocating 'trialogue'. When, in 1997, Sigi, together with Sheikh Dr Zaki Badawi and the Rev. Dr Marcus Braybrooke, set up the Three Faiths Forum with the aim of 'encouraging friendship, goodwill and understanding amongst people of the three Abrahamic monotheistic faiths in the United Kingdom and elsewhere', Shipton was appointed coordinator and charged with the responsibility of turning the concept into a functioning organization. Years later, in September 2004, at a meeting of the Ealing Council of Christians and Jews, Shipton expressed regret that the CCJ was still unable to form a partnership with the Three Faiths Forum, particularly as both organizations were affiliated to the International Council of Christians and Jews. As the CCJ was beginning to hold dialogue with Muslims in its own capacity, the apparent rivalry between the organizations threatened to make the Forum's interfaith activity less effective. Even so, Shipton pointed out that the Foreign and Commonwealth Office was using the Forum as a role model for visiting delegations.

At its outset, the Three Faiths Forum was established as a charity limited by guarantee and dependent on donations in order to carry out its work. One project donor was the City Bridge Trust, a branch of Bridge House Estates which is in charge of the maintenance of four London bridges – Blackfriars Bridge, Tower Bridge, Southwark Bridge and the Millennium Bridge. Another prominent project donor was the Pears Foundation, a charitable foundation created in 1992 with the prime objectives of supporting young people and communities, the prevention of genocide, international development, philanthropic work and charities in Israel. The Sternberg Foundation, which Sigi set up in 1986 to support inter-religious and inter-communal activities and projects for reconciliation was a third donor. The Forum, based in Star House, which houses the Sternberg Foundation and other organizations with which Sigi is involved, is also supported by funds from central government and from the Ealing Council for its numerous projects, in particular its work in schools.

Shipton also lobbied the government to take note of the forum's concerns and spread its message at conferences around the world. In March 2005 he was the only participant from Britain at a NATO Advanced Research Workshop in Lisbon on 'Security and Migrations in the Mediterranean', held under the auspices of the Portuguese National Institute of Defence.

Shipton made a presentation on the activities of the Three Faiths Forum to a seminar of academics, ambassadors and military officers and also met with leaders of the Christian, Muslim and Jewish communities in Lisbon, who agreed in principle to establish a Three Faiths Forum in Portugal.

Further afield, in Tunisia, an interfaith dialogue group involving the three Abrahamic faiths was becoming a reality following Sigi's second visit to that country in January that year. His visit was the outcome of a conference held under the auspices of the Tunisian President, Zine El Abidine Ben Ali, at the El Manar University, on 'The Abrahamic faiths and a vision of peace and tolerance'. Professor Mohammed Hassine Fantar, holder of the Ben Ali Chair in Interreligious Dialogue, discussed with Sigi the possibility of holding future conferences together with groups in the UK, and Sigi invited the professor to participate in the ICCJ conference to be held in Chicago later in the year. Sigi also met Oussama Romdhani, director-general of the Tunisian External Communications Agency, and invited him to a conference at the British Embassy in Paris the following month on strategies for tackling religious tension in Britain and France.

Already in 2004, the Three Faiths Forum, together with the Muslim Council of Great Britain, had issued a protest at proposals instigated by French President Jacques Chirac to ban French schoolchildren from wearing symbols of their religion – the hijab or headscarf worn by Muslim girls, the kippah or skull cap worn by orthodox Jewish boys and the cross worn by devout Christian girls and boys. 'Such restrictions violate the human rights of children and do a disservice to the French Republic's long-standing belief in equality, liberty and fraternity', the Forum's statement declared. And a month earlier, in December 2003, the advisory board of the Forum had passed a statement expressing sadness and distress

> at the senseless haemorrhage of blood that is taking place in the Holy Land ... Jews, Christians and Muslims regard human life as sacred ... We therefore condemn unreservedly all acts of violence by those who claim to act

in the name of or with the justification of a religious faith against civilians, especially those targeting women and children and the innocent. Neither the suicide bombers nor the raids by tanks and airplanes are going to engender security to Jews or Arabs.

Another country where an interfaith association was likely to be set up was Cameroon, following a meeting that the High Commissioner, Samuel Libock Mbei, held with Sigi and Shipton in April 2005. After hearing about the work of the Three Faiths Forum, the minister said he was sure his government would welcome such an initiative. Indeed, the launch of the Forum's international activities had been announced by Shipton at a meeting in November 2004. 'Following meetings with ambassadors based in London and our relationship with the Foreign and Commonwealth Office, we are now meeting foreign delegations and making presentations to them on our work.'

In October that year, when Sigi and Hazel were in Rome for ceremonies marking the fortieth anniversary of *Nostra Aetate*, Sigi also instigated discussions to explore the possibilities of a partnership between the Three Faiths Forum and the Italian Section of the World Conference of Religions for Peace. Sigi and Hazel were the guests of the British ambassador, Sir Ivor Roberts and his wife. The couple, deeply committed to interfaith dialogue, organized a dinner and several breakfast meetings in the Sternbergs' honour attended by Jewish, Christian and Muslim leaders including the Chief Rabbi of Rome, Dr Riccardo di Segni. During Sigi's visit to Rome, at a meeting with Cardinal Walter Kasper, President of the Pontifical Commission for Relations with the Jews, it was announced that Rabbi David Rosen would be awarded the order of Knighthood of St Gregory.

In the domestic arena, Sidney Shipton was constantly engaged in promoting the Forum's message. In early October 2004, a church in Winchester was the venue for a gathering of some 200 people from as far afield as Portsmouth, Southampton, Bournemouth and Basingstoke who were eager to explore questions of dialogue between the three faiths. Topics raised at the meeting ranged from terrorism to practical ways of developing dialogue. Later that month, Shipton spoke at a church in Mill Hill, following a simple meal of foods symbolic to each of the three faiths – dates eaten at the breaking of the Ramadan Fast, simulated Greek bread representing Lent and Easter and fruit symbolizing the Jewish festival of Succot. Also that month an important meeting of the Forum was held at the East London Mosque. Opening the meeting, Sigi declared that the mosque was a 'prime example' of the Forum's work. The mosque's director, Dr Dilowar Khan, then spoke of the good relations the mosque had always had with the Fieldgate Street Synagogue at the rear of the building, while the synagogue's Vice-President, Mr N. Roos, confirmed how cooperative the mosque had been in suspending building works for the construction of a new centre adjoining the mosque during the whole of the Jewish High Holy Day period.

In November, Shipton attended the Evensong Service at Canterbury Cathedral and later addressed a meeting of CANDIFA, Canterbury and District Interfaith Action, on the subject of whether Muslims, Christians and Jews could speak to each other. He referred to a recent visit of four members of the Iraqi Institute for Peace under the Forum's auspices and to the fact that the Muslim College, the Iraqi ambassador's residence and the West London Synagogue were the three venues for breaking the Ramadan fast, concluding that 'this is a good example of how the Three Faiths Forum operates'. At the end of November 2004, Shipton, together with Marcus Braybrooke and Imam Mohamed Ovaisi, represented the Forum at a seminar held at Chelsea Methodist Church on Concepts of Interfaith, British Citizenship and Religious Discrimination. Shipton pointed out the anomaly in the racial discrimination laws that protected Jews and Sikhs but not Muslims and welcomed the proposed new legislation against religious discrimination. A few months later, he and Sigi met a delegation led by Sheikh Yahaya Amin from the Islamic Foundation for Peace and Development, founded in Ghana in 2003, which was visiting London under the auspices of the Foreign and Commonwealth Office and had expressed the wish to learn something of the Forum's work in promoting dialogue between faiths.

Among the more unusual meetings Shipton organized and chaired was one at the Globe Theatre early in 2005 called 'Islam meets Shakespeare' – not such a strange subject, as he explained good-humouredly in an introductory speech: 'Whilst there was no truth in the suggestion that Sheikh Spear was an Arab, Shakespeare refers to Muslims in four of his plays, namely Othello, who is referred to as the Moor, the Prince of Morocco in The Merchant of Venice, Aaron in Titus Andronicus and possibly Caliban in The Tempest.' Sigi continued the theme. 'It's a curious fact that while Shakespeare built one of his most famous plays round the character of a Jew and has passing mention of Jews in at least another six of his plays, it is quite unlikely he ever met a Jew. On the other hand, Shakespeare probably knew of, even if he was not acquainted with, many of the Muslim faith.' Sigi went on to acknowledge a statement of a leading Muslim who said that Islam had no place for those who taught hatred and destruction. 'Declarations such as this are the pillars on which we seek to build relations within our society and to which Shakespeare's Globe is making so major a contribution in hosting this festival. I have no doubt at all that, were the Bard among us today, he would salute and celebrate this enterprise.'

Another unusual event organized by the Forum was the visit of the Duke of Gloucester, together with several ambassadors and diplomats, to the Holocaust Exhibition at the Imperial War Museum in September that year. Welcoming the Duke, Sigi mentioned that he was following 'in the most distinguished footsteps of the Queen', who had opened the exhibition five years earlier:

> At a time when there are prominent voices rejecting the basic facts of the Holocaust and pressing for the abolition of Holocaust Memorial Day, the Imperial War Museum provides a powerful corrective. The main purpose of the Three Faiths Forum, which I helped to found some nine years ago is to promote better understanding and dialogue among members of the three great Abrahamic traditions … Today we would like you to leave this museum not only better informed about the terrible history of the Nazi Holocaust; we would like you to take with you the lesson

20. Tamirs and Sternbergs: Left to right: Elinor, Hazel, Ruth, Sir Sigmund, Deborah, Noam, Jonathan. Copyright John Rifkin.

21. Sir Sigmund with George Carey, Archbishop of Canterbury. Copyright Susan Greenhill.

22. Sir Sigmund with Prime Minister Tony Blair at the Labour Party Conference. Copyright Gus Campbell.

23. HM the Queen and Sir Sigmund at the unveiling of the Wallenberg Memorial, London, 26 February 1997. Copyright Paul Mellor.

24. Presentation of the Templeton Award to Sir Sigmund at Buckingham Palace by HRH The Duke of Edinburgh, 15 May 1998. Copyright Official Templeton Foundation Photographer.

25. Sir Sigmund with Oscar Scalfaro, President of Italy, January 1999. Copyright Official Quirinale Palace Photographer.

26. Sir Sigmund presenting HRH The Duke of Edinburgh with a photograph of the tree planted at Yad Vashem in honour of his mother, Princess Alice, who was named a Righteous Gentile, Buckingham Palace, October 2002. Copyright John Rifkin.

27. Sir Sigmund presents the Interfaith Medallion to Mary McAleese, President of Ireland, 6 March 2003, Dublin. Copyright Official Photographer of Irish President.

28. The Three Faiths Forum at Mansion House, 16 May 2003. Left to right: Rev Dr Marcus Braybrooke, Sir Sigmund, Alderman Sir Gavyn Arthur, Lord Mayor of London, Sheikh Dr Zaki Badawi, Sidney Shipton. Copyright Lewis Photos Ltd.

29. Visit of HRH Prince Michael of Kent to the Sternberg Centre, 4 May 2004. Copyright John Rifkin.

30. Inauguration of a new Sefer Torah in Israel, 2005, in memory of Henry and Joseph Perlman. Left to right: Robert Perlman, Suzanne Perlman, George Perlman.

31. Visit of the Papal Nuncio HE Archbishop Faustino Sainz Munoz to the Sternberg Centre, 11 October 2005.

32. HRH Prince Charles planting a tree in memory of his grandmother, Elizabeth the Queen Mother, at the Sternberg Centre, 22 June 2006. Copyright John Rifkin.

33. Foreign Secretary David Miliband unveiling of a plaque in honour of British Diplomats who saved lives during the Second World War, Foreign Office, 20 November 2008. Copyright C. Marten.

34. Pim Waldeck, Suzanne Perlman and Sir Sigmund at the Presentation of the Royal Order of Merit to Suzanne Perlman, Embassy of The Netherlands, 29 April 2009. Copyright John Rifkin.

35. Inauguration of the exhibition of the eighteenth-century synagogue Tzedek ve-Shalom from Suriname at the Israel Museum, Jerusalem, May 2010, made possible by Suzanne Perlman in memory of her husband Henry Perlman. Left to right: Robert Perlman, Louis M. Perlman, George Perlman, Suzanne Perlman, James S. Snyder (Director of the museum).

36. A selection of Sir Sigmund's medals: Left to right: Order of St John; Defence Medal; 1977 Silver Jubilee Medal; Légion d'Honneur; unknown; Spanish Order of Merit; Austrian Order of Merit; German Order of Merit; Order of Honour Greece; Hungarian Order of Merit; Morocco Order of Merit. The Star is the Vatican Order of St Gregory.

that the way forward in preventing the recurrence of genocide and hatred is through dialogue and understanding.

The importance of interreligious dialogue in the wake of tragedy was emphasized at a dinner hosted by the Chargé d'Affaires at the United States Embassy in June 2004 for members of the Three Faiths Forum to meet Dr Judea Pearl, father of the murdered *Wall Street Journal* correspondent, Daniel Pearl, and Dr Akber Ahmed, Professor of Islamic Studies at the American University. The two men were in the UK to speak about the Daniel Pearl Muslim-Jewish Dialogue programme, set up in memory of the journalist whose murder in Pakistan in February 2002, while investigating the alleged links between Richard Reid, the 'shoe bomber', and Al-Qaeda, had shocked the world. While various members of a conspiracy had been tried for the murder and one of them sentenced to death in March 2007 at a closed military hearing at Guantanamo Bay, Khalid Sheikh Mohammed said he had personally beheaded Pearl. Welcoming the discussion 'with our honoured guests', Sigi declared that 'dialogue is the only way', while David T. Johnson, the Chargé d'Affaires, expressed the embassy's appreciation of the efforts of the Three Faiths Forum and its admiration for Dr Pearl and Dr Ahmed. Closing the discussion, Sidney Shipton pointed out that ignorance of the other could only be overcome by personal contact at grass-roots level, which was where the Forum operated, and stressed that only by increasing the dialogue between the three Abrahamic faiths could the two guests of honour really be thanked.

Another particularly relevant meeting was held on 7 April 2005 at St Ethelburga's, a Church of England church located at Bishopsgate in London. The church also houses a Centre for Reconciliation and Peace. Arranged by the Wyndham Place Charlemagne Trust, an organization dedicated to bringing together people of different cultural, political and religious backgrounds, the subject of the meeting was 'Anti-Semitism and Islamophobia: two sides of the same coin?' Sigi was due to be the speaker for the Jewish side, with Imam Dr Abduljalil Sajid of the Brighton Islamic Mission speaking for the Muslims. Due to ill health, however, Sigi was unable to be present and Sidney Shipton spoke on his behalf. Dr Sajid had already participated in an interfaith event with Shipton the previous year when he addressed the Leo Baeck B'nai Brith Lodge in London on the work and activities of the Three Faiths Forum, the first meeting of the Lodge to be addressed by a Muslim. The intense interest displayed during the question and answer session following Dr Sajid's address at the Leo Baeck Lodge indicated that a gateway to goodwill and understanding had been opened up.

At St Ethelburga's, Dr Sajid referred to the 'roots of prejudice among Muslims against the Jewish people', pointing out that they were complex and originated from different sources. 'Prejudice can be religious (anti-Judaic), racist (anti-Semitic) and political (anti-Zionist). One prejudice does not automatically assume the other two. There may be those who oppose the political ideas of Zionism but are not either anti-Judaic or anti-Semitic.' He acknowledged that the creation of Israel 'complicates matters for Muslims' and that the distinctions were often blurred. 'Such Muslims make the mistake they accuse others of making about themselves: seeing all Jews as monolithic and threatening.' Dr Sajid also referred to the increase in both anti-Semitism and Islamophobia in the wake of the events of 9/11.

Reading out Sigi's prepared address, Shipton mentioned a number of initiatives taken by international organizations to fight anti-Semitism and drew attention to the fact that for the first time there had been recognition of the link between events in the Middle East and attacks on Jews in European countries. He emphasized that Muslims and Jews acting together could contain the virus of anti-Semitism and pointed to the work of the Three Faiths Forum. While he condemned the poisonous messages disseminated on the Internet, such as those on Holocaust Denial and the *Protocols of the Elders of Zion* posted on the Hamas website, he was encouraged by some initiatives against extremism launched by Muslim scholars around the world.

Exactly three months later the forces of moderation were once again challenged by the horrific events of 7 July 2005.

Speaking in Edgware that evening, Shipton emphasized the importance of cooperation between the faiths.

> On this day when terrorists struck at Central London, it could not be more appropriate for us to discuss if Muslims, Christians and Jews can talk to each other. It is clear that Muslims, Christians and Jews must intensify their efforts to promote good relations, respect and understanding between the three Abrahamic Faiths and unequivocally condemn the indiscriminate killing of innocent men, women and children.

Acknowledging that the war in Iraq could be seen as contributing to the outrages, he referred to the fact that the previous evening he had attended a reception at the Iraqi Embassy to mark the first anniversary of resumption of diplomatic relations with the United Kingdom. 'The terrorists are afraid that the emergence of a new Democratic Republic of Iraq could act as an example to other countries in the Middle East. The moderates of the three Abrahamic Faiths are the majority and must make their voices heard against the extremists and terrorists.' In Barnet the following week, Shipton emphasized that the Three Faiths Forum was doubling its efforts to bring the silent majority within the Muslim, Christian and Jewish communities to work together against the forces of evil. 'The reaction of the world to last week's bombs and indiscriminate murder help us to fully understand what it is like in the Middle East. No longer can apologists say that while they condemn terrorist attacks they understand the reasons for them.' A few weeks later, in early August, a Multi-Faith Service of Remembrance and Hope was held at the Al-Khoei Islamic Centre in West Hampstead.

In response to the July 7 outrage, the government put forward proposals for legislation to deal with terrorist suspects, including the possibility of detaining suspects for up to three months for questioning. Sigi, together with Marcus Braybrooke, Zaki Badawi and Sidney Shipton, issued a media release intimating that holding suspects without charge for three months would be breaching the Human Rights Convention. 'The Three Faiths Forum considers it is imperative that all communities and their respective leaderships must cooperate and work closely together to ensure the effectiveness of all proposed and existing anti-terrorism legislation', they declared in the media release, concluding that 'terrorism in all its aspects must be fought vigorously, but not at the expense of a weakening of democracy and human rights'.

Speaking at a meeting organized by Open Democracy the following year – 'The London bombs, one year on' – Shipton stated that

> suicide bombers suggesting they are acting in the name of the holy Qu'ran have opened up a new dimension in terrorism against civilians. However, such terrorist attacks purporting to be in the name of Islam are perverting a great religion. My mentor, the late Sheikh Zaki Badawi, told me quite categorically that Islam could never sanction suicide-bombing, and that, indeed, suicide is a mortal sin. I believe, too, that the vast majority of Muslims do not accept that suicide-bombers act in their name, whatever a tiny minority of misguided individuals and self-styled religious leaders might say. The Three Faiths Forum – a Muslim-Christian-Jewish trialogue – has found that the atmosphere is changing – and for the better. Most Muslims, Christians and Jews, at all levels of civil society, want to come together in a spirit of mutual respect and understanding.

Shipton went on to point out how much demand there was for the work of the Three Faiths Forum. 'We are inundated with requests for speakers and to make presentations. Our initiatives in the fields of law and education are flourishing.'

Of the numerous endeavours undertaken by the Three Faiths Forum, education is one of the most significant. Shipton's successor as director, Stephen Shashoua, underlines the importance of combating ignorance. 'Our communities are making even bigger walls and young people are, basically, the victims when communities don't get along well and don't mix because they're told something by their teachers or by their parents and they live in ignorance. Our hope is to redress that balance so that an understanding of the other side can make them fuller people.' Shashoua does not pretend that this can eradicate extremism. 'We're going to inform and address ignorance out there, rather than target extremists. It's not really helpful to offer interfaith as a solution to extremism because that's not our primary focus. It's eradicating ignorance. If addressing ignorance leads to someone not doing something bad, then great.'

Sana Saleem, who has worked since 2007 as the Forum's Muslim Education Officer, is often asked about terrorism in her work. Non-Muslim students sometimes ask her how she feels about the negative portrayal of Islam in the media. 'What I love is being able to tell them that it is not Islam which promotes violence or terrorism but it's just individuals who are misinterpreting Islam', she explains. 'It's important for them to realize this as it breaks down this stereotype created in the media.'

Sigi has long held that education, whether for children or adults, is the key to bringing down barriers. And his determination to share his conviction about the crucial importance of interfaith relations has not been restricted to gatherings and conferences exclusively involving religious leaders. He has introduced discussions of interfaith issues into sessions of the World Economic Forum in Davos, in the belief that key world problems cannot be addressed without putting religion 'in the debating mix'. His contribution to the World Economic Forum (WEF) was warmly acknowledged in a letter from the Executive Chairman, Klaus Schwab, in December 2009. 'Sir Sigi Sternberg has been so instrumental for the development of the World Economic Forum and its religious and spiritual consciousness. Thank you, Sigi, for this partnership over the last 10 years!'

In January 2005, Sigi addressed a meeting of religious leaders at the Forum on the persistence of anti-Semitism. 'It is an ever-mutating virus that can best be contained when there can be open, honest and trusting dialogue within a society.' And while he did not claim that criticism of policy of the Government of Israel was necessarily anti-Semitic, he pointed out that 'much of today's anti-Semitism is cloaked in hostility to the State of Israel – the only Jewish state in the world. No one says that the fifty

Muslim states in the world have no right to exist or that those states whose official religion is Christianity have no right to exist. It is only the State of Israel whose right to exist is challenged.' He went on to conclude that 'incitement to hatred must stop ... whether their source is some Right-wing semi-fascist party or extremist religious groups and the Left must end its dangerous flirtation with Islamic extremism'.

It was in 2001 that the WEF first invited religious leaders to share in deliberations about globalization, recognizing that 'religious traditions have a unique contribution to offer ... particularly in emphasizing human values and the spiritual and moral dimension of economic and political life'. A precedent that may have inspired this initiative was the Millennium World Peace Summit of Religious and Spiritual leaders which met in the General Assembly Hall of the United Nations in August the previous year and issued a 'Commitment to Global Peace'.

Sigi's own involvement with the WEF dates from the year 2000 when he was invited to participate in the Forum by Klaus Schwab. It was he who introduced Schwab to the Archbishop of Canterbury, George Carey. Lord Carey became the Co-Chair of the executive committee of the West-Islamic World Dialogue. At that time, the WEF had resources in a number of spheres that were not primarily business-focused; for example, cultural, academic, intellectual, literary and spiritual and the sphere of civil society. Rabbi David Rosen, who was invited to the WEF in 1997 for a session with special focus on the Balkans, recalls that he participated in the meetings together with Cardinal Roger Etchegaray, representing the Pope, Metropolitan Kyril, representing the Eastern Orthodox Patriarch and Professor Ahmed Kamal Aboulmagd from Egypt. Rosen was then invited back as a member of the faculty. At that time, the Jewish participants at the WEF got together for informal Friday night dinners, a custom set up originally by Jews from Israel and other countries in the early 1990s. Later, these dinners became more institutionalized and ritualized, with, for example, a *Dvar Torah,* a brief commentary on Jewish law and tradition, and then with obligatory speeches from celebrity guests which included Eli Wiesel and Shimon Peres. At this point, these dinners required funding and Sigi, according to Rosen, was one of the first of the principal donors. Sigi then started inviting non-Jewish leaders to the dinners, including Lord Carey and prominent Muslims, and utilized the Sabbath dinners as interfaith events, a new trend which, Rosen noted, was resented by several Israelis. Not surprisingly, Sigi's membership of the executive committee of the West-Islamic World Dialogue at the WEF is in his capacity as co-founder of the Three Faiths Forum.

While the Three Faiths Forum, which also has an associate in Israel, aims to sustain dialogue between peoples of differing beliefs and with atheists, and to improve understanding and knowledge of different cultures and religions, it also facilitates action taken together to ameliorate communities and society as a whole. In particular, its work focuses on building harmonious and durable relationships between individuals from different religious backgrounds and non-believers, so that a society can be created in which religious and cultural differences can be seen as an enhancement, rather than a problem.

As Sidney Shipton pointed out in his speech at the Open Democracy meeting in July 2006, the Forum's work continues to be in great demand. It provides advice and support to professionals, organizations, and institutions concerned with inter-communal and inter-religious questions. Its counsel has been sought by the government and the Foreign Office and, with the help of the Marshal of the diplomatic corps, the Forum organizes seminars for ambassadors. As Sir Ivor Roberts, the ambassador to Italy, pointed out in a speech in Rome on a day of interfaith dialogue in November 2005, the UK government has maintained a close relationship with the Three Faiths Forum in its endeavours to ensure good relations between the faith communities in Britain. The Forum has also been consulted by a number of public bodies, including the Institute of Education, on matters regarding faith schools and social cohesion, and the Mayor of London's office in relation to the objectives of the forthcoming Olympic Games, and it contributed to a parliamentary consultation on subjects including freedom of belief, conversion and international human rights.

The Forum is constantly expanding its programmes. It has brought together groups of professionals, in particular doctors and lawyers, from the three faith communities, who meet to reflect and exchange views on matters of topical concern, for example Sharia law or the ethics of organ transplants. This latter concern was the subject of a presentation by Zaki Badawi to the Royal Society of Medicine in November 2004 at a meeting chaired by Sigi, who declared that while he was not a doctor, he was, nonetheless, a life member of the Royal Society of Medicine. Earlier that year, in April 2004, the Forum's Medical Group was addressed by a nurse who worked for Médecins Sans Frontières and learned of the work done by MSF in eighty countries. In September that year, the group discussed the problem of mental disabilities across Central and Eastern Europe, following a speech by Oliver Lewis, Legal Director of the Medical Disability Advocacy Centre, an international organization based in Budapest, while in March the following year, Martin Aaron, President of the Jewish Association for the Mentally Ill, gave a presentation to the Forum's Medical Group on proposed new mental health legislation.

In recent years Sigi has been happy to take a backseat in relation to the Forum's activities. As he says, 'I am past retiring age'. He is proud to have founded the Forum and is always eager to hear about all its undertakings and accomplishments. He has always emphasized that he sees education as a key priority.

Local groups from the three faith communities have also been formed in various parts of the country. In October 2004, a group was inaugurated in Cardiff in the presence of the Reverend Marcus Braybrooke, Imam Mohamed Ovaisi, Imam at Heathrow Airport, and Sidney Shipton, who spoke of the need to encourage friendship and goodwill between peoples of the Muslim, Christian and Jewish faiths. In March 2005, the Surrey Branch of the Forum was launched at Guildford Cathedral with a talk by Zaki Badawi on the Trialogue between the Three Abrahamic Faiths. A special event had taken place in late October 2004 when the Eton College Three Faiths Forum was established. Speaking at a meeting with the Head of

Divinity and the Jewish and Muslim tutors, Sidney Shipton said he hoped that this would be the beginning of the setting-up of similar college forums. 'It is essential', he said, 'that Muslims, Christians and Jews, particularly from well-established educational institutions, should learn to understand and respect each other since many will find themselves in leadership positions when they reach the outside world.'

Education has certainly been a prime focus of the Forum. It has adopted the practice known as 'Scriptural Reasoning', originally established more than fifteen years ago at the University of Virginia in the USA by Jewish scholars and philosophers, who were later joined by Christians and Muslims. The groups get together to read and study texts sacred to the three Abrahamic religions and use these texts to discuss and analyse current issues. The Three Faiths Forum has set up a Scriptural Reasoning website with Cambridge Interfaith Programme and St Ethelburga's, and, through their 'Tools 4 Trialogue' programme, apply the techniques to enable young people to explore the sacred texts.

To further the aim of establishing 'trialogue' between Muslims, Christians and Jews or people with similar beliefs, the Forum has put forward a programme tailored individually to different educational establishments – high schools, colleges, universities or more informal groups of young people – together with the tools needed to enable the programme to function. The aims of the programme are to allow young people to affirm their knowledge of their own religion and traditions so that they may feel more confident about asking questions and also learn how others understand and live their faiths. Using religious texts as the basis for discussion, as in 'Scriptural Reasoning', the Tools 4 Trialogue is an interactive encounter with the scriptures, using extracts from the *Tanach*, the New Testament and the Koran on a particular theme to stimulate discussion in which participants from each faith are encouraged by facilitators to express and share their points of view. This programme has been developed with the advice and support of scholars and leaders of the three faiths.

Within the framework of Tools 4 Trialogue, various themes

have been raised, for example the Family, Relationships between Men and Women, Sickness and Health, Forgive and Forget, Poverty and Charity. Using the different religious texts, the facilitator stimulates the discussion within the group with which he or she is working, so that the pupils from the three Abrahamic faiths can be shown the common ground which exists between their different beliefs and come to understand and respect their particular characteristics and their differences. This tool can also be seen as a pretext enabling a conversation or 'trialogue' between pupils of different faiths to take place. At times, this technique has met with resistance when certain pupils refuse to read sacred texts from other religions. To confront this problem, the Three Faiths Forum's education officers have created 'Skills for Dialogue', a tool to help facilitators.

In December 2009, the Forum's educational work and the Tools 4 Trialogue in particular, received an official commendation at the Awards for Bridging Cultures, an initiative of the Institute for Community Cohesion. A statement from the ABC said that the judges, 'felt that this project successfully addressed the interlocking issues of interfaith and intercultural conflict. They were impressed with the project's reach to 5,000 people and welcomed the methodology that gives young people the tools to ask difficult and sensitive questions in a way that supports tolerance and respect.'

Mentoring is another important feature in the Forum's educational work. The mentoring programme aims to create partnerships between adults in the professions and young people, all from different cultural and religious backgrounds. Trios of students, a Christian, a Muslim and a Jew in each group, collaborate with a professional sponsor on a particular team project for several months. The projects should have a positive social impact. The 'ParliaMentors' project puts Political Science students in contact with Members of Parliament, working on a social action project together, while 'DocuMentors' involves students interested in film, making documentaries together. In one DocuMentors programme, a trio of Muslim, Christian and Jewish students with a keen interest in film were mentored by a film-maker. At the end of the year, they put together two short films with the help of another mentor. Future projects include 'Business ManageMentors', aiming to put students of Business Administration in contact with top business managers, and similar programmes are to be developed involving students in the field of international development.

The Undergraduate ParliaMentors programme was launched in 2007. Since then about 100 students from the three Abrahamic faiths and from a variety of backgrounds have developed their leadership skills and been challenged to think and act in new ways. They have been 'mentored' by over thirty parliamentarians from the three major political parties. The students have also run empowerment projects with young people and minority groups and are learning how to work together to effect change.

The Undergraduate ParliaMentors programme, which won an award for cultural innovation from the UN's Alliance of Civilisations, has been mentioned in parliamentary debates, on television and in the press. Heads of politics departments at universities have also expressed appreciation of the programme, viewing it as the only means for their students to gain access to Parliament and noting the contribution it makes to often tense relations between faith societies on campus. As one student saw it: 'Undergraduate ParliaMentors is an important programme especially now that racism and all sorts of fears against other faith groups is so widespread.' And another confessed: 'Despite starting this project as a sceptic, I found that with the support of the Three Faiths Forum we could achieve anything we set our minds to. I learned that with determination we could make a real difference in the community.'

Mentors have included former Transport Minister Sadiq Khan, former Shadow Justice Secretary Dominic Grieve, now Attorney General, and Liberal MP Lynne Featherstone, all of whom have praised the programme. Khan mentored three students who created a project teaching twenty disadvantaged Year 10 students how to effect change in Tooting, south London, where they live and which is Khan's constituency. As he puts it: 'Undergraduate ParliaMentors is a fantastic initiative. Young adults of faith are having their views heard at the very heart of government.' Grieve's mentees worked with faith schools to understand young people's attitudes to other communities and develop strategies to address conflict in the classroom. 'I have no doubt that this year's class will go on to play important roles in the future – both in their local communities and maybe even on the national or international stage', he declared. The three students mentored by Lynne Featherstone spent their year identifying the impact of policy on refugees and asylum seekers. With her support, they were able to overcome serious tensions and conflict within the group. As she explained: 'My trio had started barely being able to talk to each other – and now they are inseparable friends. **The understanding that we all, as humans, have far more in common than we have in differences will stay with them all their lives.'**

A special end of year graduation ceremony for students on the DocuMentors and Undergraduate ParliaMentors programmes was held at the House of Lords in 2009. Baroness Hayman, the Lord Speaker of the Upper House and a benefactor of the Three Faiths Forum, presided at the reception. Twenty-seven students from the three Abrahamic faiths who had worked together within nine different teams, presented their project to their Lordships. In the course of the year, the teams had been helped by Members of Parliament who were present at the event. The teams had also worked with some Non-Governmental Organizations (NGOs) with the aim of creating projects for social action.

The goals of the project were to support students from the three faiths preparing for a political career by enabling these future leaders to understand their role at the heart of a professional political environment. The project also focused on suppressing religious barriers, thereby facilitating cooperation between young adults belonging to the three faiths, with the aim of forming a network of students from the three faiths working in the political sphere.

Another event late in 2009 saw Undergraduate Parlia-Mentors and alumni of the programme addressed by John Denham, the Secretary of State for Communities and John Bercow, the Speaker of the House of Commons, whom Sigi had met while both he and Bercow were assisting the Royal College of Speech Therapists. As Stephen Shashoua, the Forum's Director, explains: 'How did we get John Bercow there? Sir Sigmund had asked him to be a patron of the Forum. We couldn't have done this four years ago. We were able to do it because we're the Three Faiths Forum who have been around for twelve years that Sidney worked on and Zaki worked on and Marcus. We are a grass roots organization and we can link directly to the policy makers and decision makers.'

An unusual event, organized as a response to the economic crisis and the global collapse of the markets, was a conference held at the London Central Mosque in June 2009. Entitled 'Faith in Capitalism', a hundred or so professionals working in the financial milieu were brought together to reflect on how to engage in a worthwhile task while earning money at the same time and to view financial investment from the perspective of faith.

Another new project is 'Faith and Fashion', which works with five traditional Muslim schools in London and Birmingham to explore questions of identity and faith within a scriptural-based framework.

The Three Faiths Forum worked with children in five schools in Ealing in the course of the academic year 2008/09, with the aim of exploring questions of belief and identity in the different faith communities. Ealing Council and the council's Community Safety team supported the project, which focused on dissipating the myths and fixed ideas commonly held in regard to religious belief, particularly but not exclusively the Muslim faith. For this to work, it was necessary to create an environment conducive to approaching different beliefs in a way that helped young people gain a better understanding of the subject, a safe space in which it was possible to discuss questions of religious tolerance and intolerance, hate crimes and the limits of what was acceptable in terms of beliefs and behaviour within British society. At an 'Ealing Celebration Day' held at the end of the year to celebrate the work, pupils from the five schools met in a hall rented by Ealing Council to take part in different workshops focusing on the theme of identity and three principal questions: Who am I? Who are you? How can we work together?

As Debbie Danon, one of the Forum's education officers puts it:

> All young people have a lot of questions about people who are different from them that aren't being answered – not through RE, History or the media, for example. The danger is that we see adults around us who are very afraid because they have not had answers to their questions or a safe space in which to discuss matters where they feel they are not being judged or made to feel ignorant. The aim is to get to young people before they become frightened adults. That is the bottom line of our work.

When Debbie joined the Three Faiths Forum in 2007, the Forum's staff had to 'cold-call' faith schools, offering to work with them. By 2009, there was no more need for 'cold-calling'. Many schools got in touch. Indeed, not only faith schools but mainstream schools, too, want the Forum to work with them.

Debbie and her colleagues create and run workshops in the schools. First they introduce the concept of interfaith – how we should all understand and respect each other's religion and what is different. Ground rules then need to be set but it is the students who set them and agree to abide by them. After that the workshop can begin.

Debbie is well aware that, for the education officers and presenters, it is necessary to devise a particular line to follow in the event that controversial issues should arise. Some may choose to ignore them but Debbie prefers to deal with them. A not infrequent topic of controversy is the situation in the Middle East, which is particularly important for Jewish and Muslim students. Debbie believes it is necessary to validate the motivation young people have for asking questions and then try to answer them without going into politics. She recalls a young Muslim student asking her, very respectfully, 'How do you think the conflict can be resolved?' Well aware that politics often uses religion to further its ends, she answered unequivocally that there was nothing in the religions which stated that the conflict could not be resolved, whereupon the young man thanked her, saying, 'You've solved a lot of my misconceptions about Judaism.'

Rachel Heilbron, the Forum's Deputy Director and Programme Director since mid 2008, has had similar experiences. An example of the Shared Futures programme, funded by the Pears Foundation, was the first linking of a Muslim primary school and a Jewish primary school. When the children were asked: 'What have you learned that's new?', one child replied: 'That we can be friends, even if we have different religious beliefs'; another said: 'If someone has a different religion, you can still be friends with them and work with them'; while a third gave this answer: 'Meeting the children from the other school made me think that it does not matter what religion you are. You're still similar in lots of ways.'

Sana, the Muslim Education Officer, has been gratified to observe the reaction of the students to the guest speakers the Forum's education officers bring in to the schools. 'It's really refreshing when young people are surprised by our guest speakers. Young people come with a lot of stereotypes and assumptions. You can see the surprise on their faces when these assumptions are challenged.'

Debbie points out that Sigi still likes to be updated about their work. 'He's very proud of what we are doing – engaging young people on a daily basis, unlike most interfaith organizations', she explains. Rachel is also appreciative of Sigi's support.

> None of this would be possible without his involvement. We've inherited an organization which already had a strong name. Sir Sigmund has let us take the organization in the direction we believe it should and given us a lot of freedom and stability in terms of the support of the Sternberg Foundation, which has supported the core Three Faiths Forum organization, giving them office space, for example.

Stephen Shashoua is also eager to acknowledge Sigi's contribution: 'He's given us pretty much *carte blanche* to do what we think is right. He's put a lot of trust, a lot of faith in us. He likes what he sees and encourages it.'

Rachel also emphasizes that the organization embraces different faiths and beliefs beyond those of the three Abrahamic religions. There have been Buddhists working in the Forum, as well as Hindus and Sikhs, and also people who were non-religious. 'We see the office as a faith project and the atmosphere is very important,' she says, adding that the work needs to reflect people of different faiths and beliefs in society. She is quite aware, too, that fear of an agenda regarding interfaith is common to all communities. Nevertheless, the growth of the organization and the expansion of its work is something she can point to as a tangible achievement. The Forum has gone from a programme that worked with a few hundred people four years ago to one working with approximately 8,000. 'When people talk about when progress in the interfaith world really started they invariably say after 9/11 or after the disturbances in the Northern towns or after 7/7. These incidents', she acknowledges, 'have served as triggers'. And, as Sana adds: 'it is always great for young people to see a Muslim, a Christian and a Jew standing together. It's a symbolic message that faiths can work together whereas young people so often believe that faith always creates conflicts.' Debbie looks at the work from the angle of the individual: 'What it's really about is human interaction, emotions, and helping people feel validated,' she explains.

Validating others as opposed to dictating to them is a key element in the work of the facilitators of the Three Faiths Forum. Eric Muther, a French graduate student who spent some months in 2009 working as a volunteer and an intern at the Forum, compares the empathic approach used by the Forum's facilitators to the methods advocated by Carl Rogers, one of the founders of the humanistic approach to psychology. Rather than being seen as the person who has all the knowledge, the facilitator follows the personality of each person he or she is working with and adapts their contribution to what each individual needs, as if they were 'walking side by side'. Through their workshops at schools, they try to develop the tolerance and understanding of each pupil and encourage the pupils to be aware of their multiple identities and the connections this can open up with people they initially viewed as different from themselves.

Stephen Shashoua is keen to point out the importance of human interaction as an essential element of the Forum's programmes. 'Once you humanize, then you have to start building something.' He pays tribute to Sigi, Sidney Shipton, Zaki Badawi and Marcus Braybrooke for bringing interfaith into the mainstream. Where there used to be a handful of interfaith groups, by 2009 there were over 200. This is the background against which the Forum is able to develop its programmes. In one instance, the Forum's leaders brought together three single faith organizations which work with young professionals, Art and Christianity Enquiry, the Jewish Community Centre for London (JCC) and the Radical Middle Way, a Muslim group. One project was for Muslim, Christian and Jewish artists to look at the artist as social change maker and what can be done to break down barriers between communities. The artists decided they would like to take over a space together to do a showcase of their work both for themselves and for the general public. Stephen Shashoua recalls:

> We couldn't find a residential space but we found basement space, a warehouse in Shoreditch. We decked it out, made it really funky, cool, made it look like a lounge and we put the artists' work on the walls. One corner was given to architects from the three faiths, who put together a video on their plans for London as a multi-faith city. They were actually drawing a link between Bevis Marks Synagogue, the London Central Mosque and St Paul's Cathedral. It was a wonderful presentation.

Another series of events brought together musicians from the faiths – more Muslim and Jewish than Christian. There was a Klezmer group and a Muslim Hip Hop group. Both groups wanted to collaborate with someone so Stephen Shashoua suggested they collaborate together and now they are a band called 'Yalla' and have played to large audiences. As he puts it: 'At the end we had all these different people coming together, celebrating together, talking together, discussing relevant issues and, in a sense it normalized interfaith.'

Welcoming the new decade, Shashoua's New Year message for 2010 referred to the seismic events of 9/11 and 7/7 and 'other harsh challenges to our search for an open, tolerant and peaceful society', as well as the prevalence of Islamophobia and anti-Semitism. 'We must urgently move from a decade that was focused on "us and them" and embrace the "we"', he continued. 'We can only root out extremism, fear and ignorance if we act together. Talking together is a vital part of the healing process but talk alone without commitment, without action, is ineffective.'

Shashoua urges people not yet involved in interfaith activity to join in: 'We need your energy, your concern, your urge for justice to help us make positive change. Alone, we will be overwhelmed. Together we can do it.' He pays special tribute to Zaki Badawi who had said, 'We do not want interfaith as an "add on". We want it to be part and parcel of society.'

That the Three Faiths Forum has played such an important role in fulfilling this aspiration of the late Dr Badawi, is a source of considerable gratification to his co-founder, Sigi. And his own, unique contribution is clearly recognized. Stephen Shashoua puts it aptly: 'We're here because of Sir Sigmund.'

11 The Sternberg Centre

Finchley's original manor house, known as Bibbesworth, was built in the mid-thirteenth century but destroyed by fires in the fifteenth and sixteenth century. The house known today as the Sternberg Centre was built in 1723, with only a ditch or moat remaining from the earlier building. From the mid-fourteenth century until the tenure of the last Lord of the Manor in 1936, Courts Leet and Baron were held there, and for some forty years during the nineteenth century the house was used as a boys' school. The legal connection was expanded during the latter years of the nineteenth century when the house was the residence of a magistrate, who used the main hall to hear cases.

Until the beginning of the twentieth century an oblong pond with a central island existed opposite the manor and was known as the 'moat'. It is likely, however, that these were fish ponds or openings created by the extraction of clay for making bricks.

The principal lord of note was William, Lord Hastings, a prominent Yorkist nobleman during the War of the Roses whose family held the manor until 1527. Another lord, possibly the successor to the Hastings family, was executed in the Tower for an alleged affair with Anne Boleyn. From 1622 until 1830, the manor was controlled by the descendants of Edward Allen, a London merchant, and it was the Allen family who built the house that stands today. East of the manor house was Manor Farm where Dante Gabriel Rosetti painted some details of his work known as *Found*.

Between 1921 and 1981 the Manor House was used as a girls' school by the order of St Marie Auxiliatrice. And it was from this order that the site was purchased in 1980/81 for the sum of £850,000 by a consortium of organizations including the Reform Movement, Leo Baeck College, a new progressive Jewish day school called the Akiva School, and a Masorti Congregation known as the New North London Synagogue. The Westlon Housing Association was also part of the consortium and all the concerns put up funds. The Reform Movement was, at the time, undertaking a major fundraising appeal and used the funds it had acquired for the purchase.

Peter Levy, a former chairman of the Institute of Jewish Policy Research and also of *The Jewish Chronicle*, negotiated the purchase on behalf of the consortium. Mr Levy, who has had a long career of involvement in the Anglo-Jewish community and who has been praised for his 'ethical commitment to public service' was awarded the OBE in 1991 for his work with the Cystic Fibrosis Trust. During the process leading to the successful purchase, the consortium was competing against a consortium headed by the orthodox United Synagogue, which wanted to use the site for Jews' College and a primary school.

It was shortly after this that Sigi became involved. He had joined the Reform Synagogues of Great Britain, as the Reform movement was known then, shortly after his marriage to Ruth was dissolved. For a long time he had felt uncomfortable being obliged to keep up the pretence of orthodoxy, when orthodox observance was not something he could subscribe to in his heart. In deciding to move away from orthodoxy, he may have been unconsciously influenced by the precepts of his father. While Abraham Sternberg had been scrupulously orthodox in his own observance, he had been essentially liberal in his principles. He had wanted his children to be knowledgeable in matters regarding Judaism and Jewish culture but always let it be known that they should then make up their own minds as to the direction they wished to take. Sigi later became the President of the Movement for Reform Judaism. Interestingly, however, Rev. Simon Hass, the former cantor at the Central Synagogue and the father-in-law of Sigi's nephew, George, has often told Sigi: 'You may belong to the Reform but your heart is orthodox.'

By chance, or perhaps providentially, Sigi happened to be sharing the cloakroom at the North Western Reform Synagogue in Alyth Gardens on the Day of Atonement with Neil Benson, a Vice-President of the Movement for Reform Judaism. Mr Benson has also been awarded an OBE for his services to charity. Like Peter Levy, he has worked with the Cystic Fibrosis Trust and his other involvements have included the Foundation for Liver Research and the Royal Shakespeare Company. Sigi was aware that Benson was active in fundraising for the Manor House project and asked him how he was getting on. Benson told him they needed a main sponsor to whom they would be prepared to give the name of the centre. Sigi and Benson decided that they would talk about this at some point in the future and they eventually did.

At the outset of their agreement, Sigi contributed £300,000 and the Sternberg Centre for Judaism came into being. So attached is Sigi to the site that he has acquired a burial plot there for Hazel and himself.

Peter Levy remained chairman of the Manor House Trust until Sigi took over some twenty years later. The Trust bought the freehold to the property and the trustees were representatives of the various organizations that participated in the purchase. The Trust owns the freehold and each organization has a long leasehold.

The new centre was opened by Prime Minister Margaret Thatcher in 1984 and has hosted a large number of distinguished visitors over the years. It is the largest Jewish cultural centre in Europe. As well as organizations involved in the consortium, which share the site, there are numerous organizations and programmes emanating from the centre. Rabbi Dr Tony Bayfield, the centre's director, was awarded a Lambeth degree by the Archbishop of Canterbury. He is proud that the centre contains a cultural society which mounts art exhibitions and holds musical recitals, a bookshop, a library and a cafeteria used by an educational programme for young people with learning difficulties. The centre also houses an educational agency, an outreach organization for students at university, and a programme of training for volunteer carers who visit the sick, comfort the bereaved and help the elderly in Jewish communities throughout England. There are a number of social clubs based at the centre and also initiatives in the fields of medical ethics and business ethics. The centre boasts a biblical garden and until 2007, was the site of the London Museum of Jewish Life, originally known as the Museum of the Jewish East End.

Interfaith activity has been a principal focus of the centre, and Sigi, who has made regular contributions to the centre since his initial involvement, donated the major part of his Templeton Prize award towards the furtherance of the centre's interfaith work.

Indeed, from the centre's first days until the early 1990s, a group of Jews and Christians known as the Manor House Group would meet regularly at the centre. Members included orthodox rabbis Norman Solomon and Jeremy Rosen and several progressive rabbis – Tony Bayfield, Albert Friedlander, Jonathan Magonet, Colin Eimer, Julia Neuberger and Alexandra Wright. Hyam Maccoby, the distinguished author and lecturer and librarian of the Leo Baeck College, was also a member. Prominent Christians included Marcus Braybrooke and Alan Race, both Anglican clergymen, Richard Harries, then the Bishop of Oxford, another Anglican bishop, Kenneth Cragg and Sister Margaret Shepherd, then education officer of the Council of Christians and Jews, as well as John Bowden, the Managing Director of the SCM Press and himself an Anglican clergyman. And in 2000, a three day conference attended by forty-four Catholic and Jewish scholars was held at the centre.

The Leo Baeck College, too, holds annual interfaith seminars for Christian, Jewish and Muslim students and an annual Christian-Jewish bible week, as well as a wide-ranging programme of Jewish studies, including rabbinical training. Student rabbis are made aware of the importance of interfaith relations and are taught by Christians and Muslims, as well as Jews.

The centre has hosted many distinguished visitors including members of the Royal family. Prince Philip visited the centre in 1996 and Prince Charles planted a tree there in memory of his grandmother, Queen Elizabeth the Queen Mother, in June 2006. Prior to the tree planting ceremony, the Prince of Wales attended a rabbinic class at the Leo Baeck College. Welcoming Prince Charles, Sigi spoke of his grandmother's interest in the Royal College of Speech and Language Therapists of which she was a patron. Two years earlier, in May 2004, the Queen's cousin, Prince Michael of Kent, had visited the centre and another distinguished visitor at the end of that year was the President of Latvia.

Many important church leaders, including Lord Carey, the former Archbishop of Canterbury, have also visited the centre. In 2005, to mark the fortieth anniversary of the Vatican document *Nostra Aetate*, two events were held at the Sternberg Centre. On 30 September, Sigi hosted a lunch for Father Norbert Hofmann, Secretary of the Pontifical Commission for Relations with the Jews, and Oded Ben Hur, Israel's ambassador to the Vatican. Also present was local MP Rudi Vis and representatives of the local Muslim and Christian communities as well as a number of Reform rabbis. They continued discussions on 'Nostra Aetate: Building on a Sound Foundation', the theme of a seminar held the previous day; 'a remarkable occasion', as Sigi saw it. '*Nostra Aetate* is a seminal document for our times', he continued. 'I am looking forward to going to Rome later this month for the Vatican's official commemoration of the fortieth anniversary. I shall be urging the Pope to designate a specific day each year to commemorate the anniversary of *Nostra Aetate*.'

The following day, Father Hofmann attended a special interfaith service at the West London Synagogue to mark the fortieth anniversary. And ten days later, on 11 October, when the Papal Nuncio, Archbishop Faustino Sainz Munoz, paid his first visit to the centre, Sigi reiterated his wish that an official *Nostra Aetate* day should be designated, in the course of a round table discussion.

In July 2009, the recently appointed Archbishop of Westminster, Vincent Nichols, visited the centre. Welcoming him to the 'premier Jewish campus in Europe', Sigi expressed his gratification that Archbishop Nichols had 'found time for this visit so early in his service at Westminster. I am very glad that in your new capacity, you are joining the illustrious list of those who have come to the Centre, such as Cardinal Arinze, Cardinal Kasper, Cardinal Glemp, Cardinal Cormac Murphy-O'Connor, the late Cardinals Lustiger and Hume, and others', he continued. Sigi referred, too, to the Pope's recent encyclical, *Caritas in Veritate*, which, he said, addressed 'some of the most pressing problems of the age. It is a thought-provoking document which, I know from my personal conversations, is engaging the close scrutiny of Her Majesty's Government and of the World Economic Forum.' Sigi said, too, that he was looking forward to hearing Archbishop Nichols address some of the problems raised 'over the coming weeks'.

In his speech, Archishop Nichols recalled one of his 'most important' interfaith experiences which had occurred while he was Archbishop of Birmingham. He had invited Rabbi Leonard Tann, the late minister of Singers Hill Synagogue, to teach Hebrew to students at the local Catholic seminary in Oscott, where the rabbi made a discovery. He found a Torah scroll at the bottom of a cupboard. 'And then unfolded a rather marvellous story', the archbishop continued. It transpired that a priest in Oscott had taught German prisoners of war who were also students of the priesthood. One of them who became a major scripture scholar had gone to Jerusalem and acquired a Torah scroll. When he died he left it to the Oscott seminary. Later, the scroll was formally presented to Rabbi Tann's synagogue. The archbishop's visit to the Sternberg Centre was also notable for having attracted both John Bercow, the newly elected Speaker of the House of Commons, and his counterpart in the Lords, Baroness Hayman.

Archbishop Nichols' predecessor, Cardinal Cormac Murphy-O'Connor, paid another visit to the centre in December that year to present Sigi with a Star to be added to his Papal Knighthood. The presentation ceremony was preceded by performances about Chanukah and Christmas from children of the Akiva School and children from the neighbouring Catholic school, St Theresa's.

Following the presentation, Rabbi Bayfield, the centre's

director, spoke of Sigi's tireless work to promote interfaith relations. Both the Papal Knighthood and the Star, rare awards for a Jew to receive, were in recognition of Sigi's work in forging understanding and friendship between Jews and Catholics. In his response, Sigi again referred to the importance of *Nostra Aetate*.

> I have been especially encouraged these past forty years by a special decree issued by the Vatican Council in 1965, wiping away centuries of accusation and suspicion against the Jewish people and pledging to work for good relations with people of all faiths. I understand that is what the children of Akiva and St Theresa's are also doing – working for good and friendly relations with all peoples whatever their religion or their colour or their origin.

Sigi reiterated his call to the Catholic Church to declare an annual *Nostra Aetate* day. 'I am sure it would be a valuable addition to the tools we have created for promoting closer relations between Catholics and Jews. It would also surely be welcomed by Muslims, who are included in this declaration.' Lord Carey, who was also present, praised the efforts Sigi had made to encourage dialogue between Christians, Muslims and Jews.

Sigi has also entertained a number of his friends and acquaintances in the diplomatic service at the centre, as well as several foreign ambassadors. The Hungarian ambassador paid a visit to the centre in March 2008 and two special dinners were held there later that summer. In May, Sigi hosted a farewell dinner in honour of Sir Anthony Figgis, HM Marshall of the Diplomatic Corps and in June he hosted a dinner in honour of Francis Campbell, the British ambassador to the Vatican. This was a special multifaith occasion with guests including Zaki Badawi's widow and son, the Bishop of London, Richard Chartres, Lord Hameed, a Patron of the Three Faiths Forum, Raj Loomba, Chairman of the Friends of the Three Faiths Forum, Timothy Livesey, Secretary for Public Affairs at Lambeth Palace, the Chairman and Secretary of the Papal Knights Association, Sir Swinton Thomas and Leo

Simmonds and Rabbi Marc Saperstein, principal of Leo Baeck College. Among the other guests were Sir Ian Blair, then the Metropolitan Police Commissioner and his wife who is on the advisory board of the Three Faiths Forum, Catherine Pepinster, the editor of *The Tablet* and Sigi's sister, Suzanne Perlman and other family members.

Another important visitor to the centre that summer was Professor Klaus Schwab, the founder and Executive Chairman of the World Economic Forum, who gave a talk on the essence of the Forum's work. He explained the process of addressing the shared problems of diverse and often opposing interests around the world – working together, identifying common problems, finding solutions and putting them into practice. This was what the Forum saw as a 'bonding process'. Introducing Professor Schwab, Sigi recalled how he had approached him to add a religious component to the Forum's annual meeting. 'Since then over 100 religious leaders have participated in the deliberations of the annual meeting at Davos', he said.

Professor Schwab's talk was attended by a number of ambassadors representing countries all around the world and also by many Christian, Muslim and Jewish leaders active in interfaith relations. The meeting was chaired by Rabbi Tony Bayfield, who spoke of the history of the Sternberg Centre and the Manor House, and George Mallinckrodt KBE, President of Schroders PLC, gave the vote of thanks, pointing out how much the success of the World Economic Forum was due to Professor Schwab's capacity to facilitate intellectual talent. Before leaving the centre, Professor Schwab planted a crab-apple tree in the grounds in memory of his parents.

A very different visitor a year earlier was Ken Livingstone, then the Mayor of London, who was attending a meeting organized by the Movement for Reform Judaism with regard to the proposed academic boycott of Israel, which was being considered that day at the annual conference of the University and College Union. Livingstone confirmed his opposition to the boycott, saying that such a move would undermine efforts to restart the peace process. He reaffirmed his support for a two state solution and stated that he would have advised Yasser Arafat to accept the proposal for the settlement of the Israel/Palestine conflict put forward by President Bill Clinton at Camp David. He also said that it was a mistake to consider Zionism to be racism. Following his speech, Livingstone underwent an hour's close questioning from a 250-strong audience, during which he attempted to draw a line under past disagreements with the Jewish community and spoke of the need to build a shared agenda. Welcoming the Mayor, Sigi was not afraid to raise controversial issues.

> Someone with strong views about Israel, such as those Mr Livingstone has expressed from time to time, is bound to get under the skin of those of us who know that Israel can only lose once to lose everything. And we have questions about those avowedly anti-Israel spokesmen he invites to London. But criticisms hurled from afar are useless when compared with the opportunities for understanding offered by dialogue. And it is my absolute conviction that talking through problems is more likely to yield positive results than punching your way through.

Summing up the meeting, Rabbi Tony Bayfield proposed that the Mayor should make a contribution to the prospects of peace in the Middle East by hosting a meeting of Jewish and Muslim Londoners in City Hall, under the auspices of One Voice, an organization of Israelis and Palestinians dedicated to giving a voice to the majority of moderates on both sides who wish for peace and prosperity in the region.

As the largest Jewish cultural centre in Europe, the Sternberg Centre is constantly used as the venue for a huge variety of functions. In 2009, the British Friends of the Hebrew University put on a summer concert there and the B'nai Brith 1st Lodge held their annual function there. Obviously the various participating organizations use the venue for their special events, for example the annual Leo Baeck lecture. In 2006, the college held a special ceremony for Leo Baeck honorary doctorate and degree holders and in 2008 hosted a Leo Baeck Founding Patrons lunch and a book launch for Professor Marc Saperstein. In July 2008, the New North London Synagogue held a memorial lecture in honour of Rabbi Dr Louis Jacobs, as well as a portrait unveiling ceremony. The centre was also the venue for a memorial service for Sidney Shipton in February 2008.

An unusual event – 'The Rabbi, the Priest and the Couch' – was hosted by Rabbi Tony Bayfield at the centre in October 2007 in honour of the Raphael Jewish Counselling Service. This was a reception and panel discussion on 'Therapists and their Religious Commitments'. Proposing a toast to the Raphael Service, Sigi described it as almost the 'secret service' of Anglo-Jewry. Launched in 1960, it had grown from its original function as a counselling service for rabbis in the Progressive movement to being, as Sigi put it, 'a primary instrument of care for almost the entire community'. While Sigi regretted that the Service was not openly supported by the ultra-orthodox community, it enjoyed the patronage of Rabbi Bayfield, the Chief Rabbi, Sir Jonathan Sacks, and Rabbi Dr Abraham Levy, spiritual head of the Spanish and Portuguese Jews' Congregation. In his response, Jack Lynes, the Chair of the Raphael Service, referred to Raphael, the healer, and likened Sigi's work with the Three Faiths Forum to that of Raphael.

Sigi has also celebrated several of his birthdays at the centre. For his 75th birthday in 1996, the centre brought out a tribute book. Among the numerous tributes were those from prominent political figures including James Callaghan, Margaret Thatcher, Margaret Beckett, Tony Benn, Neil Kinnock, Betty Boothroyd , David Amess and Mary Wilson, widow of the former prime minister; leading members of the clergy including George Carey, then Archbishop of Canterbury, and his predecessors, Lord Runcie and Lord Coggan, whom Sigi had presented with a tribute book on the occasion of his 80th birthday in 1989, Cardinal Hume, Cardinal Cassidy, Archbishop Barbarito, Archbishop Gregorios, Bishop Richard Harries and Bishop Charles

Henderson; Chief Rabbi Jonathan Sacks, his predecessor Immanuel Jacobovits and the Sephardi spiritual leader, Rabbi Dr Abraham Levy; the ambassadors of Hungary, Greece, Austria, Israel, Switzerland and the Indian High Commissioner; the Duke of Norfolk, Lord Weidenfeld, Lord Wolfson, Sir John Templeton, Sir Martin Gilbert and Victor and Lilian Hochhauser; several progressive rabbis including Hugo Gryn, a personal friend; Zaki Badawi and Marcus Braybrooke, with whom he was to found the Three Faiths Forum and many of the people who had worked with him in his multiple endeavours including David Rosen, Ron Kronish, Ruth Weyl, Stanislaw Krajewski, Oliver McTernan, Michael Seed, Peter Bander van Duren and Professor Beno Rothenberg from the Institute of Archaeo-Metallurgical Studies.

On a more personal note, the 'Last Word' was from Hazel, who pointed out that Sigi was

> a very private man, even to the point of reticence. He is also his own man, and never gives his point of view without first applying his powers of critical judgement. Some difficult experiences in his early life taught him to rely on himself and this gave him his impressive self confidence ... He is also helpful to many people who come to him in times of crisis and reaches out also to those who are reticent to ask ... His family have watched with awe, and sometimes trepidation, his forays into new, unknown territory ... As the senior male in the family, he has become the Rock to so many people besides us. We have all been touched by sadness and struggles and we do not allow him to be ill ... He has great pride and pleasure in his children and grandchildren and, like many grandfathers, is enjoying being one step removed from day to day worries. As a husband he is caring, loyal and patient.

Ten years later, a special celebration was organized for Sigi's 85th birthday and the twenty-fifth anniversary of the inauguration of the Sternberg Centre. Sigi invited all the staff and volunteers who had contributed to the work of the centre over the years to celebrate with him and to thank them for their contribution. Peter Levy and Neil Benson spoke about the enormous influence the centre had had, both as the central site for Progressive Jewry in Europe and for Interfaith Relations. Rabbi Tony Bayfield contrasted the vibrancy of the centre and all the organizations based there with what the site had been twenty-five years before:

> It's hard to imagine Anglo-Jewry without the Sternberg Centre. Twenty-five years ago, the Manor House Complex was a run-down convent with a Roman Catholic Secondary School ... Today New North London Synagogue is an example of the vitality of Jewish life; the Leo Baeck College is the only mainstream rabbinic train-ing college in the UK; Akiva School has the largest waiting list of any Jewish school in the country; the Jewish Museum houses part of its collection on the site and RSGB [the Reform Synagogues of Great Britain] has become the Movement for Reform Judaism – an essential part of the mainstream of British Jewry ... The develop-ment of the Centre over twenty-five years to its current position in Anglo-Jewish life has been a truly amazing achievement and, although many people have contributed, it would not have been possible without the support and dedication of Sir Sigmund Sternberg.

Sigi, the President of the Movement for Reform Judaism, responded that it was fortuitous that the celebrations were taking place when Rabbi Bayfield had just been awarded the Lambeth Degree by the Archbishop of Canterbury. He paid tribute to Hazel, his hard-working wife, and to all those who had worked with him and commented that, 'The Sternberg Centre has been a place where many diplomats and religious leaders from all over the world have visited. I hope this will continue in the future.'

12 Who is Sigi?

So who is Sigi? What is the human face behind the multiple achievements? A hospital visit in January 2010 revealed how difficult it was for him to leave behind the world of work and focus on a matter that was out of his hands. As Sheilagh Viviers, his housekeeper, who accompanied him, recounts:

> It was the first time in his life he had been in hospital as a patient and it was a very traumatic experience for him. His first encounter was with a nurse who was waiting to do his blood pressure and he stopped her and took out his card and handed her a brochure. He was struggling to accept the instructions as to what he could or couldn't do and was talking on the phone to the office while an orderly was waiting with a wheelchair to take him for a chest scan. The day following the procedure he was on the phone again.

Sigi's virtual inability to relax was something the late Lord Coggan, who used to travel quite frequently with Sigi, had also noted: 'I doubt that he enjoys a holiday. Could he ever lie back with a novel for any length of time? Not worry about a newspaper, London, the world – let the world go by and relax! I've never seen him do that.'

While it might surprise many who have observed his virtual addiction to his work, however, the birth of his first great-grandchild in March 2009 showed another side to Sigi. His granddaughter, Rachel, speaks of his devotion to her young son, Jacob, and is happy that she and her grandfather have become even closer since Jacob was born. Sigi came to see her and the baby in hospital before Jacob was forty-eight hours old and held the baby, 'very excited and loving'.

'Grandpa Sigi', she says, is always phoning her to see how she is. 'I think we loved each other very much before but the arrival of Jacob has made this even stronger.' Jacob started walking at nine months and has become more interactive, communicative and affectionate and Sigi enjoys playing with him. Rachel recalls a visit to Branksome when there was a large photo of Sigi and Hazel against the wall and Jacob went up to it and kept pointing at the faces.

Rachel is also greatly appreciative of how supportive her grandfather has been of her relationship with her husband, Chris, who is not Jewish. The couple met before they both went up to Cambridge University. Sigi helped to involve them with the Liberal Jewish Synagogue in St John's Wood, where they were able to receive a mixed faith blessing. 'He's always been very inclusive of Chris and invited us to Friday nights and Seder nights', she says.

Before Jacob was born, one of the happiest aspects of her relationship with Sigi, Rachel feels, is how he has always been keen to involve his family in his work. She has particularly enjoyed the presentation ceremonies for the Three Faiths Forum award and the Interfaith Gold Medallion at the National Portrait Gallery when all the family were present. 'It was something really lovely. It was nice to see his work and what he was doing for the community, which I really appreciate. It was also nice to be able to catch up with members of the family.'

Many distinguished personalities have been the recipients of these awards, including Lord Carey, the former Archbishop of Canterbury, Bishop Richard Chartres of London, Bishop Richard Harries of Oxford, Sheikh Zaki Badawi, Rabbi Lionel Blue, Lord Coggan, Cardinal Hume, Rabbi Hugo Gryn and Rabbi Albert Friedlander. In 2005 there were two recipients: Dr Khalid Hameed, Chairman of the Commonwealth Youth Exchange Council and the Asian Policy Group, which advises ethnic minorities and George Mallinckrodt KBE, President of Schroders, former Chairman of the Council of the World Economic Forum, Trustee of Christian Responsibility in Public Affairs and a patron of the Three Faiths Forum, while in 2006, the award was presented to Dr Edward Kessler, Director of the (then) Centre for the Study of Jewish-Christian Relations.

Sigi's work for the community was recognized in September 1998 when he received the first Community Service Award from the Board of Deputies of British Jews. At a gala dinner at Lincoln's Inn organized for the launch of the award, Sigi was presented with the Silver Medal by the then Home Secretary, Jack Straw, who praised his interfaith work, particularly his founding of the Three Faiths Forum. Others at the dinner who praised Sigi's contribution included the then President of the Board, Eldred Tabachnik, who spoke of Sigi's 'unique contribution to interfaith relations', Chief Rabbi Jonathan Sacks who saw Sigi and Hazel as 'an indefatigable force for peace and mutual respect between faiths', and Rabbi Tony Bayfield who lauded Sigi's 'tireless vision and profoundly effective work in interfaith dialogue' as being 'without equal'. Sigi continues to be proud of his involvement in the building up of the Board of Deputies and welcomes the publication in 2010 of a book celebrating the Board's 250th anniversary.

A more unusual award in 2003 was the prestigious French Légion d'Honneur, which he received from the French Ambassador. The award was presented to honour Sigi's achievements within the British Jewish community and his open and tolerant approach to religious and political questions. In particular, the French Government recognized his accomplished work in so many different aspects of interfaith relations and greatly appreciated his open and sympathetic attitude towards France. Many ambassadors were present at the reception, as were the Papal Nuncio, Archbishop Pablo Puente, Rabbi Dr Abraham Levy, Rabbi Tony Bayfield and Rev. Malcolm Weisman. Accepting the award, Sigi said: 'I have a long-standing relationship with France, both as a British citizen and as a Jew. I appreciate the firm commitment of the French authorities to combat racism and anti-Semitism ... France has given much to the Jewish people in terms of freedom of religion, opportunity and self-expression. This is an honour I will wear with pride.'

Henry Grunwald QC, then newly-elected as President of the Board of Deputies, said that he felt privileged to be present on this 'unique occasion. Sir Sigmund's work has been recognized both here and abroad in many ways and the award of the Légion d'Honneur has now added France to the long list of countries who have rightly honoured him for all his important interfaith work'.

It was for his interfaith activities, as ever, that Sigi was decorated a few months later with the Order Francisco de Miranda (First Class) by the Venezuelan Ambassador, Alfredo Toro-Hardy. This award earned him considerable praise, including a spoken tribute from Jack Straw, at that time Foreign Secretary, and a message from Prime Minister Tony Blair who said he was delighted that Sigi's pioneering work in interfaith dialogue was being increasingly recognized around the world. 'Diversity is now everyday and commonplace rather than the exception. That is why it is all the more important that understanding grows between people of different nationalities and different faiths and that knowledge of the "other" is enriched.' Jack Straw said that the award 'justifiably recognizes Sir Sigmund's efforts in promoting dialogue between the religions and in bringing together existing interfaith groups across Latin America'. Other tributes were paid by Henry Grunwald, Aubrey Rose, Oliver McTernan, no longer a priest but an author, and Sidney Shipton.

Ambassador Toro-Hardy announced that the city of Caracas was to honour another of Sigi's activities by naming a square The Raoul Wallenberg Square. Sigi paid special tribute to the ambassador for the interest he had taken in promoting interfaith relations and also to the ambassadors of Latin American countries who attended the ceremony and in whose countries interfaith dialogue groups were actively engaged.

'I do feel a little uneasy about taking an award for something that I so enjoy doing', he said. 'Bringing people together, bringing religions together, bringing nations together – that has been my obsession and also my pleasure over the past decades.' Sigi's self-appraisal is endorsed by Rev.

Simon Hass, former cantor of the Central Synagogue, who has known him for many years. 'He's a great human being. He believes people should respect each other. That's his life.' Hass also praises Hazel, Sigi's 'life partner', as 'someone special'. Lord Greville Janner, co-founder of the Co-existence Trust, sees Sigi as a 'great leader' of the British Jewish community. 'I have long worked with him and for him and his organizations and have the greatest admiration for his untiring and enthusiastic efforts. He certainly deserves the awards he has received.' Lord Janner is also Chairman of the Holocaust Education Trust and he and Sigi have worked together in furthering the memory of the Holocaust in countries throughout the world.

Sigi's support for the foundation of a Jewish museum in Turkey in 2005 was greatly appreciated by the museum's curator, Naim Guleryuz. And he has had close relations with representatives of the Moroccan government for several years. The former Moroccan ambassador in London, Mohammed Belmahi, who was awarded the Interfaith Gold Medallion in January 2009, was introduced to Sigi and to Rabbi Dr Abraham Levy eight or nine years earlier by Sidney Assor, the founding president of the Moroccan Jewish community in Britain. Lord Janner, too, played an active role in their relationship. Both Belmahi and Sigi were decorated with the Royal Order of Francis I, the multi-faith arm of the Sacred Military Constantinian Order of St George, at Westminster Cathedral by the Duke of Calabria. Belmahi has spoken with admiration of the vision Sigi had had when he became active in interfaith dialogue some thirty years earlier, at a time when very few people believed in this aspiration which, now, has come to fruition. He and Sigi grew closer when both became involved in the setting up of the Sacred Texts Exhibition at the British Library in 2007.

Morocco, which, from the Hebrew script on a tomb, can trace a Jewish presence of some 2,400 years, has historically been active in interfaith relations, with the monarch officially the protector of all faiths. During the Second World War, no Moroccan Jew was killed, imprisoned or sent to the gas chambers. King Mohammed V refused to provide the Vichy regime with details, stating that Moroccan Jews were the same as Muslims. And two days after the atrocities of September 11 2001, an ecumenical prayer service for all who had suffered was organized in the Catholic cathedral in Rabat, in the presence of the leading Jewish rabbis, the archbishop of the cathedral, many members of the Moroccan government and all leading representatives of the Muslim faith.

It is not surprising, then, that Sigi's first award from a Muslim country should come from Morocco. In December 2009, he was presented with the Alawite Order Wissam, conferred upon him by King Mohammed VI, by Princess Lalla, the new Moroccan ambassador in London. Princess Lalla spoke of Sigi as

> an exceptional man who has dedicated his life to fill up the gaps of difference and indifference, which have separated Jews, Christians and Muslims; a refined diplomat who has worked relentlessly behind the scenes to resolve conflicts within or between religions. Sir Sigmund exemplifies the finest qualities of leadership, personal integrity, entrepreneurship and generosity. His outstanding and fascinating achievements are known and praised worldwide ... The bestowal of this award to you, Sir Sigmund, is a symbol of our joint commitment to place interaction between our faiths and civilizations at the heart of the debate in today's world, where risks of exclusion, ostracism, terrorism, Islamophobia and anti-Semitism are becoming more and more exacerbated ... It is our duty today to promote constructive and positive interaction between different faiths and different civilizations and stand up against those who fan the flames of extremism through the alleged 'clash of civilisations'.

If an award from a Muslim country was something special, so too was the FIRST Lifetime Achievement Award for Responsible Capitalism Sigi received a year earlier from the Foreign Secretary, David Miliband. FIRST, a multidisciplinary International Affairs organization, was founded in 1984 with the aim of enhancing communications between leaders in industry, finance and government worldwide and promoting strategic dialogue. In 2000, the organization instituted the International Award for Responsible Capitalism to honour business leaders who have excelled both in commercial success and social responsibility. At the special award ceremony in Marlborough House, Dr Mo Ibrahim, founder of Celtel Corporation, received the Responsible Capitalism Award for 2008 and Lord Dahrendorf received a Special Award. On presenting the awards, the Foreign Secretary said:

> It is an important time to be recognizing the importance of responsible behaviour in business. As the global economy faces serious challenges, it has become increasingly clear that success depends on more than short-term profit. If we make the wrong choices, then the long-term consequences – whether environmental, social or ethical – will catch up with us. So I am delighted to be able to pay tribute today to the winners of this important award.

Sigi received his award for having 'exemplified the qualities of social responsibility and dedicated service, working tirelessly to establish interfaith and inter-communal cooperation through both the Sternberg Foundation and the Three Faiths Forum'. In his response, he said: 'I am very conscious of the immense honour you do me with the Lifetime Achievement Award, which is based on the belief that responsible capitalism has a moral as well as an economic quality.'

A few months earlier, in July 2008, Sigi set up, in conjunction with *The Times*, a new award, The Times/Sternberg Active Life Award, to celebrate the achievements of people over the age of 70. The concept of the award had arisen the previous year during discussions at the World Economic Forum in Davos. Commenting on the prize announcement in an article in *The Times*, Michael Binyon wrote:

> Sir Sigmund Sternberg ... is still tirelessly promoting dialogue between the three Abrahamic faiths ... He goes to his office daily and travels to conferences at the age of 88. Sir Sigmund has now proposed an annual award, to

be given to the older person who, in the opinion of the public, has done most for society and for good causes in old age. He, himself, would probably be a fitting first winner.

Sigi, Binyon explained, was on the board of Age Exchange, a voluntary body championing the rights of the elderly and the exchange of experience between older and younger generations. In a letter to Sigi in 2009, Lord Heseltine, recalling their 'very satisfactory involvement' while he was Secretary of State for the Environment, commended him for recognizing 'the invaluable role the elderly play in today's world'. The first winner of the award was, in fact, Helen Bamber, founder of the Medical Foundation for Care of Victims of Torture. The second was Phoebe Caldwell, awarded for her work with people suffering from severe autism. 'She has changed the lives of hundreds if not thousands of people', Sigi said, on presenting her with the prize.

Sigi, too, has changed people's lives, both in his contributions to worthwhile causes and through his vast network of contacts in all spheres. Ben Helfgott, the Chairman of *Polin*, the volumes of scholarly papers published by the Institute for Polish-Jewish Studies, is grateful for the help both *Polin* and the Institute have received from him. Sigi was invited in 1995 to become president of *Polin* and has always shown great interest in its work, which deals with anything in connection with Polish-Jewish relations, as well as promoting literature and publishing a book every year. It was originally formed in 1983 after a conference about Polish-Jewish Relations at Oxford University organized by Antony Polonsky and Felix Scharf. *Polin* also works very closely with Polish ambassadors and, together with the Polish Cultural Centre, has put on a large variety of events promoting an informed understanding of the Polish-Jewish past and fostering dialogue between Poles and Jews with a view to encouraging a new generation to respect the heritage of 900 years of Jewish life in Poland.

Polin and the Polish Cultural Centre have also played a major role in helping many Holocaust survivors from Poland to come to terms with Poland as it is today. A former Polish ambassador, Ryszard Stemplowski, invited a large group of members of the Second Generation who were about to visit Poland to a reception at his residence. One son of a Holocaust survivor was so moved by the ambassador's words that he could hardly reconcile what he had just heard with the terrible things he had learned from his father about Poland. Helfgott emphasizes how important Sigi's support has been and in his opening remarks to the annual conference in December 2009, launching the twenty-second volume of *Polin*, Sigi praised the 'depth and intensity' of the relationship between Poland and the Jews and marvelled that the relationship continued to yield material relevant to the long history of the two 'incredible peoples'.

Sigi has been a longstanding member of the Council of Management of Keston College, which was founded by Canon Dr Michael Bourdeaux in 1969 for the purpose of studying religion and communist countries. Sigi's aim was to promote knowledge of Jewish religious life in Russia and Eastern Europe and the difficulties Jewish religious leaders have had to contend with. Canon Bourdeaux pays tribute to Sigi as 'one of those supporters who has stuck with us through thick and thin'. He appreciates Sigi's valuable advice regarding the organization's financial 'ups and downs', his generous contributions to various initiatives that have been undertaken, his regular attendance at meetings and his readiness to be actively involved at times of crisis despite his own 'exacting timetable'. 'He kept us up to the mark with his constant good humour and was always understanding of our failings. No one could have wished for a wiser colleague.'

For much of the time Sigi was the only Jew on Keston's Council – although Chief Rabbi Jacobovits had also been a patron of the institute – and, Canon Bourdeaux believes, the trust Keston has experienced from within the UK's Jewish community was due, in no small measure, to Sigi's personal endeavours.

Sigi's close association with ambassadors of many countries led to a special visit in December 2006 of the former German ambassador, Wolfgang Ischinger, to the North

Western Reform Synagogue in Alyth Gardens, where he delivered the sermon. This was particularly poignant as many of the synagogue's founding members were refugees from Nazi Germany and a number of former refugees were among the congregation. Ambassador Ischinger spoke movingly of the influence in today's Germany of Rabbi Dr Leo Baeck, the synagogue's first president, and of his pride in the resurgence of Jews in Germany in recent years. He referred, too, to Germany's support for Israel. Thanking the ambassador, Rabbi Mark Goldsmith also expressed his gratitude to Sigi for making the visit possible. 'The ambassador's sermon demonstrated a deep understanding of issues within our community. He set out his commitment to encouraging Jews to get to know today's Germany without putting aside our duty to remember Germany's past and the German people's duty to combat racism of all shades.' In 2010, the current German ambassador also spoke at the North Western Reform Synagogue, while the same year the Papal Nuncio spoke at the West London Synagogue, the first time a Papal Nuncio had spoken in a synagogue.

Sigi's ability to use his powers of networking has impressed many who have worked with him. As Rabbi Mark Winer puts it: 'He is utterly boneheaded about bringing people together and relentless in pursuing peace.' And Rabbi Tony Bayfield affirms,

> I know of nobody who has been able to open more doors, to build more bridges, to make more connections than Sigi. Therein lie his genius and his great achievements ... Sigi has always needed other people to go through the doors, to work with the connections, to provide substance to the contact ... I can testify just how much he's persuaded me to do when it's not been my job and in a sense I hadn't wanted to do it, but I found he was right in the sense that the doors he opened for me, many of them were extraordinarily worthwhile and valuable.

The same point was also put forward by the late Lord

Coggan: 'He is shrewd, very shrewd, in enlisting people to his causes. He gets the right man and holds on to him and if I use the word "uses" him it's with no evil content to the word because the cause is good.'

Clive Marks OBE can point to a similar experience. A trustee of the Stone Ashdown Trust, a patron of the Friends of Israel Educational Foundation and the London Philharmonic Trust and a founder and patron of the London Jewish Cultural Centre, he has also been actively involved in philanthropic ventures for many years. He recalls Sigi telling him in the early 1990s: 'Clive, you have got to run the Spiro Institute.' Marks protested that he was too busy but Sigi was undeterred. As Marks recalls, Sigi gave him no option, explaining that financiers and accountants were trying to run the institute and they had no idea of education. He then persuaded Marks to accompany him to a board meeting, which was being held by a distinguished member of the Jewish community who had always been a good friend to Marks. 'Half way through Sigi brings me in and says, "I want Clive to chair these meetings". I sat down and, to my eternal shame, didn't argue and the then chairman very politely made way for me.' Marks was astounded by the politeness with which he was received and explains that it was because of Sigi that he has always been closely associated with what is now the London Jewish Cultural Centre. 'The amazing thing was, had anyone else "parachuted" me in, I'm sure there would have been civil war, but Sigi's great brilliance and tact was welcomed without a murmur, something unprecedented in Anglo-Jewish relations.'

Paul Winner, who had formerly worked in public relations, attributes much of his success as an artist to Sigi's support. The two men originally met on a mission to Israel in the early 1970s and Sigi soon spotted Winner sketching in a corner. As it happened Winner was working on one of many sketches he had done of Sigi himself and when Sigi saw the sketches 'his face lit up with a mischievous twinkle', as Winner recalls. Sigi then invited Winner to join the Rotary Club and the Council of Christians and Jews. At that point, Winner feels, his life had been transformed. He had been 'anointed with the Sigi symbol – his "service before self" Rotary philosophy – and was in the "charmed circle": Sigi was introducing me to everybody as a wonderful artist.'

Winner duly joined the Rotary Club and the Council of Christians and Jews and was later on the Advisory Board of the Three Faiths Forum, of which he was a founder member. He recalls that Sigi invited him to go and see the Pope in 1994. 'On arriving at the hotel in Rome, I see a gentleman whom I assume is the hall porter in a funny hat and uniform with big gold buttons all the way down. It was Sigi in his papal knight's uniform!' The following day Winner was introduced to the Pope by Sigi and presented the Pontiff with half a dozen 'lightning sketches' with a bit of colour. The Pope then told him 'But Mr Winner, we do have other artists here in the Vatican' and pointed to a painting by Leonardo da Vinci.

On another occasion, Winner was attending a meeting of the Three Faiths Forum in the House of Commons. Knowing that Sigi had received many awards, as a light hearted joke he presented him with a 'Winner Award' of a picture of Petra he had been commissioned to do by the Jordanian Tourist Board. Sigi was happy to accept the award! At that same meeting, after the 'presentation', Winner was approached by a Mr Sharif Horthy, a member of the Three Faiths Forum. A grandson of Admiral Horthy, the former Governor of Hungary – an admiral in a country without a fleet – Horthy was a member of the World Conference on Religion and Peace. Winner then found himself to be the artist in residence at the Seventh World Conference on Religion and Peace, all thanks to Sigi.

'Sigi in his generous way of always introducing everyone to everyone else introduces me to the beautiful ambassador of Bosnia at the ceremony when he received the Légion d'Honneur and I was sketching the scene', Winner recalls. He was then invited to be the artist for the new bridge at Mostar in 2004. Also thanks to Sigi, who officially opened Winner's exhibition at the Board of Deputies in 2003, Winner was invited by the Home Office to be the artist at large for Holocaust Memorial Day in 2004. Winner is impressed and moved by Sigi's generosity of spirit. 'He is thinking of everyone else while helping the world.'

George Mallinckrodt KBE, President of Schroders Bank and a former Chairman of the Council of the World Economic Forum, who has known Sigi for some ten years, enjoys a 'wonderful friendship' with him and admires his persistence. 'He doesn't let go, he is very dedicated. He lives with his dedication. There is a feeling of 24-hour commitment on his part.' Mallinckrodt has been involved in interfaith activity since 1979 when he was present at an initiative launched by the Queen and Prince Philip at Windsor Castle. He believes wholeheartedly in the work of the Three Faiths Forum, of which he is a patron, and is glad the Forum has extended its activities to include other faiths, for example Buddhists and Hindus. Mallinckrodt sees the way Sigi operates as both 'political and not political, because in order to achieve his goals he activates various talented people and makes use of his good connections'. While admiring Sigi's respect for and loyalty to his own Jewish faith, Mallinckrodt appreciates the fact that Sigi is not 'trying to sell his own religion' and is sufficiently independent to be critical when it comes to the political side of the religion. Sigi, Mallinckrodt feels, 'has made a considerable difference. In today's world people who can make a difference really count.'

One example of Sigi's connection with people outside the three Abrahamic faiths is the friendship he enjoyed with the late Dr L.M. Singhvi, a former Indian High Commissioner in London. In a letter in 2007, Dr Singhvi wrote: 'We dreamt many dreams together. You and Hazel filled our hearts with the joy of true friendship. Time and distance have separated us but the memories of both of you are green and vibrant in our hearts.'

Henry Grunwald, former President of the Board of Deputies, has known the Sternberg family for a long time. He was joint best man, together with Sigi's nephew, George Perlman, at Michael Sternberg's wedding. In fact he had known Michael's wife, Janine, and her family for some time before Michael and Janine met. Grunwald recalls a special reception hosted by Her Majesty the Queen at Buckingham Palace in 2001 for leaders of all the faith communities in anticipation of the Jubilee year. It was also Prince Philip's 80th birthday that day. As Grunwald recalls: 'A group of us were standing together, most of us Jewish, when Prince Philip came over to us. He spoke to us all and we thanked him for sharing his 80th with us. He went on to say, "Do you know Sigi Sternberg?" I said, "Very well". Philip continued: "He keeps telling people we were born in the same year."'

Indeed, both Sigi and Prince Philip were to celebrate their 90th birthdays within days of each other in June 2011. To honour the Prince, Sigi wrote to the *Daily Telegraph*, pointing out that Prince Philip's important charity work had not been given sufficient emphasis in the paper's tribute to him. The Prince, Sigi noted, had lent his name to more than 700 charitable causes, most notably the Duke of Edinburgh award that helped more than 275,000 young people every year. He had also presided the previous week over the presentation of the Templeton Prize at Buckingham Palace. 'I really think that the Duke of Edinburgh should be counted among our national treasures', Sigi's letter concluded. A few days later, Sigi received a letter from the Prince:

> Dear Sir Sigmund,
>
> Thank you so much for your good wishes for my birthday. Quite how I have managed to keep going to this great age is a mystery. I was delighted to see you again, briefly, the other day. It was kind of you to write the letter to *The Daily Telegraph*.
>
> Yours sincerely,
>
> Philip

The Prince had signed the letter in his own hand.

A few days later, Sigi wrote to *The Times*, praising the 'comprehensive and well-merited reporting of the very full life' of the Prince but mentioning that the fact that Philip had been the first member of the Royal Family to visit Israel had been omitted. 'Prince Philip went there in 1994 to visit the grave of his mother, Princess Alice of Greece, who died in 1972 and is buried in Jerusalem.' Sigi went on to mention that Princess Alice had been named as one of the 'Righteous among Nations' by the Yad Vashem National Holocaust Memorial for having sheltered a Jewish family at her home in Athens during the Nazi occupation.

> During his visit, the Prince planted a maple tree in his mother's memory in the Yad Vashem memorial garden. He said that his family had never known and his mother never mentioned the fact she had hidden Jews during the occupation. A member of the hidden family who was introduced to the Prince was so overwhelmed with emotion that he could not make the intended short speech of appreciation.

Sigi's abstemiousness is an important factor that has contributed to his indefatigable energy. He follows the news constantly and is quick to write a letter to a newspaper about any matter that he feels needs addressing. Indeed, he has written more letters to *The Times* than any other correspondent. An article about him in *The London Rotarian* commented that in his letters to the press 'he opines on everything from ageism in the workplace to … a Simpsons-style comedy cancelled by the BBC'. In August 2005, he wrote to *The Daily Telegraph* in the context of the debate about A Level examinations to propose the art of interfaith dialogue as a new subject for the curriculum, while in June 2008, after Bishop Michael Nazir-Ali wrote an article blaming the decline of Christianity and the rise of liberal values in the United Kingdom for creating a 'moral vacuum' that radical Islam was filling, Sigi, together with Marcus Braybrooke and Imam Maulana Shahid Raza, Zaki Badawi's successor at the Three Faiths Forum, wrote to *The Daily Telegraph* stating that such a vacuum could only be filled with the assistance of the great faiths affirming their shared moral values. 'The Three Faiths Forum, through its work with young people and its medical ethics and lawyers' programmes brings together Jews, Christians and Muslims to address the social evils that the bishop highlights.' And the following month, at a party to mark Father Michael Seed's departure from Westminster Cathedral, Sigi was commenting to a journalist about his doubts as to whether Tony Blair, who was involved in so many ventures since stepping down as Prime Minister, could really devote enough attention to the Faith Foundation he was setting up. However, he remained optimistic, seeing Blair as a 'miracle worker' who had a chance of achieving his aims.

The compliment has been reciprocated. Answering questions from readers of *The Jewish News* in June 2010, Tony Blair spoke of the parallels between his Faith Foundation and The Three Faiths Forum, particularly between the Forum's Shared Futures Schools Linking Programme and the Foundation's Face to Faith schools project, and acknowledged the expert facilitation provided by a member of the Shared Futures' team for the Face to Faith project. Sigi, he said, has been 'an inspiration and wise adviser' to the Faith Foundation since its inception and he looked forward to the two of them continuing to work together.

If Sigi, himself, has not been seen as a 'miracle worker', many who have worked with him over the years have praised him as little less. Rabbi Mark Winer, who worked independently but in cooperation with Sigi on some of his most significant endeavours – the accord between the Vatican and the State of Israel; the resolution of the conflict at Auschwitz between the Carmelites and their supporters and world Jewish opinion; the importance of extending interfaith dialogue to the Muslim community – is particularly emphatic: 'He is and has been the foremost lay interfaith activist in the world, a model of the way lay people can be religious leaders and transform religious action.' While Winer is quite content with what he sees as Sigi's 'self-promotion', one particular area in which he believes Sigi deserves all the acclaim and awards he has received is in his recognizing early on that the most critical relationship that needed mending was with Muslims. This became especially important after 9/11. Till then, Winer felt Sigi's was 'a voice in the wilderness', even though the Three Faiths Forum had already been set up. Winer recalls how he and Sigi had to argue their case 'against a whole slew of rabbis' who wanted to restrict interfaith dialogue to Jews and Catholics. He feels Britain is fortunate in having Sigi, as there is no parallel lay leader in America. 'He's done more to bring people of Great Britain and the religions of the world together than anyone on the planet.'

Winer's words are echoed by Gillian Walnes, Co-Founder and Executive Director of the Anne Frank Trust, of which Sigi was one of the founders. The Trust has its office in Sigi's Star House. She sees Sigi as a 'maverick, the kind of maverick society needs, who was active in interfaith relations when hardly anybody else was and this kind of work wasn't even regarded as important'. Rather than being embittered by the legacy of Nazi brutality which seared his youth, Walnes praises Sigi's awareness of the importance of bringing people together to explore their common heritage as human beings, rather than to focus on their differences, and his tenacity in sticking with his mission for so long, with Hazel's invaluable support.

Sigi is very appreciative of many of the people with whom he has worked or who work in related fields and, as Gillian Walnes confirms, is eager to ensure that 'the right people are recognized for their efforts'. Walnes herself was awarded the MBE in the 2010 New Year Honours, while Rabbi David Rosen was awarded a CBE for his contribution to interfaith relations in the Middle East. In 2005, Rosen was the first orthodox Jewish rabbi to become a Papal Knight when he was invested with the order of St Gregory the Great. Sigi was happy to put his name forward, as he was to put forward Rabbi Tony Bayfield's name to receive a Lambeth Doctorate from the Archbishop of Canterbury in 2006. Sigi had also put forward Sidney Shipton's name to receive an OBE.

Sigi was also influential in the appointment of Francis Campbell as Britain's Ambassador to the Vatican in December 2005. Campbell, who was only 36, was the first Catholic to be appointed to the Vatican embassy since the Reformation. He had most recently served at 10 Downing Street as an advisor on Europe as well as on faith and religious issues and had cooperated with Sigi during his time in Downing Street. On presenting his credentials, Campbell expressed Britain's appreciation of the Pope's commitment to dialogue between the Church and other faiths and to search for the good of human beings and society. 'We know from experience that it is only through meaningful dialogue over time that old suspicions can be transcended', he declared. Sigi described Campbell as 'an excellent choice' and praised the unusual appointment of so young an envoy, who was also a committed Catholic as 'very imaginative'. Responding to Sigi's wishes for his birthday in April 2011, Campbell wrote: 'It is lovely to hear from you, Siggy. Please know that I will always remember your kindness and friendship. You are a wonderful friend and I promise I will be in touch when I am next in London. Take care and God bless.'

One key aim of Sigi's that has not yet been achieved but which he continues to urge with all his remarkable energy is the establishment of a world faith day to be known as *Nostra Aetate* Day, in honour of the seminal Vatican document in 1965.

Nevertheless, recent years have provided Sigi with much gratification, as well as times of sadness. The death of his colleague, Zaki Badawi, in January 2006, evoked a moving tribute: 'Islam has lost a dedicated leader and spokesman, the world of interfaith endeavour has lost a prime advocate of respectful and purposeful dialogue and I am bereft of a friend and colleague of many years, one who can never be replaced', were Sigi's words on hearing the news. On a more cheerful level, he has seen members of his family succeed in many varied endeavours. Michael, his son, as well as becoming a grandfather, was appointed a QC in 2008, while Frances, his daughter, has a flourishing career as an artist. Sigi's grandson, Daniel, is now a practising barrister in a prestigious chambers and his granddaughter, Sarah, a first-class graduate who has just completed her Masters' Degree, is particularly interested in Jewish history and will ensure that the family ties with Jewish tradition are maintained. Their sister, Rachel, an actress and a playwright, is, of course, the mother of Sigi's great-grandson, Jacob. Her play, *Negative Space*, co-written with Jemma Wayne, was well received when it opened at the New End Theatre in 2009.

Sigi's 90th birthday in June 2011 was also an occasion to celebrate. The Board of Deputies of British Jews held a special reception in his honour and one of the many distinguished guests was the Chief Rabbi, Lord Sacks. The London Rotary Club also honoured him with a reception, while Sigi and Hazel hosted a buffet supper for family and close friends at Branksome on the day itself. Sigi is also awaiting an Honorary Fellowship from the Hebrew University in Jerusalem, due to be awarded to him in the autumn of 2011. In recent years, Sigi has arranged an interfaith lecture every year at the university. Particularly gratifying, too, is the publication of the letter to Sigi from Klaus Schwab, founder and executive-chairman of the World Economic Forum in the recent book about the Forum's activities, *A Partner in Shaping History – The First Forty Years*, which thanks Sigi for his invaluable contribution to the religious and spiritual consciousness of the Forum and for his partnership over the previous decade.

Suzanne, Sigi's sister, has also received a number of distinguished honours. In 2009, she was awarded an Honorary Fellowship of the Israel Museum, where she contributed to the reconstruction of a 400-year-old synagogue from Suriname, formerly Dutch Guyana. The unveiling of the Tzedek ve-Shalom synagogue took place in May 2010 and Suzanne received a letter from the Chief Rabbi, Lord Sacks, regretting that he could not be present but recognizing that 'it is most meaningful and fitting that this reconstruction should be attached to the memory of … your late husband … who did so much for Jewish life in that part of the world, notably, of course, in Curaçao, but also in Suriname where he attended services at this synagogue when he was there'. Also in 2009, Suzanne was decorated with a high royal honour of Oranje-Nassau, the equivalent of a knighthood, and received the Rebecca Sieff award, the international prize of WIZO. She recalls that WIZO events in Curaçao were on everybody's social calendar and Bible exhibits of all denominations were displayed, including, on one occasion, the secret collection of Jose Maduro, micro-copies of which are now found in museums throughout the world. That event, Suzanne believes, might have been the first interfaith event in the Americas, very much in Sigi's spirit.

She remains grateful to Sigi for taking care of her three sons while they were in Carmel College and stayed with his family during their half term holidays. Sigi, she says, was always very solicitous about their welfare and must, she trusts, feel gratified at their success after leaving school. Louis represented his university in the European Parliament, George was awarded a scholarship for a BSc degree and gained an Honours Degree in Law in the USA while Robert, the eldest, was elected President of the Cambridge Union. Robert's eloquence was evident later in life on many occasions and Suzanne recalls one instance when Sigi took her and her husband to the celebration of the twenty-fifth anniversary of Carmel College when the Prince of Wales was the guest of honour and Robert gave the keynote speech. Several years later, Sigi and Hazel took Suzanne to a grand anniversary reception of the Board of Deputies that took place at Hampton Court. They were seated together and the Prince of Wales was to shake hands on one side of the room and Princess Diana on the other side. When Prince Charles came over to their table, he shook hands with Sigi, with whom he was well acquainted and Sigi then introduced Suzanne to him. 'We've met before', the Prince told her, recalling the occasion at Carmel College. 'Your son made such a memorable speech.'

Suzanne recalls an episode which shows his compassionate nature when Sigi took her to visit Robert at Carmel College. Robert was waiting for them at the gate and a much smaller boy was waiting next to him. As they walked away, with a large tuck box they had brought along, they turned back and saw the boy still standing at the gate, all alone. Sigi suggested they go back and see whether there was some problem and they found the boy with tears in his eyes as nobody had come to visit him. Robert offered him half his tuck box and they took the boy with them for a delicious tea so he could forget his missing visitors.

Sigi's portrait painted by Valerie Wiffen was presented to the National Portrait Gallery by Michael and Frances. The tie he is shown wearing in the portrait is covered with hats. As he explained to a journalist from the *Financial Times* in 2006, this is 'because I wear many hats'.

A fascinating appraisal of Sigi, which reflects his capacity to wear many hats and lauds his 'formidable' contribution to humanity was made by Lord Frank Judd:

> For many years I have watched with fascination the operations of 'Sigi'. To say he is a complex man would be an understatement. He is a dynamic enigma. Naive? Probably. Ambitious? Very. Warm? Definitely. Generous? Without a doubt. Kind? At times beyond measure. Sensitive? Not always to those nearest to him, but often impressive. Imaginative? To a fault. Contradictions? Full of them. A risk taker? And how! Own goals? Quite often. Courage? A challenging example. Effective? Overall, very; indeed very, very.

Recalling the time they worked together for Oxfam, Lord Judd commends as 'outstanding' Sigi's 'tireless work for inter-faith understanding and cooperation and his commitment to reconciliation and mutual understanding'. In a similar vein, John Bercow, Speaker of the House of Commons, comments,

> Sir Sigmund Sternberg is one of those life forces who feels an absolutely restless and insatiable desire to try to bring about change and in particular betterment in the relations between communities. He will not consider his own work completed until he feels those relations are appreciably better than they are at present. He has devoted himself to supporting a vast array of good causes over the decades and that's something I much admire.

One of Sigi's more unusual 'hats' was as a member of the international advisory panel of CEANA, the Commission of Enquiry into the Activities of Nazism in Argentina. Sigi was invited by the Argentine government in July 1997 to be one of the eleven members of the panel, which included Lord Dahrendorf, Edgar Bronfman and Walter Laqueur. Two years later, in May 1999, the Argentine Foreign Minister, Dr Guido Di Tella and the ambassador in London, H.E. Rogelio Pfirter, were awarded the ICCJ's Interfaith Gold Medallion. Speaking at the ceremony at the Argentine Embassy, Sigi praised Dr Di Tella's work in advancing the image of Argentina as a forward-looking democratic nation and emphasized the work of CEANA and the unveiling of the memorial to Raoul Wallenberg in Buenos Aires. At a dinner at the Argentine Embassy in Sigi's honour later that year, Ambassador Pfirter announced that Sigi was to receive the Order de Mayo al Merito en el Grado de Gran Official in Buenos Aires the following month. In his response, Sigi urged the Argentine Government to continue its probe into its Nazi past, which, in some areas, was not yet complete. He also recalled the bombing of the Jewish community headquarters in Buenos Aires some five years earlier and hoped that those responsible would yet be brought to trial. In January 2000, responding to the approaches of four Jewish leaders, Sigi, Judge Richard Goldstone, Lord Greville Janner and Samuel Kaplan, the President of B'nai B'rith's Latin American Section, Argentina's new president, Fernando de la Rua, agreed to renew CEANA's mandate so that the Commission could complete its work. Sigi announced that he was delighted that President de la Rua had so positively demonstrated his support for CEANA's important work and that Argentina had chosen to join the Task Force for International Cooperation on Holocaust Education, Remembrance and Research.

Another 'hat' to which Sigi can lay claim is his endowment of the annual Sternberg Interfaith Lecture at Leicester University. Zaki Badawi was the lecturer in 2000, speaking on Islam in a Multi-faith World, while Bishop Malcolm McMahon of Nottingham, lecturing in 2005, urged faiths to find a common morality of life and recalled that while Jews had been expelled from Leicester in the thirteenth century, they had later returned to make a significant contribution to the city's growth, leading it to become a city of racial, cultural and religious harmony and an appropriate setting for the Sternberg Lecture. In 2007, the tenth Sternberg Lecture was given by the Moroccan ambassador, Mohammed Belmahi, while in 2011 the lecture was given by Baroness Sayeeda Warsi, co-chairman of the Conservative party.

Sigi's involvement together with Rabbi Dr Abraham Levy, Spiritual Head of the Spanish and Portuguese Jews' Congregation, in the events commemorating the quincentennial year of the expulsion of Jews from Spain in 1492 is yet another of his 'hats'. Rabbi Levy recalls that before 1992, his community was approached by the Spanish Embassy with the aim of establishing better relations between Christians and Jews in Spain. He and Sigi provided facilities for a number of activities both in England and also in Spain, with the participation of ambassadors, to highlight successful Christian-Jewish relations. An important element of their work was to bring Christians and Jews in Spain to a closer understanding by drawing attention to the important contribution made by Jews in Spain before the expulsion. For example, Jews had been active in the fields of medicine, logic, mathematics and astronomy; celebrated Jewish poets of the era included Yehuda Halevi and Solomon Ibn Gabirol; the *Zohar*, the most famous work of the *Kabbalah*, was revealed to the Jewish world in the thirteenth century by the Spanish rabbi, Moses de Leon, who attributed it to the mystical writings of the second-century rabbi, Shimon bar Yochai.

One significant result of Sigi's and Rabbi Levy's efforts was to obtain a formal apology for the expulsion from the Spanish Primate, Cardinal Marcelo Gonzales Martin, Archbishop of Toledo. And in recognition of their achievements, they were honoured by the Spanish government, together with the late Hayim Pinner, President of the Board of Deputies, who had also been involved in the quincentennial commemoration. All three were awarded the Knight Commander (Encomienda) Order of Civil Merit.

Rabbi Levy, who admires Sigi's pragmatism, sees him as 'our Jewish ambassador at large'. Indeed the late Lord Jacobovits had called him 'our foreign minister'! As Rabbi Levy puts it: 'He has a sort of *weltangschaung* – there's no doubt about it – and has a tremendous gift for making contact with ambassadors. He's a man who keeps his contacts in constant repair. If there's a function, he invites ambassadors and they come. I think it is terribly important from a political point of view and a Jewish point of view that he does get on very, very well with these people.' While Sigi is a committed Reform Jew, Rabbi Levy appreciates the fact that he recognizes that all branches of Judaism must work amicably together. The most rewarding example of this cooperation was a service at Bevis Marks Synagogue in 2006, celebrating the 350th anniversary of the resettlement of Jews in Britain, when, as Rabbi Levy explains, 'we were able to bring under one roof all the different sections of Anglo-Jewry together'. Although Rabbi Levy is aware of Sigi's desire for publicity for himself, he believes he has still done a lot of good and sees the resolution of the Auschwitz Convent imbroglio as his crowning achievement. The rabbi's wife, Estelle, meanwhile, respects the fact that while Sigi 'dignifies every occasion, he is as much at one with the common man as with anyone of importance. Everyone really loves him because he relates to them'. This is something with which Sigi's stepdaughter, Ruth, would concur. As she says, 'he loves all the attention but has spent all his life thinking of others'.

Another person who remains very grateful for Sigi's kindness to her is Ruth Edith Weisz, the former wife of Sigi's cousin, George Weisz. As a small child, Ruth Edith had come to England as a refugee from Vienna with her Jewish father and Catholic mother through the good offices of James Parkes, the distinguished Christian clergyman, scholar of Judaica, early advocate of Christian-Jewish relations and passionate adversary of anti-Semitism. The family had settled in Barley, a village near Cambridge where Parkes was living. In 1960, Ruth Edith met Sigi's cousin, Olga Kennard, née Weisz, who was determined to introduce her to her brother,

George. Their father, however, was a very strict man and quite opposed to his son geting involved with a 'shiksa', whose mother was a Christian. Sigi, whom she met at the time, was very sensitive to her situation. Ruth Edith 'slogged through a very orthodox conversion' and the couple were eventually married in Olga's garden by Sigi's and George's cousin, the 'joyous, huge-hearted, orthodox but flexible Solly' (Solomon Schonfeld), who, Ruth Edith recalls, also offered hospitality at his home to mixed-faith couples. When Ruth Edith moved from Cambridge to join her husband in London, Sigi, she says, 'took every opportunity to show me kindness and acceptance'. On one occasion he took her to an evening at the Cambridge University Union, where 'his brilliant nephew, Robert' – then President of the Union – was speaking. Ruth Edith is sure Sigi told Robert, 'Be nice to Ruth Edith in London; she might feel lonely', because Robert did get in touch with her and invite her out to lunch and showed her round the offices of *The Economist*, where he got his first job. Ruth Edith also appreciates Hazel's kindness to her and feels that Suzanne, Sigi's sister, was 'adorable' to her and asked her to her art shows. George, her husband, was away a great deal on business.

Sigi then found Ruth Edith many things to do, to make her feel a *mensch*, she believes, since she was so denigrated by many of her husband's close family. He 'roped me in to join his good works at the Howard League – befriending lonely prisoners and helping them when they were out again, giving me the feeling that I was a *mensch*'. Sigi also 'roped her in' to 'his new interest' – Christian/Jewish relations. After the birth of her daughters, Rachel and Minnie, he continued to be kind and solicitous. Something Ruth Edith says she will never forget is the 'big gesture' he made after her mother died. 'Sigi knew that George's father never accepted my mother at all so he got his driver to bring him up to Cambridge for my mother's Catholic funeral and stood in for him, so to speak, here in Cambridge for the day, desperately busy though he was. I learned later that he had cancelled a major appointment in London to do it.' Ruth Edith greatly appreciates Sigi's inviting her to all his festivities, 'especially since I was divorced'. She was particularly touched that he and Hazel came up to Cambridge for her grandson's first birthday, even though it was Sigi's own birthday that day. As she sees it, 'he was and remains the kindest of men'.

Lord Coggan, too, pointed to examples of Sigi's great kindness: 'Under protest from me, when I was 80 he organized a party for me to which he invited all kinds of people who had touched my life at various points and it was a very kindly act. Not content with that, he put all the tributes into a book and had a sort of leather-bound copy done for me.' Lord Coggan also appreciated Sigi's ability to remain open minded: 'I think the nice thing about him is that if you disagree with him on a matter of policy and you are open with him and tell him so he never holds it against you and the friendship is not broken because you differ from him.'

Frances, his daughter, recalls various instances of Sigi's great concern for her. One instance was after the death of Annely Juda, the art dealer and gallery owner, with whom she had formed a close relationship. Frances was told of Annely's death by her son, David Juda, but Sigi was so concerned that she would be upset that he hid all the obituaries of Annely. Eventually Sigi confessed: 'I didn't want you to know'. 'I was at the funeral', Frances replied.

Another instance of Sigi's somewhat excessive concern was when Frances's mother, Ruth, was dying and the family were all together at her bedside. It was the first time in thirty years Frances had been with her parents together. She was sitting on a chair eating a packet of crisps. 'Don't eat those, Frances, they're really bad for you', Sigi told her: 'Stop eating them.' Then Ruth 'piped up': 'Leave the child alone, she's enjoying herself.'

Ruth, clearly, had a good sense of humour. Once, after she and Sigi were divorced, she phoned Sigi's office and spoke to a new PA called Ruth Silver. 'Oh dear, your name is Ruth and you work for Sigi. Your life must be very difficult', she told her. Indeed, Sigi has a joke of his own. He is known to say that he has never been 'Ruth-less'. 'What does Ruth-less mean?'

Frances recalls her grandmother, Sigi's mother, asking him. 'It means without a Ruth in my life', Sigi explained.

Indeed, while other Ruths have played an important part in his life, Sigi still cherishes the memory of his first Ruth. At his 88th birthday party in 2009, the first year that his great-grandson, Jacob, was present, he was overheard saying, after introducing the baby to the guests: 'I am thinking this moment of my dear Ruth and that she can't be here and I wish she could be here.'

It was when he was married to Ruth and just over 30 years old that Sigi told his sister something that was to represent the essence of his life. They were going up in the elevator of a skyscraper on New York's Fifth Avenue when he said:

> Suzi, to make money can never be an aim in itself. Yes, I want to make money, but only with a different aim. My money must aim to help people of different religions to respect and understand each other, to eliminate the ignorance of the faith of the OTHER. We must achieve knowledge and trust to eliminate hatred that can result in war so that we can, by understanding each other, achieve a peaceful co-existence between man and his neighbour so that, as the Scriptures say, the wolf can lie down with the lamb without fear of the OTHER. This is purely the essential aim of my life. To make money is only good if you can USE it for the good of HUMANITY. Everything I will do and achieve, and any decorations and distinctions I may get, will have this sole aim for me.

But he couldn't have accomplished all he did without his helpmeet, Hazel.

Glossary

Bimah	A platform in the centre of a synagogue from which the Torah is read
Chumash	Book containing the Five Books of Moses
Gemara	A rabbinical commentary on the Mishnah
Kabbalat Shabbat	A synagogue service to welcome the Sabbath
Kaddish	Memorial prayer for the dead
Mensch	A person of integrity and honour
Meshuggas	Madness, nonsense, irrational idiosyncrasy
Mitzvah	One of the 613 commandments; a good deed
Seder	Ritual service and dinner on Passover
Sedra	Weekly portion of the Torah read in Synagogue
Shul	Synagogue
Siddur	Prayer Book
Succot	The Jewish festival of Tabernacles held in the autumn
Talmud	The Mishnah and the Gemara
Tanach	The Hebrew Bible comprising the Torah (Five Books of Moses), Nevi'im (Prophets) and Ketuvim (Writings)

Index

INDEX

Sir Sigmund Sternberg in *Who's Who*

STERNBERG, Sir Sigmund, Kt 1976; JP; Chairman, Sternberg Charitable Foundation, since 1968; b Budapest, 2 June 1921; s of late Abraham and Elizabeth Sternberg; m 1970, Hazel (née Everett Jones); one s one d, and one s one d from a previous marriage. Chairman: St Charles Gp, HMC, 1974; Inst. for Archaeo-Metallurgical Studies. Hon. Life Pres., Labour Finance and Industry Gp, 2002– (Dep. Chm., 1972–93); Life Vice Pres., Royal Coll. of Speech and Lang. Therapists, 2002– (Sen. Vice-Pres., 1995–2002). Life Pres., Movt for Reform Judaism (formerly Reform Synagogues of GB), 2011– (Pres., 1998–2011); Patron, Internat. Council of Christians and Jews; Mem., Board of Deputies of British Jews (Patron, Charitable Trust, 2005–); Governor, Hebrew Univ. of Jerusalem (Hon. Fellow, 2011); Life Pres., Sternberg Centre for Judaism, 1996; Co-Founder, Three Faiths Forum (Christians, Muslims & Jews Dialogue Gp), 1997; Sen. Religious Advr, World Econ. Forum, 2002–. Life Mem., Magistrates' Assoc., 1965. Mem., John Templeton Foundn, 1998– (Templeton Prize for Progress in Religion, 1998). Founding Patron, Anne Frank Trust, 1991–. Vice Pres., London Jewish Cultural Centre, 2006–. Hon. Vice Pres., Inst. for Business Ethics, 2010. Mem., Court, Essex Univ., 1976–2009. Vice-Pres., Keston Inst., 2003–. Freeman, City of London, 1970; Liveryman, Co. of Horners. JP Middlesex, 1965. Hon. Life Fellow, Inst. of Dirs, 2007. FRSA 1979. Life FRSocMed 2002; Hon. FCST 1989; Hon. Fellow, UCL, 2001. DU: Essex, 1996; Hebrew Union Coll., Cincinnati, 2000; DUniv Open, 1998; Hon. LLD Leicester, 2007; Hon. DHLitt Richmond American Internat., 2008. Paul Harris Fellow, Rotary Foundn of Rotary Internat., 1989 (Rotary Internat. Award of Honour, 1998); Medal of Merit, Warsaw Univ., 1995; Wilhelm Leuschner Medal, Wiesbaden, 1998; (jtly) St Robert Bellarmine Medal, Gregorian Univ., 2002; (jtly) Dist. Service Award, Internat. CCJ, 2005; Lifetime Achievement Award, First, 2008. OStJ 1988. KC*SG 1985; Order of Merit (Poland), 1989, Comdr's Cross, 1992, Comdr's Cross with Star, 1999; Order of the Gold Star (Hungary), 1990; Commander's Cross, 1st cl. (Austria), 1992; Comdr of the Order of Civil Merit (Spain), 1993; Comdr, Order of Honour (Greece), 1996; Comdr, Royal Order of Polar Star (Sweden), 1997; Order of Commendatore (Italy), 1999; Gran Oficial, Orden de Mayo al Merito (Argentina), 1999; Grand Cross, Order of Bernardo O'Higgins (Chile), 2000; Order of Ukraine, 2001; Order of Merit with star (Portugal), 2002; Officier, Légion d'Honneur (France), 2003; Order of Madara Horseman (Bulgaria), 2003; Order of White Two-Armed Cross (Slovakia), 2003; Order of Francisco de Miranda (Venezuela), 2004; Comdr's Cross, Order of Merit (Hungary), 2004; Knight Grand Cross, Royal Order of Francis I, 2005; Knight Comdr's Cross, Order of Merit (Germany), 2006 (Comdr's Cross, 1993); Comdr, Order Pentru Merit (Romania), 2007; St Mellitus Medal, 2008; Officer, Order of Wissam Alouite (Morocco), 2009. Recreations: reading the religious press, swimming. Address: Star House, 104 Grafton Road NW5 4BA. Clubs: Reform, City Livery.

From 2012 edition of *Who's Who*, published by A & C Black Ltd.